Social Collateral

Social Collateral

*Women and Microfinance in Paraguay's
Smuggling Economy*

Caroline E. Schuster

UNIVERSITY OF CALIFORNIA PRESS

University of California Press, one of the most
distinguished university presses in the United States,
enriches lives around the world by advancing scholarship
in the humanities, social sciences, and natural sciences. Its
activities are supported by the UC Press Foundation and
by philanthropic contributions from individuals and
institutions. For more information, visit www.ucpress.edu.

University of California Press
Oakland, California

Library of Congress Cataloging-in-Publication Data

Schuster, Caroline E., author.
    Social collateral : women and microfinance in
Paraguay's smuggling economy / Caroline E. Schuster.
        p.   cm.
    Includes bibliographical references and index.
    ISBN 978-0-520-28704-4 (cloth, alk. paper) —
    ISBN 978-0-520-28705-1 (pbk., alk. paper) —
    ISBN 978-0-520-96220-0 (electronic)
    1. Microfinance—Paraguay.   2. Microfinance—Social
aspects—Paraguay.   3. Businesswomen—Paraguay.
4. Women-owned business enterprises—Economic
aspects—Paraguay.   5. Smuggling—Economic
aspects—Paraguay.   I. Title.
    HG178.33.P33S38   2015
    332—dc23   2015014471

Manufactured in the United States of America

24   23   22   21   20   19   18   17   16   15
10   9   8   7   6   5   4   3   2   1

In keeping with a commitment to support
environmentally responsible and sustainable printing
practices, UC Press has printed this book on Natures
Natural, a fiber that contains 30% post-consumer waste
and meets the minimum requirements of ANSI/NISO
Z39.48-1992 (R 1997) (*Permanence of Paper*).

Contents

Illustrations

Acknowledgments

This book would not be possible without the ongoing collaboration and friendship of many people in Paraguay whose lives and livelihoods are described here, most of whom do not appear by name. Since 2006 they have contributed their support, care, and intellectual generosity during my trips to Asunción and Ciudad del Este. I would especially like to thank Martín Burt and the dedicated staff at Fundación Paraguaya. Martín's enthusiastic support of my research gave me a crucial window onto the microcredit world. His staff at the Asunción head office was incredibly warm and welcoming. I would also like to acknowledge the deep debt I owe to the NGO workers at Fundación Paraguaya in its Ciudad del Este branch. Most have since left for other careers in the financial services industry; I wish them best of luck in their new jobs. While our discussions of microfinance were memorable, the best times were spent juggling *terere* in the car, sipping Brahma beer at office parties, and watching the Paraguayan *selección nacional* hurtle toward the quarter finals of the South Africa World Cup. It was wonderful sharing many laughs alongside loan documents and *comité* meetings.

Along with the staff of Fundación Paraguaya, I would like to thank the borrowers, activists, friends, and neighbors of the neighborhood I call Ciudad Jardín. Their tutorials in plant husbandry, community bake sales, and neighborhood organizing inspired my thinking about social obligation. I was captivated by their vibrant projects, which kept drawing me back to the neighborhood. And importantly, my life in Ciudad del Este was profoundly influenced by the serendipity of coming to live with Modesta, Lucia, and the whole family—a happy accident that made my time there joyful. Thanks to Carmen and Ana for lots of laughs. Juan and Luz, our friendship is a blessing.

I owe much to Christine Folch, Gustavo Setrini, John Tofik Karam, Kregg Hetherington, Fernando Rabossi, Jennifer Tucker, and Juan Carlos Cristaldo for lively discussions during fieldwork in Paraguay. Putting Paraguay on the research map has always been something of a puzzle, and I am immensely grateful to find myself in such good company while undertaking that task. Directora Adelina Pusineri and Vicedirectora Raquel Zalazar at the Museo Etnográfico Adrés Barbero provided excellent archival resources and institutional support for research in Asunción. I benefited also from extensive conversations with researchers working in the tri-border area, especially at the Seminário Pesquisas na Tríplice Fronteira organized by Fernando Rabossi and hosted at the UNIOESTE campus at Foz do Iguaçu in 2009. I would also like to thank Ariel Wilkis for organizing a wonderful panel on economic anthropology at the Reunión Antropológico Mercosur (RAM) in 2009. The Grupo de Estudions Sobre el Paraguay (GESP)—headed by Magui López, among others—has built exciting research collaborations, and I hope to see the network of scholars flourish.

This has been an extended writing project that I began at the University of Chicago. Jessica Cattelino has taught me—over many years—the conceptual power of anthropology. Jessica, I aspire to your analytic precision, critical stance, and intellectual generosity. And I treasure our friendship. I would also like to thank John Comaroff for his ceaseless support of this research and his constant encouragement to think boldly and write clearly. Julie Chu pushed me to unexpected places, and Alan Kolata encouraged me to puzzle over development. At the University of Chicago I would also like to thank Joe Masco, William Mazzarella, Shannon Dawdy, Judy Farquhar, Karin Knorr Cetina, and Susan Gal for their commentary and suggestions throughout. Jennifer Cole provided critical insight in her patient reading of drafty drafts of early writing. I greatly benefited from the chance to share early versions of chapters in several workshops at the University of Chicago, including the Gender and Sexuality Studies Workshop, the Law, Culture and Society Workshop, and the Money, Markets and Consumption Workshop. At the Center for the Study of Gender and Sexuality (CSGS), Linda Zerilli has been a tireless advocate of graduate student research on the politics of gender. I enjoyed being a part of the Sawyer Seminar on International

Women's Human Rights, both as a dissertation fellow and as a participant in the events and faculty seminar, at which Agnes Lugo-Ortiz, Charlotte Walker, Lauren Berlant, Leela Gandhi, Rochona Majumdar, and Tara Zahra offered helpful comments. Thanks to Gina Olson and Sarah Tuohey at the CSGS and all the participants at the Gender and Sexuality Studies Workshop for thoughtful feedback. Julia Kowalski read and commented on written versions of the argument, and I benefited from our deep discussions. Duff Morton helped me clarify the argument of the first chapter of the book. Thanks also to George Paul Meiu, Sarah Luna, Monica Mercado, Zahra Jamal, and Larisa Reznik at CSGS. Adam Sargent, Brian Horn, Betsey Brada, Ender Ricart, Erin Moore, Gabe Tusinski, Kate McHarry, Jay Sosa, Mary Leighton, Duff Morton, and Malavika Reddy have been great intellectual companions.

I would like to thank Bill Maurer for his generous commentary at two annual Institute for Money, Technology and Financial Inclusion (IMTFI) conferences. I workshopped early drafts of writing at the Irmgard Coninx Stiftung "Financialization of Everyday Life" roundtables chaired by Jane Guyer and Susanne Soederberg. I also benefited greatly from participation in the Futures of Finance conference in April 2012, hosted by the Institute for Public Knowledge at New York University. For my archival research on Paraguay's financial history, I would like to thank Michael Tomz at Stanford University for a wonderful introduction to Latin American political economy. A large portion of the archival work from the Corporation for Foreign Bondholders is based on reels of digitized microfilm that Mike generously shared with me when I left for graduate work at Chicago. At the Weatherhead Center for International Affairs at Harvard University I made extensive use of Harvard's archival sources on Latin America. Throughout, I received invaluable feedback from anonymous reviewers at several scholarly journals. The comments and critical suggestions pushed me to refine the argument and clarify my analysis.

This research was undertaken with the support of the University of Chicago Century Fellowship for graduate research, the Jacob K. Javits Fellowship from the U.S. Department of Education, and FLAS Title VI funding for Guarani language training at the IDIPAR language institute in Asunción. Field research was supported in part by the Institute for Money, Technology and Financial Inclusion at University of California, Irvine. I also received support from the Fulbright-Hayes DDRA program and the Wenner Gren Foundation to conduct fieldwork in Paraguay. I would like to acknowledge the support of the Center for the

Study of Gender and Sexuality at the University of Chicago during dissertation write-up. Further fieldwork funding and research support came from the Harvard Academy for International and Area Studies.

This book really took shape while I was in research residence at the Harvard Academy for International and Area Studies in the Weatherhead Center for International Affairs. Jorge Domínguez was the intellectual center of the Harvard Academy and pushed me to find the "hummable tune" for the manuscript. I benefited from discussions with fellow researchers, including Jesse Driscoll, James Long, Pablo Querubin, Gabi Kruks-Wisner, Nur Amali Ibrahim, Noora Lori, Naor Ben-Yehoyada, Jeffrey Kahn, Timothy Noonan, and Kerry Chance. Lively discussions with Sohini Kar still inspire me to think through comparative analysis on financial inclusion. I owe a very special thanks to the generous scholars who reviewed portions of the book manuscript at an author's conference symposium organized by Larry Winnie and the Harvard Academy. Julia Elyachar, Gustav Peebles, Steve Caton, Michael Chu, Diego Abente Brun, Fernando Rabossi, and Jorge Domínguez all offered a very close reading of an early draft and gave exceptionally thoughtful suggestions for revision. The early review of the manuscript draft and lively discussion at the symposium were of incalculable value. I also benefited from the support of my colleagues at the Australian National University for their feedback and suggestions at the final stages of revision. I would like to say thank you to John Cox, Simone Dennis, James Flexner, Catherine Frieman, Patrick Guiness, Christine Helliwell, Nicholas Peterson, Andy Kipnis, Francesca Merlan, Sverre Molland, Alan Rumsey, Laurajane Smith, Trang X. Ta, and Ashley Carruthers. Thank you to Shiori Shakuto for index assistance.

Reed Malcolm at University of California Press shepherded this project into book form. The manuscript benefited immensely from his feedback and critical commentary and his unflagging support for the underlying research. I would like to thank the editorial team at the Press, as well as the reviewers, including Kregg Hetherington, whose clear-sighted comments pushed me to write a better book.

I am especially indebted to my core academic (and life) support network: Alex Blanchette, Tatiana Chudakova, Kate Goldfarb, and Elayne Oliphant. They are the "hive mind" whose collective contribution to the writing and analysis of this project cannot be overstated. Thank you also to Peter Hepburn, interlocutor throughout the writing process. Eliza Ridgeway and Megan Kemptson have been an amazing resource in the process of writing a book that is actually nice to read and remembering to have a good time while doing it. And an enormous thank you to my family for advice, encouragement, and humor throughout. Sue Schuster and Kristen Schuster are an endless source of inspiration and joy. Thank you to my grandma Aba Schuster who printed out every email and blog post from the field. Randy, Ana-María, Tracy, Rafa, and Claudia all offered unceasing support from Davis. Timothy Hermanas deserves more recognition and gratitude than I can express here. I am so thankful for a partner who insisted that I see this project through wherever it took me, even if it meant five-thousand-mile and nine-thousand-mile commutes.

At last, a huge thank you to the women who borrowed as Committees of Women Entrepreneurs in Paraguay and who continue to be a source of inspiration and awe. I am deeply grateful for the patience and perseverance of all the women who shared their economic travails with one another and with me. They helped me see the fragile connections and enduring bonds that hold together Ciudad del Este. This book is dedicated to them.

Introduction

Ña Fabiana stacked the plastic bags full of clothes on a chair as we discussed the final items that remained from her investment the previous year. She spread out the last of her inventory: soft microfleece gloves for children and adults, brightly colored striped socks with individual toes, winter coats, and children's turtleneck shirts. Some of the clothing had become stained in storage over the past months, though it still had its original tags. The sun shone brightly on her shaded patio and Fabi and I were in shirtsleeves,[1] though it was already late fall and Paraguay was due for a cold snap in the coming winter months. Fabi tried—mostly in vain—to persuade her neighbor that buying in advance made good economic sense. She was selling these last items at a steep discount, and she expected the prices for winter clothes would go up when the weather turned. "Look at this," she said, pulling out a light jacket that she had purchased for about $20 in one of the shopping gallerias made famous by Ciudad del Este's vibrant[2]—and largely duty-free—import-export economy. On the Paraguayan side of the triple frontier with Argentina and Brazil, most residents found their livelihoods bound up in some way with Ciudad del Este's cross-border trade and special customs zone. Fabi started a sales pitch: "For you, I'll sell it at $12. I need to recover some of my investment. I need movement." The neighbor sent her daughter next door to fetch $5 to purchase a lavender-colored long-sleeved shirt with embroidered flowers around the collar. When the little girl returned with only a fraction of the money her mother scolded her and marched her back to find the correct amount.

While we waited another woman drove slowly along the dusty road on Fabi's block of the housing settlement in the periurban outskirts of Ciudad del Este, pulling up in a small blue hatchback car and kicking up a cloud of red dust. She was selling Sawary brand jeans that she had brought from São Paulo, Brazil. Ciudad del Este's unusually open customs regime makes this sort of business trip quite lucrative for those with the means to finance the journey and buy merchandise in bulk. Announcing that she would be willing to collect payments in installments, the woman added the duffle bag of fashionable Levanta Bum Bum body sculpting jeans to the pile of Fabi's clothes on the table. Fabi took a few pairs into her house to try on but did not find any that fit to her liking. "If you find a pair like this in my size," she said holding up a pair of jeans with zippers on the pockets, "then I would be interested." Looking wistfully at the little hatchback car, driven by the saleswoman's husband, Fabi commented, "I'd really like to work like that. Not wasting time." Three years ago she had cosigned a loan to purchase a motobike with her husband, which they paid off in twenty-four monthly installments. However, he used it every day to drive the six kilometers to the transport business where he worked as a driver and mechanic. Fabi sold her wares mostly to neighbors, and made investments with specific buyers in mind since she had come to know the intimate details of their tastes and needs. But to expand her sales network, reliable transportation would be a tremendous asset.

Selling clothing was one of several ventures that Ña Fabiana had undertaken in recent years. And these income-generating activities overlapped intermittently with a microcredit program, among other sources of credit, which animated some of the economic "movement" that sustained her and her family. For several years Fabi had been the treasurer of a Committee of Women Entrepreneurs at Fundación Paraguaya, a local microfinance nongovernmental organization (NGO). During that time she had also raised decorative plants, a pursuit that she obviously enjoyed. Since I had known her, the spacious patio in front of her small two-room home had always been full of orchids, other flowers, and fruit trees (fig. 1). While she focused on flowers, Fabiana also occasionally negotiated business partnerships to expand her clothing sales, several of which ran into difficulties at the interface of credit and repayment. She had invested in merchandise to stock a neighbor's small store but never managed to recover either profits or her original wares. At around the

FIGURE 1. Ña Fabiana's patio, which doubles as a plant nursery.

same time she had offered a loan to one of her wholesale suppliers in the city market. Although it had seemed like a successful business, the owner had been slow to pay her back. Despite these business troubles, her husband's steady salary and Fabi's various projects helped her meet all of her obligations, from bills and payments to daily expenses.

It had been four years since I first visited Fabi's home in the periurban settlement,[3] and there were markedly fewer terracotta pots and fewer seedlings in black plastic containers ready for sale. This was due in part to the chicken-raising venture that had occupied a few months of her attention since I had last seen her two years before—and that had unintentionally turned many of her plants into chicken feed. But, she explained, she had "lost it all" with the plants, unwinding her story while plucking orange blossoms from one of the few remaining trees to flavor our cold yerba mate tea. "After you left I invested good money in my plants. Each one of these planters cost almost $2, and first I was selling them in front of the grocery shop, there downtown in front of Fundación Paraguaya." The investment in and prioritization of a single venture among many was made possible by her regular participation in Fundación Paraguaya's small-scale lending targeted at women, since the movement of credit was linked to the movement of her income and labor. Fabi continued, "And Abuela, the old woman from here in the settlement, she was helping me. But by October I was ill and spending all of my time at the doctor. My credit counselor for the Fundación even called and wanted me to show my plants as part of their Expo for Microenterprise, but I told her I couldn't because I was sick and I did not want to deal with transporting all those planters." Her story of the Microenterprise Expo concluded with the NGO branch manager eventually bringing his truck to help her transport them there, but she faced the unanticipated extra expense of having to pay a driver to bring the unsold plants all the way back to settlement where she lived, which all but erased her profit. In a twist that is emblematic of the unevenness of the economic pathways of microfinance, her participation in the Expo helped get her product to market but left her waiting at the curb, as it were, when she needed to get home.

Fabi's story looped back and forth between unexpected successes and setbacks. She said that she continued to build the flower business, even managing to work out a deal with the pharmacy next door to the microcredit office. The owners offered to let her sell her orchids every day and agreed to store them in their small warehouse overnight. But, she said, as her health deteriorated she missed a few days at the pharmacy. And while she was away a different security guard took over at the warehouse, and her arrangement for storing the plants imploded. When her health improved and she finally returned to tend her plants, she discovered that all of her stock had been thrown away, and not even the planters were left. "I really felt for my plants," she said. "I'm telling you about what I invested [financially], and on top of that I had my orchids. The orchids were what I felt most." Although her feeling for her plants was surely connected to her sense of place and belonging in her luscious garden and by extension in the wider neighborhood, Fabiana's financial loss was also bound up with the gendering forms of investment that were subtly encouraged by the Committees of Women Entrepreneurs program. Her entrepreneurial risks were inextricably linked to her work—albeit fleeting—as the "flower lady," as her NGO credit counselor enthusiastically described her. Despite her financial troubles, the staff considered her a poster child for the feminine entrepreneurial spirit valued by the organization.

Nã Fabiana brightened, though, when she stored away the last of her unsold winter wares and pulled me inside her house to show off the unexpected windfall from her newest venture. She had taken on work as a cook and housekeeper for the family of her husband's daughter from a previous partnership. Her new employer sent her home with leftover food, including most recently three rabbits that Fabi was eager to make into a traditional stew. Fabiana called the younger woman Madam, or la Señora, as a mark of deference rather than by more familiar kinship terms commonly used for a stepdaughter; proximity and distance were reckoned along lines of socioeconomic class.[4] La Señora's husband and his brothers worked as private contractors in cross-border trade as customs dispatch agents. They made heady profits managing more or less licit transportation logistics in Ciudad del Este's transborder commercial economy. La Señora's husband drove an impressive late model pickup truck, and the family lived in a spacious and well-appointed compound not far from Fabiana's neighborhood in an informal housing settlement where basic utilities and housing titles were still being negotiated with the municipality. The lucrative dispatch work was also intermittent, entrepreneurial, and opportunistic but, unlike Nã Fabiana's flower business and clothing sales, had the potential to make staggering profits; value unspooled from the unusual regulatory regime of the Paraguayan "special customs zone." If "the central task for everyone," as Keith Hart (2000: 177) has argued of informal economies, "was to find a reasonably durable basis for livelihood and even for accumulation, a stable core in the chaos of everyday life," then commercial society on the border offered up that stable core more readily to some than to others.

Ña Fabiana's account of her daily economic life shared many similarities with the lives and livelihoods of low-income Paraguayan women who were clients of the grassroots microcredit NGO Fundación Paraguaya. Their financial practices open a window onto the prosaic ways that people cohabit with debt in their daily lives in Paraguay. In development studies, microcredit is told as a before-and-after narrative of financial inclusion, with a transformative arc (for better or worse) for women who borrow. From the diversity of ways that people lived on credit in Ciudad del Este, it soon became apparent to me that microcredit was not positioned in predictable or straightforward ways relative to the myriad lending and borrowing practices that were so central to commercial society in the tri-border area.[5] The excess of credit on Paraguay's frontier illuminates the specificities of microcredit within the credit systems of Ciudad del Este, as well as the regulatory work of credit and debt in shaping daily economic practice in a zone made famous by its long history of experimenting with nonregulation and free trade. While Fabiana's efforts to bank on her relationships with family, friends, and neighbors had mixed results, it became clear to me from our discussions that she treated the boundaries and terms of her debts as open questions. Microfinance practices reshape notions of obligation as well as what it means to be both a woman and a borrower.

In Ciudad del Este, a city of about 350,000 on the Paraguayan side of the frontier with Argentina and Brazil, relationships of economic obligation permeate everyday life, and they seem to reach into the minutia of daily routines. Most people pay for both small and large purchases on installment plans, like the saleswoman selling stylish Sawary jeans in Ña Fabiana's neighborhood. From buying one diaper at a time on a store tab from the local shopkeeper to paying for jeans in monthly quotas, these constant running tabs and bills—talked about locally as *cuentas*—are ubiquitous in Paraguay. The small scales of credit and debt emplace debt in the small scale of the everyday. The movement of credit, too, traces quotidian paths throughout the city and its outskirts. Rather than instantaneous wire transfers or mobile banking, these payment schemes are often facilitated by the work of moto-riding bill collectors who make house calls to collect cuentas. Fabiana and her neighbors make mortgage payments to a local *cobrador* for the land development company when he visits every month and sets up his till on the patio of a neighborhood home. These visits are of course unnecessary when credit comes from the many small local shops—often operated in homes—selling goods to neighbors and family. Foot traffic that winds through the streets of local communities suffices to service those obligations. However, even the powerful vice president of Paraguay's private sector credit scoring company, Informconf, had to excuse himself during an interview to make a payment to a bill collector for the new flat-screen TV that he had purchased to watch the 2010 World Cup soccer matches. Circuits within commerce, to borrow the sociologist Viviana Zelizer's term for these economic pathways,[6] are literally carved out of the ruts and grooves of motorcycle tires and the networked cell phone discussions that flow—or more properly, bump and bounce—across the commercial economy of Ciudad del Este.

Many people in Ciudad del Este relied on the common phrase "bicycling (*bicicleteando*) loans" to describe their relationship to credit and debt. They kept up with the never-ending payments by repaying one loan with the next. The work of pushing the pedals around, the common phrase implied, was driven by ever increasing cycles of debt. Tellingly, Fabiana thought a great deal about "movement" and turnover in her merchandise. She described bicycling as an economic lifeline. However, she was less sure about whether such movement could be equated with a forward trajectory.[7] That tension was even built into the naming conventions of the microfinance Committees of Women Entrepreneurs, which commonly took the moniker "Women's Progress" or "Women Advancing," even as the groups routinely found themselves grappling with payment problems and repeating cycle upon cycle of borrowing.

I first heard the term *bicycling* at a finance seminar run by Gustavo, vice president of Informconf. The company deals with myriad facets of the financial services world in Paraguay, from telemarketing to debt collection to credit scoring. The seminar on credit risk where Gustavo warned participants about the perennial "problem" of bicycling debt was attended by a cross section of financial professionals working in Paraguay's banking sector. Standing in front of a PowerPoint presentation that depicted overindebtedness in bland charts and graphs, Gustavo brought the concept alive, his hands whirling round and round to evoke the spinning pedals of the credit bicycle. For conference-goers making use of Informconf's data services—and navigating a financial context awash in credit—paying careful attention to the life cycles of loans, especially their rhythms and movements, was key to managing debt. Financial actors within Paraguay's credit markets were themselves asking, Exactly what kind of economic mobility did pedaling debt imply? What sort of transactional order was sustained on the credit bicycle, and with what scope? This book considers how microcredit compared to and intersected with the multiple financial obligations that many Paraguayans pedaled on a daily basis.[8]

MICROFINANCE, VILLAGE BANKING, AND SOLIDARITY LENDING

Despite microcredit's seeming novelty and specialized place in antipoverty development aid, Ña Fabiana's vivid account of the omnipresence of credit and debt in Ciudad del Este underscores the fact that it was not just microcredit development projects that made use of unconventional forms of guarantee for loans. Fabiana's installment plans, her bill collectors, and her own efforts to collect on the debts owed her by others mixed physical and social assets, contractual liability and mutual obligation. From these overlapping regimes of debt, methodologically we might ask how microcredit differs substantively from the social practices that sustained credit relationships for countless years before the global microcredit boom. How does microcredit selectively incorporate and exclude that range of economic relationships?

In practice, these many different forms of credit share a common feature that goes to the heart of microcredit's framing and justification in global development circles and importance to anthropological theories of value: *social collateral*. Most formal financial institutions in Paraguay and elsewhere require some form of physical guarantee in order to secure a loan. Assets like a salary contract, property, inventory for a business, insurance, and a guarantor or cosignatory often serve as physical collateral on a bank loan. As I prepared to conduct research on microcredit loans, the differences between physical and social collateral came into view in my own financial life—from asking my mother to cosign my student loans to drawing a boundary around my household to report income on credit card applications. Social collateral does away with the income and asset requirements for borrowing by shifting what I term the *social unit of debt*. Rather than lent to individual borrowers and their guarantors, microcredit loans are shared among groups. Fabiana was the treasurer of her group and relied on about fifteen neighbors—some close friends and family, others strangers—to maintain her line of credit through steady collective repayment and from one credit cycle to the next. Although the specific requirements vary from organization to organization, many of these solidarity loans (*préstamos solidarios*), as they are referred to in the microcredit world, are for groups of ten or more women who collectively pledge to pay it back. If one woman is unable to make her weekly payment, then her group members will have to come together to pay her share or risk being penalized as a group. Penalties take the form of lowered loan ceilings in the next cycle of borrowing or, in some cases, exclusion from further borrowing altogether. Creditworthiness in the formal financial system turns in large part on the physical assets that the bank reckons to be available to collateralize the loan—subject to seizure—in the event of default.[9] Creditworthiness in microcredit solidarity lending turns instead on social assets like peer pressure, shame, mutual support, and reciprocity to collateralize the loan. Indeed, microcredit is even thought to build social capital among members through group meetings, mutual support, and a shared path toward financial literacy.[10]

After the inaugural 1997 Microcredit World Summit,[11] where world leaders debated the promise of microcredit as a development tool, small-scale lending went from a visionary call for pro-poor financial programs to a mainstay of development policy. Indeed, later that year the merits of microcredit as foreign aid were debated on the House floor of the U.S. Congress. Within a decade, microcredit became a central pillar of international development and ultimately was the basis for the Grameen Bank's Nobel Peace Prize in 2006. Currently, microcredit is seen by many scholars as a global comparative project analyzed by means of a series of case studies that pit communities and organizations against one another to compare results to a global model. This has become an especially powerful analytic approach made possible by large-scale randomized control trial (RCT) studies like those undertaken by the *Portfolios of the Poor* project and research collaborations at institutes such as the Jameel Poverty Action Lab at MIT.[12] Indeed, the Institute for Money, Technology, and Financial Inclusion (IMTFI) at the University of California, Irvine, with which I have been involved over a long period, takes such a broad and comparative view of new financial technologies in its many different manifestations globally. Researchers and policy makers fine-tune the organizational structures and methods for implementing these programs and debate the successes and failures of each case study, all of which signals the almost total incorporation of microcredit into a global development framework. My aim is not simply to add Paraguay to the list of cases. Rather, this book builds outward from the conditions of credit in a specific—and in many ways unusual—context in order to theorize social collateral and its importance to anthropological studies of value and in the wider world today.

Microcredit organizations were certainly not the first to notice that collateral requirements excluded large swaths of potential borrowers. Self-organized rotating savings and credit associations (ROSCAs) have for many decades been used by communities to gather and distribute the lump sums needed for investments in businesses but also in important life cycle events like weddings and funerals. Participants would all pitch in an agreed-upon amount, and the collective pot would rotate among members of the group for their own use. Anthropologists have been charting the contours of ROSCAs at least since the work of Clifford Geertz (1962), and forms of community credit were a mainstay of early debates in economic anthropology about modernization, development, and cultural change.[13] In the 1970s two development organizations began experimenting with small-scale lending requiring minimal collateral. Acción International in Latin America and the Grameen Bank in Bangladesh emerged as global players, pioneering institutionalized banking services for rural communities with few links to formal banks or finance companies. Both organizations drew inspiration for their Village Bank programs from community financing schemes that relied on group solidarity and peer pressure for credit and repayment. In Paraguay, microfinance has long been allied with the commercial banking system, and especially local finance companies (*financieras*) that offer a suite of financial products to the working class. However, not-for-profit development organizations like Fundación Paraguaya continue to rely on the Village Bank model, despite the fact that microfinance has increasingly shed the mantle of specialized aid and moved into the wider sector of commercial credit.[14] For Fundación Paraguaya, requirements like face-to-face meetings among group members and NGO staff, home visits, and group payments all ingrained social collateral in the very fabric of its lending program.

This book considers the stakes of collective forms of debt in Latin America at a moment when microcredit enjoys unprecedented success, both in articulating humanitarian antipoverty goals and driving the everyday operations of hundreds of nonprofit and commercial microfinance institutions throughout the region and around the world. These development initiatives are noteworthy on their own terms for drawing together global and regional financial systems, from the account books of Paraguayan shopkeepers to the balance sheets of Citi Group International and from the commercial hub of the tri-border area to the development hub of Kiva.org's Bay Area offices. But microcredit also invites analysis of more general questions about interdependency and obligation at the root of social collateral. Building outward from women's antipoverty programs in Paraguay, microcredit lending can serve as a framework for rethinking core assumptions in development policy and anthropological theory on poverty, women's wealth, and the social meaning of money and markets. I suggest that social collateral is a good tool to think with, beyond the intimate debts of microfinance and their expression in Paraguayan development. In fact, at a moment when, as Melinda Cooper (2010: 168) suggests, "through the act of fiat debt creation the US is effectively . . . inspiring the practical if not willing confidence of the world's investors,"[15] something that looks a great deal like social collateral—the interdependency of joint obligation and mutual guarantee—is becoming the basis for the distributional order of global finance. "Too big to fail" notions of overly dense financial entanglements among the biggest banks in the global financial system now share remarkable similarities with "too small to fail" logics of microfinance and their intimate economic ties of joint liability. This is an important context in which to consider new forms of collectivity and cohesion bound up by shared debts, as well as their potential futures.

The politics of interdependency in financial systems—and the social collateral that sustains it—is the central puzzle of this book.

THE LIFE CYCLES OF LOANS

Microcredit is part of a global trend of financial inclusion that brings banking services, and especially credit, to the world's poor. Ña Fabiana's account of the opportunities and pitfalls of financial inclusion resonate with concern in both anthropology and wider public debate about the troubling consequences of debt, as the world of commercialized finance reaches further and further into the livelihoods and communities of people least able to shoulder financial risks.[16] However, focusing exclusively on the material effects of microcredit—whether it works or doesn't, and by what criteria—can obscure other ways that microcredit shapes the inner workings of financial institutions and is situated within a complex system of financial instruments and economic practices in Paraguay and globally. One way to understand the tensions and asymmetries that generate specific material consequences of indebtedness is to set these relations in motion.[17] This book tells the story of the life course of loans and the people attached to them, including the lenders themselves. In many ways, the liveliness of loans[18] would seem to be at odds with what Bill Maurer has critiqued as common presumptions about the coldly impersonal and standardized logics of capitalism.[19] By focusing on the mobile "grip and slip" of interdependency across the unfolding life course of loans,[20] I take a feminist approach to how capitalism is generated.[21] As I argue, the hard edges of debt need not function purely through abstraction and quantification of modern money, and liability is not only dictated by a contract.[22] Tellingly, this is especially the case in Paraguay's raucous free trade zone—the pinnacle, in many ways, of abstract commerce.

Because the binding ties of social collateral take hold in everyday practice for borrowers and lenders alike, this book follows credit between the microfinance institution and the neighborhood. Building out of classic work in economic anthropology that takes a longer view than transactional exchange relationships, I am interested in the movement of credit and repayment across its social life or cultural biography.[23] Arjun Appadurai has framed his analysis of the "social life of things" in terms of regimes of value, which he describes as coordinated systems that organize and constrain the paths commodities take as they are exchanged.[24] However, my narrative of the pathways and dynamics of loans across their life cycles departs in important ways from studies of the circulation of objects through structured and stable regimes of value.[25] Instead, the moving connections of credit and debt—penciled in notebooks, carved in rutted roads, made intimate and familiar in weekly meetings—stitch a city together into temporary alignment that, over time and through cyclicality, enacts modes of financial regulation in a nonregulated place.[26] These moving connections of credit can be thought of within a wider anthropological conversation about value refracted through the lens of movement, or what Nancy Munn has famously termed "spatio-temporal extension."[27] Julie Chu's study of the desire for mobility tracks how the unstable temporalities of debt might point us back to the forms of social difference at the root of many of these binding relations of mutuality.[28] As I argue here, these asymmetries also make themselves felt in the cadence and rhythm of lending and borrowing rather than preceding and determining the paths credit takes.

The story of life on the credit bicycle cannot be told without an interwoven account of the gendered dimensions of development lending. As loans move between the promises of entrepreneurship to the hard edges of liability and between the office of Fundación Paraguaya to the homes and business ventures of women who borrow, their life course is also the story of how feminized social collateral became the basis for creating value in the financial world of microcredit and beyond. Why, in other words, do women and microcredit seem like such a natural fit? Why are women like Ña Fabiana seen as such good candidates for— and so likely to benefit from—these sorts of highly regulated and deeply social loans? And beyond the economic projects of Committees of Women Entrepreneurs that take on collective debt through development lending, what might the movement of loans reveal about the lenders as much as the borrowers, in the lives and labor of the young women who oversee loan portfolios at the NGO and the high-level managers who are themselves theorizing social collateral?

Variously, explanations have been pinned on one or the other of those terms: women, microcredit.[29] Development economists have placed the explanatory weight on the hypothesis, "It's something about women," and offered surprising and perceptive insights about metrics for economic improvement that are also sociologically linked to durable forms of social marginalization and misogyny.[30] Alternatively, critical feminist and anthropological studies have focused on the hypothesis, "It's something about microfinance," and have developed a theoretical vocabulary to track the ways microcredit extracts financial value from the dispossession of the social networks and caring relationships of women.[31] Instead of starting with either of these propositions, my ethnographic account focuses on how credit creates its social units, and thus is a fruitful site to rethink the social writ large.[32] Importantly, it goes beyond positing a formation of gendered economic sociality that preexisted and was transformed by microfinance.[33] It also goes beyond theorizing how microcredit assumes and banks on women's solidarity. Rather, microcredit helps us identify the social processes by which credit and debt—and especially social collateral—produce gendered sociality in ways that structure global inequality and opportunity. Building outward from women's endless borrowing usefully points us back to the power effects of microloans not just in terms of downward spirals of overindebtedness or uplifting stories of entrepreneurialism.[34] Being in debt, as Ña Fabiana's bumpy path through microcredit shows, is not a trajectory but rather a repeating condition that tracks her relationship to the terms of credit.

While economic anthropology has long shown how even the most abstruse and high-flying forms of finance are deeply social,[35] microcredit *begins* with the premise that collateral is social and proceeds to institutionalize solidarity lending in highly regulated, calculated, and instrumental ways. Through the lens of microfinance, looking at economic obligation where it seems most natural can help us identify how the seemingly obvious social embeddedness of women is produced,[36] and understand better its consequences. By focusing on obligation where it seems most apparent and taken for granted, this book uses the interdependency of debt as a methodological approach rather than a theory of value.[37] Interdependency offers a way of tracking the conditions under which people living and working in Ciudad del Este are drawn together or held apart—from borrowers, lenders, kin, neighbors, business partners, and clients—by the terms of credit. Drawing on scholarship in feminist political economy,[38] I argue that patterns in economic interdependency offer a window onto an economy of gender in microfinance and in institutionalized forms of credit more generally. Social collateral does not just produce financial revenues, commission bonuses, and organizational sustainability for Fundación Paraguaya. Nor does it only trace a straightforward course to business success or personal debt spirals for women who borrow. Social collateral also produces the very flexible and obligated borrowers to which these programs seek to appeal. Ña Fabi's many cross-cutting obligations—her credit counselor, the branch manager, her neighbor Abuela—got her flowers to the

Microenterprise Expo and were also key to making her into the flower lady. And perhaps more to the point, her story about having to use her own resourcefulness and relationships to get her products home again might epitomize the ways social collateral reaches past merely debt service. More surprisingly, social collateral was also the basis for creating value in unexpected places in the microcredit world, from the gendered division of labor of NGO staff to the overall mission of the organization. Thus social collateral is a deeply gendering form of social cohesion that fixes formations of gender—from financial femininity among credit counselors to Fabiana's entrepreneurial identity as the flower lady—everywhere it reaches.

I suggest that microfinance involves a *crediting of gender* in a double sense. First, gender difference serves as the basis for entrepreneurialism and creditworthiness for the thousands of women who enrolled in the Committees of Women Entrepreneurs program. But also, second, gender is simultaneously framed by borrowers and lenders alike as a force, and it is credited with certain effects, including a repertoire of economic practices at the heart of social collateral. This double crediting of gender is what makes the common question in development circles, But do these loans actually work for women?, especially vexed. This is because the very category "woman" is refracted through the terms of credit. Gayle Rubin describes these power effects of sex/gender systems best in her analysis of "the traffic in women."[39] As she writes, "The subordination of women can be seen as a product of the relationships by which sex and gender are organized and produced. The economic oppression of women is derivative and secondary. But there is an 'economics' of sex and gender, and what we need is a political economy of sexual systems" (Rubin 1975: 177). Ña Fabiana's account of living on credit already hints at some of the key terms for an "economics" of sex and gender in the microcredit world, and the particular repertoire of economic practice it creates.[40] Microcredit is awash in two linked forms of economic agency: entrepreneurship and liability. Of course, the language of agency and empowerment has long been a mainstay of international development, particularly in programs focused on women and girls. Meanwhile, liability as a form of economic agency has yet to be seriously studied in the development world and in fact remains largely invisible in studies of empowerment that focus on women's freedom and choices as both specific program goals and broader moral imperatives. In order to understand how gender is organized and produced through social collateral, both entrepreneurship and liability as regulatory forms within capitalism and development must be accounted for. The constitutive tension between joint liability and individual entrepreneurialism regulated many such processes of financialization.

Women who borrowed as Committees of Women Entrepreneurs took these entrepreneurial aspects very seriously. So did Fundación Paraguaya's own staff, going so far as to institute a training course in entrepreneurship for credit counselors and to encourage creative and flexible thinking in managing a loan portfolio. Likewise, Fabiana understood liability as a set of daily dilemmas that shuffled money and credit across obligations to fellow borrowers but also to kin, neighbors, business partners, borrowers, and creditors. In practice, liability also reached out to claim certain categories of NGO workers—particularly junior credit counselors working with women's borrowing groups—in the webs of obligation stitched by social collateral, down to the very real concerns for their monthly bonuses, job training, and career advancement.[41] Following the credit bicycle allows us to untether entrepreneurship and liability from progressive notions of economic betterment or downward spirals of dispossession. This book goes beyond noting the relationality of debt to characterize interdependence and independence as these multidimensional credit relationships are knitted and unraveled in practice. It is this near-constant regulation of the social unit of debt that gives microfinance its particular density, not the innate characteristics of borrowers or their economic worlds.

In point of fact, women had not historically been the primary institutional focus of Fundación Paraguaya. Up until the NGO reorganized in 2006, credit was evenly distributed between men and women, and all borrowers were eligible for an individual line of credit cosigned by a legal guarantor.[42] The change in Fundación Paraguaya's mission came in large part as a reaction to the proliferation of commercial microcredit loans in Paraguay, especially after a banking crisis shook the informal lending market in 1994. This was also part of a wider global trend of profit-driven financial institutions recognizing the success of the microcredit model and seeking to incorporate it into existing for-profit banking structures. Fundación Paraguaya explicitly moved in the opposite direction, reiterating its mission of poverty alleviation and collaborating with the Inter-American Development Bank to expand the program to poor women in Paraguay. Under the new initiative, borrowers formed Committees of Women Entrepreneurs composed of fifteen to twenty-five neighbors who jointly borrowed and were jointly responsible for loan repayment. If they repaid their loans successfully, the group was eligible to renew their loan in another cycle and borrow again at a higher level.

The now highly feminized microcredit program had a profound impact on how Fundación Paraguaya conceptualized and executed its development lending. In an annual report to a global microcredit financial accountability organization, Fundación Paraguaya recorded that at the end of the 2004 fiscal year only 48 percent of its clients were women; by the time I began fieldwork in 2009 this figure had risen dramatically, to 73.9 percent.[43] Members of committees borrowed as a group and repaid as a group, but the line of credit was divided among members of the lending group according to how far each woman had progressed through the cycles of borrowing. Women's loans also began very small—about $65—and the loan ceiling scaled up incrementally after the completion of each successful cycle of borrowing and repayment. Both individual and group-based clients were strongly encouraged to seek additional credit after successfully completing each cycle of borrowing.

The asymmetries of debt relations are of course part of a much bigger story in anthropological theories of value that seek to specify "money's capacity to turn morality into a matter of impersonal arithmetic—and by doing so, to justify things that would otherwise seem outrageous or obscene," especially the violence of a creditor who "has the means to specify numerically, exactly how much the debtor owes" (Graeber 2011: 14). However, many of these asymmetries and inequalities were not apparent from the creditor/debtor relation itself, or even the "strategic stances" that Janet Roitman has described people taking with respect to these arrangements[44] in an economic and moral spectrum of credit/debt relationships.[45] This book is about the set of arguments, dilemmas, opportunities, and pitched battles over when, how, and to what extent to relate to others through debt as it moves through people's lives and social worlds. Where creditors are also debtors and all are connected in flexible relationships that are then subject to the terms of credit, the subtler links to exclusion and inequality in microcredit emerge with the ebb and flow of debt, between the brackets of credit and repayment. What I have elsewhere called the periodization of obligation became an opportunity for people to debate anew the politics of interdependency in debt relations.[46]

Tellingly, anthropology has long ceased to be surprised by the sociality of economic life. Indeed, in making a broader point about the way ethics and virtue suffuses neoliberal Italy, Andrea Muehlbach (2012: 26) has argued that we have inherited Marcel Mauss's now axiomatic insight that "any socioeconomic order . . . was wrought out of both self-interest and generosity, calculation and obligation" but that his analysis hinged not on "a naïve romance of social reciprocity versus capitalist instrumentalism, but on an acute sensitivity toward the fact that any social and economic form cannot be classified as one or the other." The stories of microcredit borrowers as well as finance professionals make clear that it *matters* how and for whom social reciprocity takes hold in capitalist markets. As I argue, the broad consensus that money and markets are deeply social runs the risk of overlooking the uneven ways the social unit of debt is created and the value it is given. When does the dense sociality of markets become a structure of expectation that organizes economic access and exclusion?[47] With what effect? Social collateral offers a window onto how people construct and destroy those boundaries. These questions about microcredit policy, then, are at the core of questions in anthropological theories of value.

SOCIAL COLLATERAL IN UNEXPECTED PLACES

Even if the binding ties of collective debt appear to be everywhere once we know to look for them, microcredit seems uniquely able to capture and deploy the language of solidarity and joint obligation to anchor its claims about credit and repayment. One example of a competing model of social collateral is particularly telling, not just in terms of the contours of microcredit, but also in relation to what we can learn about economic interdependency within the antiregulatory liberalized commercial economy of Ciudad del Este.

During my first six months of fieldwork at the microcredit office of Ciudad del Este I spent a great deal of time chatting informally with clients as they waited for loan documents or queued to make loan payments. During one such conversation, a client named Mariela spoke enthusiastically about a new finance cooperative that she was eager to join because she had heard it promised very high rates of return. The program was called Elite Activity and immediately seemed to me to be a classic Ponzi scheme.[48] Mariela brought the issue up while we were talking about her loan from Fundación Paraguaya. She mentioned it primarily because she was trying to recruit me into her group. Each member had to invest $100 up front and within seventy-two hours received a return of $250. Echoing the rhetoric of the microcredit development NGO—in whose office space we were discussing this new finance cooperative—she characterized it as a great help to the poor, especially, she commented, now that there were so many people in need. "It is like a rotating credit association," she told me, drawing parallels to long-standing collective self-help groups, which were in many respects the inspiration and model for institutionalized microcredit,[49] and characterizing the program as a new type of community cooperative where neighbors helped one another.[50] When I asked about whether it was too good to be true, she responded that the "marvel" came out of the goodwill of the group. Like Fundación Paraguaya, there were minimal administrative barriers to joining the program.

The brief flurry around Elite Activity that bubbled up for a month in 2009 exemplifies the fact that many people in Ciudad del Este talked and thought a great deal about joint economic activity.[51] In other words, the process of activating social ties and transforming them into financial value was an undertaking that was certainly not unique to microcredit. Like the credit bicycle, the moving connections of Elite Activity were a powerful idiom and a practical mechanism for creating social collateral. Furthermore, one of the most interesting things about this scheme, in addition to its close resemblance to a microcredit solidarity group, was the debate and disagreement it sparked among Fundación Paraguaya's staff members. One credit counselor argued that it was not a scam because it was a "circle" where everybody has to pay, there are a fixed number of participants, and if they do not pay you are not guaranteed your profits. She drew parallels between Elite Activity and her own labor at the microcredit NGO, which hinged on very similar work: enrolling borrowers and managing their payments. Just as joint liability unified women's committees, the credit counselor reasoned, the circular relationships of Elite Activity were precisely what made the cooperative plausible and not a scam. In other words, she pointed to the fact that both the Elite Activity cooperative and microcredit group-based loans relied on social collateral. Another credit counselor retorted that profits of that magnitude were impossible, even in a place like Ciudad del Este where sizable returns on investment were often won through cross-border arbitrage and smuggling. What is particularly striking is the formal resemblance between Elite Activity and Fundación Paraguaya, to the extent that the bank's own functionaries were commenting on the resonance between joint obligation and a circle of borrowing in microcredit women's committees and this alternative type of cooperative. That is not to say that microcredit is a Ponzi scheme. Rather, this case once again underscores the hard social work of determining who gets to call which relationships debts. The debate about Elite Activity also highlights the coproduction of liability and entrepreneurship within those economic interdependencies.

This conversation among credit counselors and their clients at Fundación Paraguaya relied on and reproduced enduring narrative tropes about uneven access to economic windfalls made possible by commercial movement on the triple frontier. The Ponzi scheme took shape in a context of highly unstable valuation practices, where people struggled to pick good investments and took big risks on uncertain deals. To be sure, conditions of indebtedness have long interwoven social and economic life in the Alto Paraná region of Paraguay, from debt peonage linked to large-scale land tenure (*latifundios*) to binational loan agreements to erect the international Friendship Bridge (completed in 1965) spanning the Paraná River between Paraguay and Brazil. And living on credit is certainly not unique to Paraguay, as Clara Han's (2012) analysis of Chile's working-class credit has shown.[52] However, the excitement and uncertainty over different credit arrangements—from Fundación Paraguaya to Elite Activity—highlight a puzzle at the heart of this study of microcredit, and its particular local appeal in Ciudad del Este. These are highly regulated loans traversing a remarkably nonregulated commercial zone.[53]

Puerto Presidente Stroessner—renamed Ciudad del Este, or City of the East, after the ouster of the Stroessner regime in 1989—was officially founded on February 3, 1957. Currently, Ciudad del Este is surpassed only by the nation's capital city of Asunción in terms of urban population.[54] The city was at one point reputed to generate up to 60 percent of Paraguay's annual gross national product, although the figure has since fallen to under 5 percent as the agricultural boom of soy and other export commodities has eclipsed import/export economies as the engine of Paraguayan growth.[55] In any case, the statistics describing Ciudad del Este's economy are notoriously imprecise because of chronic underreporting of revenues, as both merchants and customers duck their tax burden and Brazilian buyers navigate the customs restrictions that are ever more strictly enforced by Brazilian border agents on imports from Paraguay.[56]

Customs officials estimate that about 162,000 Brazilian petty merchants work in cross-border trade, importing duty-free merchandise from Ciudad del Este and reselling it in Brazil.[57] Colloquially, they are called *sacoleiros*, or bag carriers, since their plastic satchels stuffed with goods are the visible sign of economic abstractions like national trade, commercial capitalism, or borderland arbitrage. Sometimes while I was waiting on the bridge to cross the frontier to Brazil, I would watch saco-leiros furtively dump their bags over the side of the bridge, to be collected by a river skiff or carried by the current to the opposite bank and thus avoid the import restrictions imposed by customs officials. But most sacoleiros could be seen waiting in the endless queue at the border checkpoint, expecting to register their $300 in tax-free imports[58] and return on long-haul buses to the towns in Brazil where they would sell the Paraguayan merchandise.[59] Congestion on the two-lane international Friendship Bridge can be so intractable that it might take hours to cross from one side to the other, especially during peak transit times. A local Paraguayan TV station offers a continuous live video feed of the bridge so that locals can judge when to attempt a crossing to avoid a miserable wait in traffic.

A cottage industry of transportation services has sprung up around the cross-border trade, including moto-taxis that will carry passengers and sacks of merchandise over the bridge, brazenly weaving through the traffic congestion in an effort to speed up the crossing. During recent renovations, the Brazilian border crossing included a special chutelike cement lane to expedite motorcycle traffic. Crossing is so common that there is usually no passport or ID card check for locals who pass back and forth on a regular basis, which also helps sacoleiros furtively move merchandise across the border without always paying customs duties on reentering Brazil. Microbuses and vans queue up at the foot of the bridge, their drivers clamoring for potential passengers and haggling over fares and their doors propped wide open advertising the space inside that might soon be stuffed with cargo to cross the bridge. Moneychangers with fat fanny packs full of Brazilian, Paraguayan, Argentine currency and U.S. dollars sit in small groups on lawn chairs set up in the median of the highway; passing vehicles will pull over to exchange handfuls of cash through a car window, seemingly unconcerned about the traffic congestion building up behind them. Street vendors make a good business from the captive audience of customers stuck waiting to cross the bridge, hawking beverages from ice chests, tubes of Pringle chips (and their off-brand Paraguayan equivalent), and plastic fans during the sweltering summers. The commercial engine of the city is so central that even hurriedly purchased snacks take the form of mass-market commodities—Coca-Cola and Pringles—rather than local street food, as is common elsewhere in Paraguay. This is a testament, I think, to the perceived translocal nature of the place and the expected forms of social interaction in the city.

Despite a long-standing policy of open markets, the founding and construction of Ciudad del Este did not chart a steady path of increasing market efficiencies, or the incremental incorporation of Paraguay into global economic regimes. It is important to tell the parallel story of how the minimally regulated economy of sacoleiro smugglers and cross-border moto-taxis came to be, to understand social collateral in the highly regulated world of microfinance. Talk of agency, empowerment, and entrepreneurship is so pervasive in the mission statements and goals of development organizations it became easy to lose sight of the fact that these were not simply program objectives or discursive frames,[60] at least not for many of the women who borrow from Fundación Paraguaya.[61] The story of what women do with their loans is interwoven with the hope of being buoyed by Ciudad del Este's prosperous commercial trade as well as the disappointment of deals going bust and an increasingly moribund downtown choked off by Brazilian trade regulation at the border.[62] Thus while microcredit often conjures an image of women's artisanal labor—producing handicrafts, tailoring clothes, selling local foods, or farming the land—entrepreneurship in Ciudad del Este is only rarely about investing in a single venture, as Fabiana's combined clothing, flower, and domestic labor ventures attest. More often entrepreneurialism is associated with "deal making" (*negociado*) and valued forms of investment "movement" (*movimiento*). In fact, women are especially involved in doing business in "ant contraband" (*contrabando de hormigas*), so named for the tiny trickle of smuggled goods carried across the border.[63] Unlike the masculine vocational labor of customs dispatch agents engaged in logistics and transport across the border, women thought of their work as "a little bit of everything" (*todo un poco*), including ant contraband traversing the triple frontier.

Scholarship on Paraguay has benefited from a recent flurry of new and innovative ethnographic research. Taken together, these recent contributions by a group of early-career scholars position Paraguay as a fruitful site from which to view broader trends in Latin America and globally, from studies of the state to indigeneity to neoliberal governance and regulation.[64] I join recent anthropological research in an effort to understand Paraguay's simultaneous centrality and marginality in regional and global regimes of political and economic interconnection. Moreover, my ethnographically grounded study of everyday economic life in Paraguay's infamous tri-border area offers a necessary corrective to sensationalist accounts of violence, lawlessness, and criminality in Ciudad del Este. My aim here is not to make the case for Ciudad del

Este as an exceptional context overdetermined by market reason, or what Marshal Sahlins has described as "negative reciprocity."[65] Instead, I take my lead from friends and contacts in Ciudad del Este who puzzled daily over how to make a living in the special customs zone. I found that participation in a Committee of Women Entrepreneurs was replete with many connotations of entrepreneurship and liability, which were especially thick with meaning on the triple frontier. I build outward from their stories of life in Paraguay's smuggling economy to theorize entrepreneurship and liability as mutually constituting regulatory forms.

AN ETHNOGRAPHY OF BANKS AND FINANCIAL PRACTICES

I began my first ethnographic fieldwork for this project on microfinance in Paraguay in 2006. It was a moment when consumer and housing credit in the United States appeared to be a mainstay of the economy: cheap, ubiquitous, and seemingly endless. When I returned to Paraguay for sustained fieldwork from February 2009 to August 2010, publics in the United States and Latin America were grappling with how to understand a profoundly changed global credit market. Surprisingly, even in the context of this financial turmoil—the ripples of which were being felt in Paraguay—my research was tightly structured by the humdrum daily grind of work at a small bank. In a practical sense, the credit crisis was visible to me only through the micro-crises of office work: rushing to compile credit scores and meeting daily deadlines for sending loan applications to the head office. More broadly, my perspective on banking practices came out of my own feminist commitments as part of a long tradition of scholarship on the invisibility of gendered labor as the basis for value production.[66] I build on the work of anthropologists such as Louise Lamphere's research on gender division and social reproduction in American industrial labor and Leslie Salzinger's pioneering research on the maquiladora shop floors on the U.S.-Mexico border, which reveals the complex and contingent formations of gender produced in the factories and management strategies that simultaneously create global commodities such as hospital scrubs and automobiles.[67] My ethnography of daily work at a branch office of Fundación Paraguaya's lending operation focused on finance capitalism as it was generated by the people—lenders, borrowers, community organizers, managers, lawyers, and development workers—whose paths crossed in the cool tile-floored bank offices of the NGO and the shaded patios of clients' homes. Importantly, the language of "the social" was just as important for the microfinance NGO as it was for my own conceptual tool kit in anthropology. A key element of studying banks and banking turned on my effort not to reinscribe dominant assumptions in anthropology of what constitutes the social. Staff at Fundación Paraguaya constantly challenged me to keep their lending and payment practices in view, which was how I came to see the social unit of debt as an object for manipulation and production in the labor of banks and banking.

I have Martín Burt, president and founder of Fundación Paraguaya, to thank for my unrestricted access to the NGO and especially the local branch in Ciudad del Este. My research on microfinance took me deep inside the NGO, as I was often recruited to consult on particular projects and mediate disagreements or snarl-ups across various levels of the organization. Sometimes I was complicit in those snarl-ups, as my background in development studies had largely been on the research side, and I was often quite hopeless (and hapless) when it came to program development and strategic vision. However, as Karen Ho has described in her work on management consulting and investment banking, *Liquidated: An Ethnography of Wall Street,* it was precisely my academic credentials—including, in my case, degrees from Stanford and the University of Chicago—that appealed to Fundación Paraguaya as a self-consciously international organization built out of a grassroots NGO. In fact, within the hierarchies that organize both development and finance I was eminently qualified to consult, even if I had virtually no practical experience with the nuts-and-bolts of development work. This book reflects my years of consulting work alongside the dedicated staff that made the NGO function on a daily basis. In fact, I never would have come to understand social collateral without having been captured by the microfinance world and its repertoire of obligations. My first three months of fieldwork were spent in the high-octane environment of the NGO central office in Paraguay's capital, Asunción. Martín immediately put me to work evaluating a new project that his top managers were developing to address women's poverty. From the NGO headquarters I discovered that Fundación Paraguaya is a thoroughly local organization with densely networked regional and global relationships. I found myself working alongside a group of Paraguayan technocrats trained in economics and business at Paraguayan universities and in some cases Latin American development hubs like the Comisión Económica para América Latina (CEPAL). As Kregg Hetherington has described in his remarkable work on transparency and governance in neoliberal Paraguay, this emerging group of elites makes up a cohort of "new democrats" committed to global standards of accountability and neoclassical economic reason.[68] By becoming a new democrat myself, including helping to design a survey instrument on poverty and consulting on the Committees of Women Entrepreneurs program, I gained new lines of sight on the everyday bank management and development work.

As my fieldwork moved to the Ciudad del Este branch of Fundación Paraguaya the grueling seven-hour long-haul bus ride back to the main office in Asunción came to stand in analytically for the gulf between policy work in the head office and the day-to-day labor of managing credit. Every time I braced myself for the overnight trip on Nuestra Señora de Asunción's double-decker bus fleet, I was reminded how the stark division of labor within the organization stratified the bank staff of Fundación Paraguaya. For about nine months in 2009 my daily routines followed the labor practices of NGO credit counselors and loan officers. I observed—and in many cases assisted them in—the practical work of selling loans to clients and managing their structured repayments. Concretely, this meant showing up as the office opened in the morning to observe, and occasionally mediate, the interactions between credit counselors and the groups of women that poured into the office for loan disbursals. I would often type up fieldnotes as credit counselors punched routine loan data into a standardized application and hurried to send the loan approval forms in to Asunción by the noon deadline. Afternoons were organized around "field visits" to microlending groups to negotiate loan renewals and troubleshoot problems. Throughout, I shared the triumphs and disappointments of the young women who worked as credit counselors. In many ways this book tells their story. And importantly, low-level staff were actually much more vulnerable than the women who made up their client base, especially when it came to sanction from the NGO. I have therefore taken extra measures to ensure the confidentiality of what these young women told me and what I observed at the office. In my ethnographic writing, I have recombined and renamed the accounts of different credit counselors to create a number of composite aliases. These include observations and interview data that were actually distributed across several separate individuals. I appreciate the difficulties of trading off the rich details of their life histories and unique personalities, which I came to know well during our shared time in the office. However, I balance that empirical specificity against the very real danger of disclosing information that might jeopardize their work in the financial services industry in Paraguay. During follow-up fieldwork in 2013 and 2015 I found that most have departed from Fundación Paraguaya, as they sought to leverage their professional credentials for other work in Ciudad del Este. However, they continue to maintain important connections with their former employer and with one another.[69]

During the final six months of my long-term fieldwork in 2010 I found myself pulled toward Ña Fabiana's settlement on the outskirts of Ciudad del Este and the more than five microcredit groups that blanketed the neighborhood I call Ciudad Jardín. Instead of going to the NGO office every day, I followed the daily routines of the women who worked in the neighborhood, usually out of their own homes, while their male partners left for day labor or structured employment. Through women borrowers, I also followed the workaday lives of neighbors and kin who left the settlement each day for wage labor downtown, impelled by their employment as cooks, cleaners, saleswomen, and sometimes smugglers. The many months of shadowing credit counselors had given me an opportunity to visit microcredit groups throughout the city and understand their variation along socioeconomic and spatial dimensions. My focused work with one neighborhood offered an in-depth look at what happened to a microcredit loan day in and day out.

Overwhelmingly, I found that the loan got paid. That is not to say that microcredit was a straightforward funding line for women's businesses that generate revenue streams that go toward the repayment of loans.[70] As others have persuasively argued, looking for women's business strategies can actually conceal more than it reveals, since few borrowers had a single revenue-generating activity that would be recognizable as "a business." Nor was this simply a matter of leveraging assets,[71] since I quickly found that assets were at the same time liabilities, depending on how the loan was unfolding in its life course and from whose perspective the debt was reckoned. Instead, I found endless opportunities to debate those assets and liabilities over the several months I spent with Ña Fabiana and her neighbors as they sent their children back and forth to the neighborhood shops, crossed the border to Argentina to buy cleaning supplies in bulk, and prepared local food like *chipa gazú* to sell at annual festivals. I came to realize that Ciudad Jardín was as important a context for producing Fundación Paraguaya's loans as the air-conditioned office buildings where their loan portfolios were made and managed. Importantly, Lamphere (1985: 519) has argued that the specific gender sociality of the industrial shop floor is "shaped by the historical development of an individual industry or occupation and by the ways in which management policy has responded to a particular phase in the development of capitalism." In the microfinance moment, women who borrowed were active in creating as well as contesting microcredit's social unit of debt, and thus their work in Ciudad Jardín should be thought of as continuous with the financial work of the branch office and the wider financial services industry in which Fundación Paraguaya was enmeshed.

In Ciudad del Este, the agonistic debates among lenders and borrowers about the role of microcredit social collateral in Paraguay's commercial economy help identify tensions between two processes, as they are described by both policy makers and scholars of financialization: (1) the form of microfinance is given surprising coherence and stability both as a global asset class and an object of development discourse; and (2) when we talk about financial instruments, we are naming a set of open-ended arguments about the value(s) and terms of the shared economic substances we call debt. Rather than try to engage in a hermeneutics of capitalist devices, or interrogate financial value as an epistemology, I suggest that a better method of understanding this tension between debt-as-contract and debt-as-argument is to approach debts—and especially microlending—with an eye to the politics of interdependency in which they participate. This is not just, or even primarily, about broadening the scope of anthropology of finance or anthropology of development. Instead, I suggest that the very project in economic anthropology of reembedding commercial capitalism—and all of its vexed interdependencies—in its social context risks overlooking how the seemingly obvious embeddedness of particular economic subjects is produced and how this hyper-obligation affects economic practice in the everyday. Ciudad del Este provides an exemplary case of the pervasiveness of credit politics in contemporary capitalism because these forms of social interdependency are a constitutive element of financial relations at the heart of its liberalized laissez-faire commercial markets.

PART ONE

Regulatory Forms

CHAPTER I

Entrepreneurship

My conversations with Martín almost always followed the same script. At first I thought I must be receiving a well-rehearsed narrative from Fundación Paraguaya's energetic, enthusiastic, and at times overwhelming founder and director. After encountering Martín in a variety of contexts and as he was addressing different audiences, I came to realize that the script was not really a reprise of his organization's mission statement, as I had assumed. More often it was a reflection of his personal management style. Martín has a politician's gift for clarity and organization in his exposition. Since I met him in 2006, a compact man in middle age and with the bespectacled intensity of a technocrat, Martín has always exuded stage presence, even when the platform was Fundación Paraguaya's modest offices or meeting rooms. He founded the organization in 1985 and has carefully cultivated its success ever since.

Despite Martín's relentless focus, I found myself a bit unmoored as we spoke. His talking points would routinely be cast adrift by anecdotes and asides describing projects and ideas that were happening *right now*. Over the past eight years of collaboration with him and his organization I have come to recognize this as a hallmark of Martín's highly effective management style. He said he "just got off the phone with Nigeria"— they wanted to implement his model for self-supporting agricultural schools. His friend just invited him to participate in Matt Damon's initiative on clean water. Just this morning, Fundación Paraguaya had added a new component to the microfinance program that would

Describing Martín

expand the savings requirement for its more than thirty thousand clients. His preoccupation with innovation did not just center on new policies and programs. I was assured on countless occasions that the latest software was being used, that contacts at Hewlett Packard would provide brand-new technology platforms, and that a new initiative would roll out surveys by cell phone. In his framing, cutting-edge trends in the development industry were quickly taken up and just as quickly shelved as the organization positioned itself as nimble and innovative.

The headlong gallop after new projects and ideas—one week it was microfranchising, then microinsurance, then child savings, then vision care—left Martín invigorated and his staff winded, struggling to match his furious pace. Of course, this had everything to do with the appearance of financial performance of his microcredit NGO, which resonates with Anna Tsing's (2000) study of economies of appearance, a sly double entendre for financial success coproduced with theatricality. In Fundación Paraguaya's economy of appearances, Martín was charged with representing the NGO's public face and brand. His emphasis on growth in the organization created a sense of seamlessness between the actions of microfinance borrowers and the actions of Fundación Paraguaya itself. Through Martín's management style, both were cast as businesspeople who are constantly innovating and taking risks in order to grow. At first I thought that this economy of appearances staged entrepreneurship for outsiders in the development world—including social scientists—who saw Martín and his NGO as a captivating spectacle.

It was Cynthia, a credit counselor in Ciudad del Este, who provoked me to reconsider what the concept of entrepreneurship achieved in the Fundación. In the sterile and utilitarian local branch office, furnished with plain desks and computer workstations, Cynthia was a force to be reckoned with, just like Martín in his realm. At the Ciudad del Este office, junior credit counselors overseeing huge lending portfolios to Committees of Women Entrepreneurs also dashed around the workplace, scrambling to get their loans processed and approved in time to achieve monthly goals, troubleshooting loans to hundreds of clients, and renewing microcredit groups in further cycles of borrowing. Like Martín, Cynthia energetically tackled the work of microlending. In her case, it was through the day-to-day managing of specialized development loans targeted at women. A tall and intense woman in her mid-twenties, Cynthia had left her family in rural Paraguay to move to Ciudad del Este in search of work. She was a bit of a fitness geek and spent what little personal time she had lifting weights at a local gym. Unlike other credit counselors, who played traditionally feminine games like volleyball and basketball, Cynthia was not into team sports. In fact, she had arrived in the city with virtually no contacts, connections, or prospects for employment. She was hired at the Fundación after rigorous screening—hundreds of young women applied for the position of credit counselor—and assiduously began building her loan portfolio.

For all of her self-sufficiency and the intense pleasure she took in the competitive professional environment of the Fundación, Cynthia constantly fretted about the aspects of her work that were utterly out of her control. While Martín's constant stream of ideas could almost instantly reorient the workday priorities of the organization's staff, Cynthia focused on maintaining the work she had succeeded at already, especially her client base that through great effort she had accumulated via personal relationships with over nine hundred microcredit borrowers. As I shadowed Cynthia and other credit counselors in the local branch office of the NGO in Ciudad del Este, these women constantly expressed worries over the volatility in their loan portfolios, especially groups of Committees of Women Entrepreneurs who unexpectedly fell behind in their payments or decided to leave the Fundación's microcredit program and not renew their loans for another cycle of borrowing. These upheavals in their routines had dramatic consequences for Cynthia and her coworkers. If credit counselors did not meet their portfolio goals, the young women who worked at the NGO would not receive their monthly commission bonus, which represented about a third of their income. The Fundación paid credit counselors a minimum-wage salary (about $400 a month), and the commission was talked about by both staff and managers as incentivizing employees to work hard and be creative in administering their loan portfolios. But the salary volatility meant that sometimes money was so tight at the end of the month that credit counselors were short even the loose change needed to buy biscuits and tea for breakfast at the office. On a long bus ride back to the office after an unsuccessful meeting with microcredit borrowers, concern was visible on Cynthia's face as she anxiously talked through her doubts about how she would pay the rent on her small flat while still sending money home to support her mother and siblings in rural Paraguay.

Innovation, competition, and rewarding risk were core precepts at Fundación Paraguaya. Martín's development mission was targeted at unlocking the entrepreneurial spirit of the women participating in his microlending program,[1] which he understood as a poverty alleviation venture. Cynthia enthusiastically modeled those entrepreneurial qualities in an effort to succeed professionally in the organization. In this chapter, I show that it is not just the microcredit Committees of Women Entrepreneurs—the subjects of development interventions—who were caught up in the project of entrepreneurialization that animated the development work of Fundación Paraguaya. Martín associated risk, competition, and agency with his development goals for the women he was trying to offer a path out of poverty through business financing. I suggest that in addition to being an outcome for borrowers—often with ambivalent results—entrepreneurialism was central to the labor practices of permanent staff like Cynthia and Martín.

In what follows, I track the development framework that moved entrepreneurialism from Committees of Women Entrepreneurs to unexpected sites within the organizational mission of the NGO. This was especially the case for feminized credit counselors who oversaw the loan portfolios of precisely those microcredit clients. I emphasize the multiple feminized subject positions produced through the forms of difference organized around workplace culture. Crucially, credit counselors perceived the promise of a feminine professional identity that was separate from the feminine subject position of the low-income women enrolled in their development projects. With steely determination Cynthia strained to contrast herself to her clients—women portrayed as impoverished and seeking development assistance—by cementing her professional identity as a financial manager at a bank. However, entrepreneurship gripped Fundación Paraguaya in a way that blurred precisely that key distinction between lender and borrower.

Might entrepreneurship be a new domain of pink-collar work in the financial services sector?[2] Further, do development workers and microcredit borrowers stabilize contrastive subject positions, which might proliferate multiple feminized entrepreneurial positions? Or might that distinction collapse altogether in the workplace practices that prioritize entrepreneurship across the whole field of microcredit, from clients to bankers to CEOs? Entrepreneurship as an integrative process made the whole field of microcredit seem the same, such that borrowers, staff, and CEOs were generally engaged in the same thing. This integrative process was in constant tension with the equally important forms of differentiation that stratified labor throughout the bank and among borrowers. These constitutive tensions go to the heart of the process of crediting gender that I trace across the microcredit world, all the way up to the central offices of Fundación Paraguaya and beyond. Entrepreneurship as a valuation practice at Fundación Paraguaya illustrates the way microfinance creates interdependence as well as independence.[3] As I argue, it is the constant knitting and unknitting of economic ties that gives microfinance social collateral its particular density. It is this through this wider field of relationships that I understand entrepreneurship to be a regulatory form that creates relations but also severs them.

It was precisely the cultivation of entrepreneurialism as a professional goal of Cynthia and her colleagues that enabled the NGO to reproduce itself as an institution with the aim of entrepreneurializing poor women. I examine how the gendering of class—for both microcredit Committees of Women Entrepreneurs and bank functionaries like Cynthia and Martín—was a generative force in processes of identity formation and workplace regulation. Rather than spontaneous emanations from the creative imagination, entrepreneurship as a form of economic agency was a project that took a great deal of institutional work. That work went to the heart of microcredit's crediting of gender.

SOCIAL DEVELOPMENT: "*IKATÚ*, YES WE CAN!"

Entrepreneurship transected all levels of Fundación Paraguaya's microfinance mission, from borrowers to credit counselors to NGO managers to top leadership. Martín was the intellectual center of the organization, as well as its ultimate authority concerning major institutional decisions. His office was fortified by a stern secretary, a cosmopolitan Argentine with extensive ties to the NGO world. Their suite of offices connected directly to a capacious seminar room equipped with an array of flat-panel screens for teleconferencing and presentations. In adjoining offices, the head managerial staff worked at desk stations in either private or collaborative workspaces, depending on their role at the Fundación. Managers at the Asunción head office commented wryly that they dreaded Martín's visits to their workstations because it meant that they might be immediately put to work on a new project.

During his enthusiastic enumerations of projects in development, which were taken as evidence of the Fundación's creative spirit, Martín often invoked Joseph A. Schumpeter's classic formulation of entrepreneurship as creative destruction.[4] Institutionally, this meant constant upheaval in the daily administrative tasks of permanent staff members, particularly in the top tier of elite managers working out of the head offices in Paraguay's capital city. And even more than the classic industrial models of progress invoked by Schumpeter, the office at Fundación Paraguaya seemed perfectly adapted to the information age, modeling

FIGURE 2. Ciudad del Este branch office of Fundación Paraguaya.

tech start-ups that invite top managers to "innovate or die." Their style of business was more reminiscent of the Silicon Valley tech world than the investment havens of Wall Street or Fordist assembly lines.[5]

Despite the frenetic office environment at the headquarters in Asunción, the majority of Fundación Paraguaya's day-to-day operations at its local branches mirrored the routinized administrative workings of a small bank. The bulk of the NGO's credit infrastructure was distributed across eighteen regional offices that dealt with microfinance clients on a daily basis (fig. 2). Although the managerial staff at Fundación Paraguaya's central office were the ultimate arbiter of credit, since they approved loan requests originating from lower-ranked employees scattered across the country, they did not handle the nuts and bolts of loan disbursal and repayment. Their task, as they saw it, was to provide direction for the organization and interface with international funders and organizations, giving a relatively obscure Paraguayan grassroots NGO considerable clout in global microcredit circles. The concept of entrepreneurship knit together these various administrative sites and projects, and ultimately it became the prime directive of the Fundación. Entrepreneurship organized the Fundación's overall development mission: from

Martín's litany of ideas and projects to the managerial strategies of the microcredit division manager, the development program of "entrepreneurial spirit," and the workday practices of the Fundación's lowest-ranked employees.

When I began my most extensive fieldwork with Fundación Paraguaya in February 2009, its leadership was sketching the contours of its latest initiative, a program that was later consolidated under the operational title "*Ikatú:* Sí se puede," Guarani for "It is possible," translated into Spanish more closely as "Yes we can." Martín expressed disappointment that the Obama campaign had popularized the catchphrase first. The Ikatú initiative was, Martín explained, conceptualized as a way to "turn village banks into poverty alleviation vehicles by correctly identifying the causes of poverty." This program was targeted at the microfinance clients who borrowed through the Committees of Women Entrepreneurs program and hence exemplified the seep of entrepreneurialism into every crevice of the NGO. The Fundación had been financially self-sufficient since it opened its doors in 1985, and in past years had seen spectacular growth with the addition of group-based solidarity loans to women. These social collateral solidarity loans were administered based on joint liability, where groups of fifteen to twenty-five women took out a loan collectively and became responsible for paying it back collectively. However, by citing the need to turn these microcredit solidarity loans into poverty alleviation vehicles, the president of the Fundación seemed to imply that as they were currently configured, the group-based microcredit loans were financially self-sustaining programs but were not working successfully on social development goals. In other words, despite the promise of microcredit as a development tool aimed at helping borrowers escape poverty, there was a general consensus among high-level staff that credit in and of itself was not sufficient to achieve Fundación Paraguaya's mission to alleviate poverty.

The perceived failure of "village banking"—a pared-down microcredit-based development model restricted to the provision of credit services—is caught up in a wider debate both among Fundación Paraguaya staff and in the microcredit industry globally. The question of whether microcredit, on its own, is enough to fulfill development objectives is the site of ongoing discussion. Some development experts argue that it is; they suggest further that financial success also indexes the wider social development successes of the tool. Others, especially the venerable Grameen Bank group, claim that microcredit is ineffective without ongoing social support and a suite of programs that offer training and assistance beyond the loan per se.[6] The *Ikatú* initiative signaled Fundación Paraguaya's ambivalent position between these two microcredit orthodoxies. On the one hand, financial measures of organizational self-sufficiency were a key element of Fundación Paraguaya's microcredit development model. Organizations like the World Bank's affiliate group Consultative Group to Assist the Poor (CGAP) have gained visibility and policy influence by focusing on the market finance fundamentals of "financial inclusion" development policies. The Fundación received a favorable score from the microcredit ratings agency MixMarket and has long partnered with Kiva.org, both of which take a close look at the successfulness of the NGO as a banking outfit, even as a not-for-profit organization. On the other hand, *Ikatú* and programs like it responded to the perceived failure of credit to achieve social goals fully.

One of the reasons *Ikatú* resonated so strongly with senior staff members at the Fundación was that the NGO had little direct role in what development workers term "capacity building"[7] among its borrowers. Other programs developed by the Fundación took a greater role in education and health outreach, but the regional branch offices focused almost exclusively on providing financial services. Within Latin American development organizations, capacity building (*capacitación*) is an indispensable aspect of development initiatives. Usually these take the form of workshops, training seminars, organizational meetings, inspirational retreats, and group-based work. They often culminate in some kind of certificate program. As a regional phenomenon, *capacitaciones* have been studied widely in the contexts of social movements and development NGOs in Latin America.[8] However, since credit counselors like Cynthia managed very large loan portfolios and received no direct compensation for undertaking capacitaciones with microcredit borrowers, they complained bitterly about the additional burden of leading seminars on topics like household budgeting, business plans, communication, prudent use of credit, and administering human resources. Boxes of unused training manuals and worksheets cluttered the upstairs storage space of the Ciudad del Este branch office.

One of the reasons the capacitaciones occupied a relatively marginal place within the broader framework of credit services was that the workshops had been modeled after the Fundación's Junior Achievement business program for elite high school age students in Paraguay. The sort of business training that might capture the imagination and attention of a youth living at home and attending a prestigious baccalaureate program in the national capital actually mapped unevenly onto the lived experience of many microcredit borrowers. And as a consequence, credit counselors generally treated the capacity-building workshops like just one more technical requirement for loan approval, having borrowers sign an attendance sheet along with other loan documents, whether staff members actually had time to conduct the capacitación or not. The net effect was that the mere fact of participating in the microcredit borrowing program was understood by NGO workers as virtually synonymous with training in entrepreneurship, full stop. NGO managers like Martín read the completion of incremental cycles of borrowing as progressive entrepreneurialization. The central office equated credit with business training partly because it was the only information that the Fundación kept about its borrowers and partly because entrepreneurial success was thought to be evidenced by ever greater lines of credit. Whether that was accompanied by business training was taken as incidental.

While the everyday management of credit was the central feature of workaday life at the branch offices, the organization's leadership conceptualized its lending and other programs under the wider umbrella of entrepreneurship. According to the board members of the Fundación I interviewed, entrepreneurship was the organizing principle for the three projects that made up the bulk of their development programming. The microcredit lending program dealt explicitly with microentrepreneurs; the financially self-sufficient boarding schools funded their programs through microenterprises run by students and school staff; and entrepreneurship was the basis of the Junior Achievement high school baccalaureate "business incubator" program. The central administrative office of Fundación Paraguaya, housed in the affluent Villa Morra neighborhood of Asunción, consisted of three separate buildings tucked away on a quiet residential street a few blocks from the main thoroughfare of the neighborhood. The administrative offices for the microcredit program, the rural microenterprise school, and Junior Achievement had been spaced out across the city until an organizational shakeup in 2002 restructured the NGO and brought the three different programs together on the same block and under the same mission statement of entrepreneurship. This complex of buildings became the policy and administrative cortex of the NGO and set the direction for the organization.[9]

In the flurry of activity and the constantly shifting rhetorical ground of self-assessment, project proposals, internal competitions to vet new projects, all in the relentless pursuit of the next big idea, it became very easy to lose track of the areas of life that seemed not to budge, especially the day-to-day administration of the organization. The permanent institutional personnel—225 loan officers, credit counselors, secretaries, bank tellers, and office managers across Paraguay—all saw remarkable consistency in their workaday lives. In other words, the rhythm of their labor practices stood in marked contrast to the spirit of innovation that gripped the Fundación's upper echelon. Bank work involved plenty of drudgery: filling out folder after folder of identical loan documents, printing credit histories, copying and pasting cells of client data from one spreadsheet to the next, calling clients who were behind on payments. Credit counselors and loan officers literally faced a wall as they worked at drab computer terminals completing electronic forms and transmitting their loans to higher-ups for approval. Everything seemed to point to an ossified institutional structure over which the entrepreneurial fervor was layered. The disjuncture between managerial identities and entrepreneurial drive went right to the heart of the Fundación's development mission.

ENTREPRENEURS AND ACTIVE AGENTS

Beyond the hum of activity at the NGO, entrepreneurship has much wider purchase in anthropological analyses, becoming central to critical social studies of global neoliberalization.[10] Building on historical genealogies of the self-improving economically oriented subject, scholars have chronicled the reconfigurations of work and social welfare that have called on individuals to embody risk in novel ways, especially in the context of transnational flows of capital and deepening global inequality.[11] Within the broader global ascendency of unfettered markets and the obsession with economic growth, Fundación Paraguaya's persistent return to the theme of entrepreneurialism—of which the *Ikatú* initiative was the latest iteration—might seem unsurprising. However, the social solidarities that were thought to anchor microcredit loans were often in tension with the individual drives and personal autonomy that Martín associated with entrepreneurial spirit.[12] This tension also has deep roots, particularly in Latin America. The *Ikatú* project did not, of course, spring sui generis from Martín's creative imagination. His commitment to entrepreneurial spirit was part of a long trajectory of development interventions in Latin America, especially as these were tied up with structural adjustment programs that shifted control of national development away from the state and ostensibly toward the market.[13] As I argue here, this model of connection between microentrepreneurs and the market is particularly vexed in the context of micro-credit: a development tool premised on social solidarity in microcredit groups that were held jointly liable for one another's loans as a condition of borrowing. Tellingly, in the Fundación's model of entrepreneurship, the cross-cutting obligations, affiliations, and relations that span and connect individual economic actors were recast as a site of anxiety when a single connection—of the entrepreneur to the market—was given absolute priority.[14]

As Carla Freeman (2007) has argued, unexpected tensions can emerge when globally circulating economic frameworks like entrepreneurialism collide with similar value systems that have their own cultural-historical conditions of emergence. She points to the overlap of neoliberal ideals of flexible risk-taking and self-fashioning, which shared contingent and unexpected similarities with Caribbean values of reputation. In her research on middle-class entrepreneurs, this confluence is particularly puzzling since the appeal of reputation in Barbados hinged on its subversion of colonial formations of hierarchy and respectability. She asks, What tensions might this overlap expose?

The polysemy of entrepreneurship in Paraguayan microfinance participates in similarly unexpected alignments and complexities. For instance, within global development frameworks entrepreneurship has played a central role in the widely influential United Nations Human Development Reports (UNHDR). Within this policy framework, women have been considered especially vulnerable to the coercive and constraining force of the cultural, social, political, and economic systems in which they were embedded. Liberation of women through the market as a mechanism for expanding freedom and choice became a central focus of antipoverty programs after the human development turn of the early 2000s. In fact, the conflation of "active agent" with "entrepreneur" built out of Martha Nussbaum and Amartya Sen's scholarship and policy advocacy on a Capabilities Approach to development,[15] conceived as an expansion of an individual's choice set.[16] In the UNHDRs, which sought to draw out specific metrics and measures from the philosophical liberalism of Nussbaum and Sen's research, the market was framed as the realm par excellence of action and choice. In fact, the connection was drawn explicitly, as the UN report that laid out a working definition of human development means was given the eye-catching title *The New Wealth of Nations.* As framed in the UNHDR working paper, "So human development empowers people to be responsible and innovative actors. Because human development views people *not as passive victims but as entrepreneurs and active agents,* it helps people to help themselves" (Alkire 2010; my emphasis).

By equating entrepreneur and active agent within the UN human development framework, it often seems as though these *qualities* are conceived of as agents of change in and of themselves but only once they are incarnated in an individual. However, in Paraguay the conflation of entrepreneur and active agent is talked about rather differently. In Committees of Women Entrepreneurs, individuals were often thought of as agents of change, and the qualities of entrepreneurship were descriptors of the person's activities. In fact, many women borrowers who were clients of the Fundación expressed their admiration of successful neighbors and family by commenting that they were "very active ladies" (*mujeres muy activas*). Being an active agent and being an entrepreneur in Paraguay drew on local tropes of the hustle and bustle of deal making in the commercial economy. Ña Fabiana, a microcredit borrower who split her time between selling clothes to her neighbors, cultivating houseplants, working as domestic labor, and selling catalog order cosmetics, among other enterprises, was described to me by both her neighbors and her credit counselor as "a very active lady." Like Martín and Cynthia, Fabi often seemed out of breath as she rushed from one task to the next. Her business activities (*actividades*) were embodied and enacted daily. Most recently, as digital media and cell phone–mediated Internet access has swept Paraguay, Fabi's Facebook feed showcased a nearly continuous stream of beaded sandals that she had decorated and was advertising for sale to her network of friends. I couldn't help but feel that the visual performance of the constantly updated social media bore remarkable similarity to Martín's constant stream of new project ideas. Fabiana's energy was infectious. It propelled her onward in her incessant search for new ventures. This sort of "activity" was particularly prominent in the border town of Ciudad del Este, where commerce was so central to everyday life. In fact, it had been built into the very fabric of the town.

When I began mapping out the many ways that entrepreneurship was invoked during my time at Fundación Paraguaya, I was constantly reminded of Paraguay's reputation as a commercial hub in the region. This idealization of commercial growth has deep roots in classical economic thinking, harkening back to Adam Smith's criticism of colonial trade monopolies. Smith's theory of trade policy—and especially the scorn he heaped on encumbered goods, taxes, and restrictions on colonial trade—was based on the maxim that commerce should generate the most good for the most people. Despite the fact that a certain class of merchants profit from these restrictions, he argued, "to found a great empire for the sole purpose of raising up a people of customers, may at first sight appear a project fit only for a nation of shopkeepers. It is, however, a project unfit for a nation of shopkeepers; but extremely fit for a nation whose government is influenced by shopkeepers" (Smith 2000: 780). Since Ciudad del Este is an important regional bottleneck in the contraband trade, as well as commercial exchange more generally, Paraguay has often been framed by its neighbors as precisely such a nation of shopkeepers.

Rather than consider creativity, innovation, and entrepreneurship transformative agents of change—as do the UNHDR reports—the free-market policies in Paraguay have long benefited those people who are already positioned to leverage their personal "activities." In fact, the political architect of Ciudad del Este, Edgar Ynsfrán, had commerce in mind when he began planning for Paraguay's expansion eastward from the capital city in the 1950s.[17] From the passenger seat of an old Catalina bomber making a reconnaissance flight of Alto Paraná in 1956, Ynsfrán, the regime's powerful minister of the interior recalled that the treetop-skimming vista "influenced [him] in a singular manner" to reconsider Paraguay's borders in terms of pathways that commodities take to the global market.[18] His aspirations for a new city in the east were already interwoven with a bigger story about landlocked Paraguay's place among regional economic powers, the politics of trade controlled (and often foreclosed) by the port authorities of Buenos Aires, and the possibilities of commercial development as a national project. Indeed, the Stroessner regime was already working to connect Paraguayan exports to the global economy. An international highway was slowly being cut through the 350 kilometers of dense forest between Asunción and the Brazilian border to the east, where it would connect with a highway to take exports overland to the port city of Santos on the Atlantic coast of Brazil. Returning to the site that he had seen in the overflight, Ynsfrán oversaw the inauguration of the city of Puerto Presidente Stroessner on February 3, 1957.[19]

The city was conceived of and built with Brasília—Le Corbusier's modernist planned city that became Brazil's national capital—in mind. Indeed, many of the engineers and urban planners that were recruited by Ynsfrán drew inspiration from modernist icon Oscar Niemeyer, whose projects were also being executed at that same time in Brazil. But Brasília was planned and built based on a theory of state-led economic "developmentalism" (Holston 1989: 18). Developmentalism was an extension of Brazil's national program of import substituting industrial (ISI) development and national integration that was inward looking, aimed at protecting budding national industrial sectors. For instance, the rattletrap 1970s-era VW Bug that I drove during fieldwork was built by the Brazilian auto industry as part of the ISI economic strategy. Following the development economics precepts laid out by Latin American thinkers including Raúl Prebsch of the immensely important Comisión Económica para América Latina in the 1950s and 1960s, Argentina and Brazil both erected high trade barriers in an effort to protect domestic industries and spur growth from within the nation's borders.[20] In keeping with Paraguay's long legacy of international commerce and economic liberalism, Puerto Presidente Stroessner was aimed instead at a model of economic development that prioritized free trade, commercial development, and *inter*-national integration.

The differences between these two models of development inspired planners to conceptualize these cities in remarkably different way. In Ciudad del Este, the actual work of planning, zoning, and building large tracks of the city was immediately privatized in 1960–61, and a major commercial interest took the lead in construction.[21] Large areas of that newly cleared land were quickly turned into a commercial barrio. In fact, Ynsfrán eventually brokered a deal that resulted in a sale of vast areas of the proto-city to Elías Saba, an important Paraguayan businessman. In the short term this was probably not a very remunerative venture, but later Saba's investment returned a veritable fortune. Thus the model of city planning was imagined by Paraguayan technocrats to be self-constituting *through* market speculation and real estate profits as the engine of both economic growth and urban development.

This model of development reached its peak with the 1970 approval of the Free Trade Zone, or Zona Franca, in Puerto Presidente Stroessner. The legal framework for the Zona Franca was debated in a special session of the Paraguayan Senate on Wednesday, December 16, 1970, some thirteen years after the city was founded. The region had long been a hub of cross-border smuggling, so the legislation did not create cross-border commerce de novo but rather was intended to channel and regulate flows that already existed. The crux of the debate was around who would control that trade, especially the provision that authorized the executive power to approve the contract and concession for the Zona Franca. Along with the legal framework for free trade, the Senate also gave a private conglomerate, aptly named Bussines [sic] Company SRL, the

FIGURE 3. "Parachutes over Pto. Pte. Stroessner. Invaders? No, duty-free zone."

right to operate the zone.[22] When other senators expressed doubts about the international makeup of the consortium, including partners from Brazil, Argentina, and Singapore, the bill's sponsor responded that "capital does not have nationality." Not satisfied, the opposing senators worried that foreign capital would serve as a "mode of penetration," relying on a clever turn of phrase linking licit and illicit business practices: "Esta no es una firma de *negocios* Company sino de *negociados* Company," which is loosely translated as "This is not a *business* Company but rather a [clandestine] *deal-making* Company" (my emphasis). "*Negocio*" was too close to "*negociado*" for the senator's comfort. This debate staged concerns about the people behind Ciudad del Este's commercial dynamism. Powerful interests like Bussines Company SRL and Elías Saba were considered agents of development—literally building the city from its foundations—but only because they were already well positioned to leverage their considerable political and economic clout (fig. 3).[23]

Against the UNHDR development model of entrepreneurship *as* an agent of change, the duty-free zone hinged on the powerful business interests that leveraged Paraguay's market-centered development policies. In fact, the Zona Franca could not parachute in to the region, as depicted in a political cartoon accompanying an editorial published in Paraguay's leading newspaper. Rather, it grew out of the existing distributional order of commercial capitalism in Paraguay. This was precisely because the alignment of private interests and state authority was hardly unusual under the Stroessner administration. In what Lambert and Nickson (2002: 167) call "the privatized administration of the state" in Paraguay, there were "strong historical links between the fledgling private sector and the state in this weakly industrialized country. The most powerful industrial groups in the country have all amassed their wealth via, rather than in opposition to, the state." This policy went well beyond political patronage and control of public sector enterprises. In a 1965 interview, President Stroessner went so far as to comment that military control of the growing contraband trade was "the price of peace," which suggested that "military discontent was lessened by the prospect of rich picking to be gained through officially sanctioned illicit activities" (Lambert and Nickson 1997: 25). High-ranking members of the Stroessner administration were caught up in drug and arms trafficking, as well as other commercial contraband, most famously in the Ricord Affair (1971–72), a weapons and drug scandal that implicated Stroessner's second in command, General Rodriguez. The military junta that profited from the smuggling trade backed Stroessner's usurper in a 1989 coup d'etat, which ultimately put Rodriguez in power as Stroessner's successor.

In effect, Puerto Presidente Stroessner's special customs zone gave duty-free status to an economy that was never regulated and did not impose customs duties in the first place. By formalizing the regulatory regime in Puerto Presidente Stroessner, the Paraguayan legislature gave minimal regulations to a zone that had been built and managed on an almost entirely ad hoc basis by politicos and technocrats at the Paraguayan Interior Ministry, in concert with the business interests of wealthy investors. The most remarkable thing about this legislation is that it named the city a special customs zone—that is, gave it a regulatory framework—even as the economic regulation of the city was being dismantled by the Bussiness Company SRL and other private commercial interests. The coincidence of economic regulation (through legislative decree) and dismantling of economic regulation is, I suggest, itself a theory of development. The development of commercial society is markedly different from either state-led development that seeks to generate economic growth through centrally planned economic policy or neoliberal development that hollows out those state-led development initiatives and opens them up to market forces.[24] Since Paraguay has long been a crucible of financial experimentation, economies of debt in Ciudad del Este can offer a preview of the shape that financial relations might take in ever more deregulated economies in the Americas and elsewhere.

With this colorful history of entrepreneurialism as a value system and development model as the backdrop to Martín's *Ikatú* initiative, we might well ask what is at stake in the union of "entrepreneurs and active agents" as an explicitly gendered phenomena centered on women's access to credit. It is important to keep in mind the important argument in economic anthropology that capabilities are not abstractions, separate from the people who embody them in particular moments, contexts, and locations. Explaining her concept of "sentiments as forces of production," Sylvia Yanagisako (2002: 11) has convincingly argued that "all human capacities that can be used in production, after all, also constrain and shape processes of production. As human capacities, they are not merely passive resources to be used in a neutral way for the sake of an acultural process of production. These human capacities, moreover, are constitutive of social actors themselves." For Saba and the Bussines Company, business acumen was thought of as a personal characteristic that they could harness to make profits or even to build a city and a region. By contrast, poor women's capabilities were positioned by the Fundación as the neutral ground on which culture and gender as difference could be framed rhetorically.

Martín's position at the helm of Fundación Paraguaya's project of entrepreneurialism is especially vexed because it is precisely his deft handling of leadership, innovation, and management that eclipsed the projects of women like Cynthia and Fabiana.[25] At first I sought to level the playing field and represent the competing entrepreneurialisms enabled by the NGO on somewhat equal terms. As I returned to my fieldnotes in search of women's voices and stories that could cantilever Martín's outsized place in the narrative, I realized I was going about it in exactly the wrong way. In fact, what I was describing was an asymmetrical phenomenon. On the one hand, I found Martín's appropriation of the vocabulary of Silicon Valley venture capitalism fascinating and compelling. He has maneuvered a grassroots Paraguayan NGO into a position of enviable policy importance on the national and international development scenes. On the other hand, his seemingly effortless mastery of the sort of entrepreneurialism epitomized by Ciudad del Este and the national development imperative of free and unfettered markets actually carved out a contrastive space of small-time activity for small-time women entrepreneurs. When "entrepreneurs and active agents" was inflected by the gender and class distinctions that stratify labor at the NGO, the apparent sameness of entrepreneurialism concealed important differences. By dint of being privileged as the marked site of entrepreneurialism, Martín's very success paradoxically served to silence the voices of Cynthia and Fabiana, who could not articulate their "activity" in his terms.

FINDING "GREEN WOMEN"

Martín was omnivorous in his consumption of materials that might offer ideas for new projects and approaches. His effort to be "disruptive"—in the idiom of venture capital—filled his bookshelf with a wide range of material. In both Spanish and English, the titles ranged from self-improvement manuals to business handbooks: Alcoholics Anonymous sat alongside New Age integral theory[26] and Peter Drucker's classic management theories. Hence, it might appear as though he was a bricoleur, scavenging a pastiche of ideas and philosophies to craft his development programming. However, part of what I think Martín was up to in his out-of-the-box thinking could be read through the lens of classic definitions of entrepreneurialism. Martín was in a position to take on the risk of profit or loss by innovating development ideas. A great deal of what he risked was his reputation by experimenting with unconventional management and project paradigms. His strategy was more TED Talk than financial expert, in line with microcredit 2.0 in the age of social media, design, and Web presence. Here I explore the tensions in this model of entrepreneurship, especially when it is applied to microcredit social collateral, a development context premised on distributing risk across a collective.

The *Ikatú* initiative at Fundación Paraguaya was part of this broader trend in global development, emphasizing the increasing freedom, choices, and personal agency of program participants. As the project got under way in 2009, Martín characterized the *Ikatú* development program as a "holistic approach to poverty alleviation." The holistic approach hinged on a nationwide survey instrument that Fundación Paraguaya was piloting to measure and assess the socioeconomic status of borrowers. The six poverty categories that he outlined corresponded to a large degree with the capabilities measured by the Human Development Index (HDI): (1) income and employment, (2) health and environment, (3) education and culture, (4) housing and infrastructure, (5) organization and participation, and (6) "interiorization" and self-liberation/motivation. Martín was most enthusiastic about the final category; he claimed that it was not just a tool for measurement. Instead, he thought that the survey would further the process of interiorization itself. Survey takers wouldn't just measure interiorization; taking the survey would actively promote it. To that end, he tasked a member of his staff with translating and editing an English-language version of the Alcoholics Anonymous handbook for overcoming addiction, citing it as a methodology that was proven to bring about a transformation of consciousness that and might help overcome poverty. In a sense, Martín started with the conceptualization of poverty established by the HDI but located the process of development or capability building in the tool or the index itself. And importantly, the interior qualities that Martín wanted to foster were grouped broadly under what he called "entrepreneurial spirit," which he defined as capacity for adaptation and innovation, autonomy, capacity to make decisions, self-esteem, and self-worth.

When I followed up with Martín about his sense of where entrepreneurial spirit comes from, he responded that women who were enrolled as clients of the credit cooperatives were already involved and self-selected since they had thought through the risks of joining the group, which shows that they were already motivated. "So they already have *the spirit,*" he suggested. In his reading, a particular economic orientation—seeking a line of credit—points to an interior progression that is already on a path to development. And this was the working assumption the Fundación was already making based on its capacitaciones for Committees of Women Entrepreneurs. By locating development in the interiority of individual women, Fundación staff would be able to read signs of internal progression by observing certain categories of behavior in the world—what the Fundación glossed as risk-taking behavior. As a consequence, *Ikatú* assumed that this association ran the other direction as well: internal transformation would have legible effects in the world, or rather the internal development of program participants and social development goals tied to the moral or ethical imperative of eliminating poverty were entailed in one another.

In July 2010, eighteen months after first articulating the methods and aims of the *Ikatú* project, Martín convened Fundación Paraguaya's fleet of nearly thirty summer interns—almost exclusively students from the United States and Western Europe—to discuss the progress made on the mission goal: eradication of poverty.[27] Throughout the discussion, Martín continually cited the need to, in his words, "change the culture" in order to eliminate poverty and succeed with the *Ikatú* initiative. He told the assembled NGO workers, "The culture has to change. It is really difficult to change the culture, but the culture exists." In opposition to abstract capabilities, Martín's framing—"the culture has to change"—posits a systemic and external force with an ambivalent relationship to personal agency. However, if culture is hard to change, individual transformations through awareness (à la Alcoholics Anonymous) are set up by *Ikatú* as a counterpoint that could provide a framework for changing culture laterally.

The key element of change, Martín suggested, was motivation and skills—the interior qualities that he associated with entrepreneurial spirit—which figured as capabilities that could be mapped *across* culture: "personal motivation and group motivation, and also structural motivation." In order to get at these motivations and drives, the *Ikatú* working group had crafted fifty indicators to measure poverty. Opening a spreadsheet on his computer and projecting it on a screen, he talked excitedly about the initial findings of the survey, conducted with twenty women in a handful of Committees of Women Entrepreneurs. On the spreadsheet women's names and microcredit committee information were listed in column headings at the top of the screen, while the fifty poverty indicators were listed in consecutive rows. The 12-point font projected on a screen at the front of the room was nearly impossible to read; we all leaned forward, squinting to decipher the minuscule text. The graphic was dizzying. But it was also a powerful visual tool. Martín explained, "We have made this 'traffic light' to see the map of poverty in this group." He continued, "And we've said that green is 'no poverty,' yellow is 'unsatisfactory,' and red is [drawing a finger across his throat] 'ghack.' [We have to have] a simple way to look at the problem, because if not, it will seem so complicated that we go back to income. . . . Everybody looks for an index, and this is the first."

Large patches of each color appeared in places, an apparent unity across people and along indicators. When one of the interns asked about a large block of green cells toward the top of the spreadsheet— nobody could read the text—Martín squinted at the computer screen and responded that they were credit and banking services, which were green because they were Fundación Paraguaya clients, so of course they would have access to financial services. He also explained that a large red block that shot across the columns of most women corresponded to documentation, including municipal permits for small businesses. "This strip of red [women] is the ones who do not have documents. They do not have property documents for their houses, they don't have commercial licenses from the municipality. They are informal. There is a problem with this, right? Their capacity to generate income is seriously limited because they do not have papers." It is actually not at all obvious that the red box (documentation) had anything to do with the capacity to generate income, since most microcredit clients do not invest in a single business per se but like Fabiana are involved in "actividades" more broadly, most of which required little licensing or regulation. And further, powerful entrepreneurs in Ciudad del Este made canny use of minimally documented trade to accumulate vast fortunes. It was their basis for negociados and profitmaking. Despite this, it was clear from the red band on the chart that it was a characteristic that most borrowers reported as having in common.

Instead of focusing on the similarities between women, however, what Martín found much more compelling were what he dubbed "the green ones" (las verdes): not the categories but the women who were green. He observed, "They all live in the same barrio, right? How is it that there are people in that same barrio, who are not poor, should be poor—what happened with her?" The conclusion that he drew is that they must be animated by a different spirit, have different motivation, have a different capacity for innovation. By way of explanation, he read the list of interior measures of poverty: "Capacity for adaptation and innovation, that is the entrepreneurial spirit. . . . And autonomy and capacity to make decisions. This is as important as having a roof, windows, food, refrigerator, documents, etc. . . . This is a fantastic experiment." He dubbed the green columns the "positive deviants,"[28] the women who, given their demographic and socioeconomic conditions, should be poor but are not. For Martín, these women were islands of green entrepreneurialism in a sea of poverty.

In the Ikatú stoplight, Martín was chasing after the elusive drives and motivations that animated a particular person to push past her "culture" to pull herself out of red and yellow and, against the odds, achieve green. Martín located these characteristics in the columns—in the personal biographies of the women who represented positive deviants—rather than in any of the rows of the spreadsheet, which tallied the broader social and economic conditions that contextualized her personal capabilities. In this sense, the *Ikatú* program "disrupted"—to borrow another tech world phrase—conventional forms of analysis. To read the spreadsheet horizontally, as most of the questioners including me seem to have done, is to conduct something of a protostructural or environmental analysis and track variation according to people's access to a particular social good. In fact, this was often the approach of classic development anthropology studies using Rapid Rural Appraisal methodologies and community mapping.[29] To read the spreadsheet vertically, however, is to insist on the coherence of the individual respondent's unique psychology and sociology. Indeed, in a later framing that circulated widely as part of Paraguay's national development initiative, that individuality became the centerpiece of the project. What I want to underscore here is the ways in which the interiorization of poverty naturalizes and individualizes capabilities, especially the categories that are supposed to be key skills to eliminate poverty.

The survey project was ongoing through the eighteen months of my fieldwork in Paraguay from February 2009 to August 2010 and appears to be ongoing up to the time of this writing in 2015. In the course of my trips back and forth between the central office in Asunción and the regional office where I conducted the majority of my fieldwork, I had many extended conversations with one of Fundación Paraguaya's interns, an American who had spent six months in Asunción working on the *Ikatú* project. He was the person tasked with developing the fifty indicators and participating in the very long interviews with borrowers that eventually yielded the traffic light map of poverty. He was finishing his master's degree in international studies at a university in Europe, and his internship at the Fundación would provide the case study that would form the basis of his MA thesis. He had recommended to Martín the American management theory bestseller *The Influencer: The Power to Change Anything* (Patterson 2008). The management gurus of *The Influencer* proposed the theory of positive deviance that later, along with integral theory, became a central pillar of the *Ikatú* project.

In our informal discussions, the intern summarized his sense of what the survey results had shown so far, or rather his gut feeling before any of it had been fully synthesized. Based on his interviews with *Ikatú* survey participants, he told me that the team had found that successful cases at Fundación Paraguaya were all women who had traumatic episodes in their past: they had to leave their husbands or their families because of abusive relationships or the death of their spouses or parents or children. They had lost everything and had moved to a different city, starting over from scratch. He observed that there must be some resilience in these women, an inner strength or spirit that other borrowers did not have. He concluded that confronting hardship had made them stronger and given them the consciousness, the perspective, to radically change their lives. This is, of course, part of a wider narrative trope in international development, especially development programs targeted at women.[30] Past crises are often invoked in the narrative of overcoming hardships. What was unique about the *Ikatú* intern's description of the green women was the tight link between entrepreneurship and past trauma that left them socially isolated and compelled them to start over from scratch.

In my conversations with the intern, I commented that what these positive deviants also seemed to have in common, aside from entrepreneurial spirit, were unique disentanglements from other social responsibilities. If microcredit is premised on social connections, then these women seemed to be free from those obligations and responsibilities. Their entrepreneurship followed the radical breaking of social ties. Like Martín's ability to risk everything in pursuit of innovative ideas, the borrowers who epitomized *Ikatú*'s success were also remarkably self-possessed. And if entrepreneurship is at least in part about the ability to take on risk (and profit by it), then the only women who seemed able to inhabit the ideal of entrepreneurship have a personal biography that can be mapped onto a spreadsheet column without other social duties and ties crowding in and muddying the crisp attribution of personal decisions and choices to economic effects in the world. Fundación Paraguaya's staff agreed and framed this as a narrative of personal triumph.

If, as Martín suggested, the first sign of entrepreneurial spirit can be gleaned from seeking out a group-based loan that relies on social collateral—social support and peer pressure to ensure repayment—then the final achievement of entrepreneurship was, ironically, profoundly antisocial. Indeed, there appeared to be a mismatch between the ideal of entrepreneurship developed by Fundación leadership and the institutional context in which it was attempting to unlock the entrepreneurial spirit of its clients: credit collateralized by social solidarity. For women borrowers, creative destruction meant that they were socially autonomous enough to be the unitary source of economic creativity and decision making. The tabula rasa entrepreneurial spirit, for Martín, was buried underneath layers of culture and sociality that needed to be stripped away to reveal the green women. In the final analysis, internal capabilities stood in contrast to the solidarity loan concept that framed *Ikatú* in the first place.

Debating the sort of person who might be considered entrepreneurial with the Fundación intern made me recall one of the major points of contestation among the project team. After looking down the list and listening to the concerns voiced by his team, Martín suggested that "we would have to go along calibrating the questions to get exactly what we were looking for." Running his finger along the list, he paused: "There are too many unnecessary questions. Are you single or married? is a foolish question. I want fifty questions that will be indicators of poverty. How poor are our clients really? Are these problems that can be overcome?" For managers on the project, then, relationships that might constrain personal choice seemed at best peripheral. By focusing on interior motivations, the connections that might dilute or destabilize the personal drive to innovation and success, responsibilities that might exceed individual economic decisions, and obligations that spill over to other realms of life—other rows on the poverty traffic light spreadsheet—threatened the sense of personhood that was both the starting place and the endpoint of the *Ikatú* program. Social connections were viewed as an opportunity but only when they could be instrumentalized to connect women as entrepreneurs to the market. By contrast, social connections like kinship ties could not, in Martín's view, be instrumentalized as an internal capability.

BORROWING AND BUSINESS

What did the economic "activities" of women who borrow—including the "green women" of the poverty traffic light—look like in the everyday? For microcredit borrowers living and working in the urban periphery of Ciudad del Este, the model of entrepreneurial independence articulated by Martín often mapped unevenly onto their daily dilemmas. In a context where humming commercial trade downtown made enterprise so much a part of daily life, a whole host of social relationships provided the contexts for—and constraints on—doing business in the city center. Rarely if ever were economic decisions made by an entrepreneur in pursuit of an innovative business idea. More often, small businesses worked in petty arbitrage, buying bulk commodities (packages of diapers, smuggled foodstuffs, designer jeans) and selling them locally. At other times, informal services like preparing and selling food, cultivating decorative plants, taking in laundry, selling cell phone minutes, or operating a small grocery shop were hooked into the cheap availability of manufactured products available in the downtown wholesale markets. The most successful businesses were deeply enmeshed in neighborhood and kinship networks rather than the result of the entrepreneurial spirit of independent and autonomous businesswomen. Indeed, there was a finely honed local discourse to talk about the edges and boundaries of these diffuse social connections. People frequently invoked the local term for "stranger," *persona ajena,* to draw the boundary of interdependence. Women discussed feeling out of place or on edge when visiting an unfamiliar home (*casa ajena*) or when people made free use of things that were not theirs (*no hay que tocar cosa ajena*) and judged neighbors who left familiar networks to visit others (*persona ajena*). Value transformations between social proximity—or its opposite, *persona ajena*—and economic resources were a practical way of materializing regimes of social obligation.[31]

In the face of these many economic interdependencies, microcredit borrowers strained to articulate and define the boundaries between business relationships and social obligations. I spent five months actively involved in one such neighborhood, Ciudad Jardín.[32] This neighborhood of about eighty households in an informal housing settlement also had several microcredit Committees of Women Entrepreneurs organized by Fundación Paraguaya. Social and economic obligations reached out to claim my time and attention for various neighborhood activities, from a local charity dedicated to preparing lunch for schoolchildren in the settlement to political efforts to formalize land titles to planning community festivals for major holidays. I, like many of my friends and contacts, soon found that my commitments far outstripped my ability to fulfill them. The obligations underwrote many financial debts. Moving beyond a narrow (and in her view, mis-)reading of Mauss's canonical study of gift exchange framed in terms of self-interest and reciprocity, Guyer (2012: 500) challenges us to rethink obligation "in the reflexive continuous voice of being tied and bonded in order to feel free to be remade by the animated things that circulate in the world." The cross-cutting obligations of Ciudad Jardín challenged me to retheorize obligation in precisely such a "reflexive continuous voice" while noting, too, that money might be one of the animated things that exerts such binding claims in social practice.

Doña Claudelina probably would have been categorized as a "green woman" if she were to have been enlisted in the *Ikatú* survey project. Her spacious brick house on a corner lot in Ciudad Jardín was ideally positioned for her to pursue her favorite pastime: exerting her influence in neighborhood life, from greeting passing vehicles to drawing people onto her porch to share the latest news. The terminus of the Ciudad Jardín bus line ended just in front of her home, which meant that she could supervise the comings and goings of people in the neighborhood. Despite being a fixture in neighborhood relations, however, Doña Claudelina told me that she had only moved permanently to Ciudad de Este later in life, having sold her father's orange groves in a rural Alto Paraná district on his death. A well-coiffed woman in her fifties who always wore tasteful makeup and a stylish haircut, Doña Claudelina was justifiably proud of her economic upward mobility. When I asked what she did with her microcredit loan she laughed, telling me that she had earned the right to relax after toiling in the countryside for most of her adult life. Her husband paid the biweekly loan installment from his income; she never told me what he did, a common omission for those with business dealings in the smuggling trade. She used her microcredit loan to secure a constant stream of revenue that was under her control while simultaneously ensuring that her husband's income was channeled back to the household. In the day-to-day management of her finances, Claudelina focused on keeping her group organized—something that she took extraordinary pleasure in—and managing her household affairs. She was widely respected, and even a bit feared, in her role as the treasurer of her microcredit group.

This is not to say that Doña Claudelina thought about her microcredit group in romanticized terms of collective belonging and women's solidarity or that she took on the responsibility out of magnanimity. In fact, she gave the impression of being utterly ruthless about her management role. In a mixture of Spanish and Guarani, Claudelina told me about payment problems within her group.

> Claudelina: Last time my associate[33] told me, "Do me a favor and make my payment with our [joint] group savings." I told her, "No! From the group savings, no way! You'll have to look around and bring your payment to me, and right away [because the group won't help]."
>
> CS: And did she find it?
>
> Claudelina: Yes, she found it. You have to find it, I told her, or go pawn your washing machine, or if not that, your television.
>
> CS: Could it be that she pawned her TV?
>
> Claudelina: Yes!
>
> CS: Seriously?
>
> Claudelina: Yes.
>
> CS: What did her husband say? Suppose he was in the middle of watching a soccer match . . .

Claudelina: "Why don't you [the husband] contribute, then?," is the question. That's my condition. Because we can't take it out of group savings, I won't touch even one guarani of the [group] savings. . . . You have to pay. The day the installment comes, we [the group] have to put down the money.

It is striking that Claudelina began her tale of accounting for the microcredit payment by referring to her group member as "my associate." It was common for borrowers to talk about their microcredit committees as business affiliates even when the group comprised close friends and relatives. Thus it is unsurprising that Claudelina's hard line on the group payment points to the priority of microcredit loans over other types of earmarking and claims on income, since the social unit of debt was the shared business association. As a consequence, though, the bill implicated not just her group member but also the member's household. And Claudelina made sure to draw the connection and make the material link explicit.

The entanglements of credit and debt were felt most acutely when there were shortfalls but were also at work when there were surpluses and excess income. Moments later in the interview Claudelina recounted a microcredit success story from her group. A member of her group used her $100 loan to buy an electric washing machine so that she could set up a laundry service at her home. With a lump sum of $100 her neighbor could buy the machine in cash rather than on the more expensive payment plan so that it was worth her while to use the Fundación's loan. When I asked what the woman's husband thought about her work, Claudelina laughed again and said that he had given his wife the matching clothes dryer as a gift. "He works at an ice-cream shop downtown. And now with the laundromat at his home, with the money from Fundación Paraguaya," she said, beaming.

What went unremarked in Claudelina's account (and accounting) was that the two domestic appliances arrived in her neighbor's house through complicated forms of redistribution, return, and repayment that coupled the money from the Fundación with the income from work downtown and then to a laundromat in their shared home. One circuit of repayment—the Fundación—took the form of regular weekly loan installments. The clothes dryer was a gift. But both were vulnerable to the forms of return demanded by the microcredit loan; either appliance might end up in the pawn shop if the debt intruded too far into the household. As Claudelina's unsentimental reckoning of the intractable payment system of the Fundación went to show, "The day the installment comes, we have to put down the money" or pawn precisely that appliance that anchored the family enterprise, or perhaps the gift it had inspired. Like Karl Marx's coat, which shuttled back and forth from the pawn shop in order to sustain his work and his household (Stallybrass 1998), the regular return of the Fundación's solidarity loans magnetized the circuits of obligation within the group and the neighborhood. Claudelina's role, like Martín's, was to make sure that accounting stayed in spreadsheet columns rather than rows. Part of being an entrepreneur entailed keeping a line of sight on individual women and their payment stories and thereby producing "active agents."

CREDIT COUNSELORS AS ENTREPRENEURS

In my eighteen months of fieldwork and subsequent years of intermittent contact with the management staff of the Fundación, *Ikatú* remained a mission goal of the organization. Martín's objective of unlocking the entrepreneurial spirit of the organization's microfinance clients remained a priority of the head office and the motivating force for numerous funding proposals, including a grant from USAID and another proposal to the Inter-American Development Bank. By 2014 Fundación Paraguaya reported that the traffic light project was being piloted in eighteen countries around the world. But with all of that, *Ikatú* did not immediately alter the daily management of credit undertaken by the regional offices. That is not to say, however, that the mission of entrepreneurship did not have important consequences for the Fundación's staff. Indeed, the Fundación was in many ways extraordinarily successful at enrolling young, socioeconomically disadvantaged women in its project of entrepreneurship. These young women were not the Fundación's clients but rather its employees (fig. 4). Here I tell the story of the tensions within entrepreneurship as it took hold of the bank work of Fundación staff and not just development interventions reshaping the subjectivities and livelihoods of borrowers.

Cynthia, the credit counselor I described at the beginning of this chapter, was one of several young women who administered the Fundación's loans to Committees of Women Entrepreneurs at the Ciudad del Este branch office. Being a credit counselor at Fundación Paraguaya involved managing dozens of Committees of Women Entrepreneurs, but the professional identity of branch manager (*gerente*) was reserved for their boss, who managed their labor and oversaw the loan portfolio of the office. The Ciudad del Este office itself managed a portfolio of

FIGURE 4. A credit counselor at Fundación Paraguaya working on the *Ikatú* project.

$600,000 of debt.[34] Seven out of ten clients were part of the Committees of Women Entrepreneurs program, but they represented only a quarter of the finance capital of the office, or about $150,000. The balance went to individual microloans in support of already existing small businesses, which were eligible for much larger lines of credit. In practice, this meant that the three young women who worked as credit counselors were tasked daily with negotiating loan contracts, completing lending documents, supervising debt repayment, and renewing loans for another borrowing cycle for a staggering number of women: between six hundred and nine hundred borrowers each.

Cynthia was an anomaly among her colleagues in the office. Intensely ambitious, she was rather a divisive figure; the others viewed her as selfish and instrumental in her everyday dealings with both clients and fellow staff members. Other staff members complained, for instance, that she took more than her share of printed forms and monopolized the time of the office secretary, who printed and collated credit scores and loan paperwork. The office politics bubbled up in part due to her success in the regional office. In fact, Cynthia was so effective at enrolling Committees of Women Entrepreneurs that she won the NGO-wide competition for best credit counselor and was ultimately promoted to the rank of loan officer in the Ciudad del Este office.

Professionalization within the organization tacitly recognized the career limits of administering credit solely to women. In other words, the professional identities of credit counselors were always marked by gendered social collateral, with the tacit acknowledgment that they were working on a specialized development product rather than being regular bank workers. Because of this, credit counselors sought ways to professionalize themselves further and move up in the office hierarchy. Cynthia and her colleagues were involved in specialized training programs aimed at fomenting their entrepreneurial acumen. In one telling instance, the Cisco Entrepreneur Institute WebEx online training program offered credit counselors modules in small business management. Paradoxically, their professional labor, their clients' businesses, their own loan portfolios, and the mission goals of the NGO all orbited around the concept of entrepreneurship, which threatened to cut across and collapse those categories. Such was especially the case because the Cisco WebEx program was vicarious entrepreneurship training that offered credit counselors training in management science. Credit counselors were not business owners or investors themselves but rather managed the loans of clients who were. What is more, the training itself closely resembled the capacity building workshops aimed at microcredit clients under the rubric of development programing, which further troubled the status of the professionalization training. Entrepreneurship itself chafed against the professional possibilities of a managerial position.

One might imagine that the stable, salaried labor position at an NGO would mean Fundación Paraguaya staff members were quite the opposite of creative risk takers and business innovators. However, the Committees of Women Entrepreneurs were in practice the locus of constant adaptation and innovation. In fact, it was Cynthia who excelled at creatively adjusting to changing market conditions, shifting risks, and intense competition. As Cynthia constantly scrambled to recruit new microcredit clients and reenlist existing clients in higher cycles of borrowing, she seemed to exhibit precisely the entrepreneurial spirit that Martín was searching for in his traffic light of poverty. However, the resemblance between credit counselors and their clients made the professional identities of Cynthia and her colleagues particularly tenuous, especially when credit counselors were called on to use their own social skills, peer pressure, and personal relationships—hallmarks of microcredit social collateral—to manage their loan portfolios. In practice, this meant that credit counselors were sociologically indistinguishable from the successful green women who were their microcredit clients and were thought of by the NGO's directors as needing development aid. Both credit counselors and their borrowers lived in the same periurban neighborhoods, rode the same buses to the city center, had attended the same public schools, and were intimately connected to local neighborhoods. For NGO staff such as Cynthia, upwardly mobile professional opportunities hinged almost entirely on their status as employees working on financial instruments.

One afternoon I shadowed Cynthia and another credit counselor, Ana, to a meeting with the treasurer of one of Fundación Paraguaya's Committees of Women Entrepreneurs. Expecting a routine discussion about loan documents and payment cycles, I was surprised to find lunch waiting for us, and a table covered with scraps of brightly colored fabric and spools of thread. Ana and Cynthia explained to me that their client decorated the insulated thermoses that were popular accessories in Paraguay, used by many people to serve tereré.[35] The microcredit borrower covered the generic plastic coolers with vinyl fabric and colorful stitching and sold the custom-colored thermoses to neighbors and friends. Cynthia and Ana wanted to learn how to make them themselves, and had arranged for their client to give them a lesson. In a surprising reversal, the credit counselors got a lesson in entrepreneurship from their own client as we spent an afternoon with sticky hands from gluing fabric and sore fingers from sewing the heavy material. Cynthia and Ana did not pay their neighbor for her time, nor did they buy one of her tereré thermoses as a template for future craft projects. They did, however, discuss the costs of investing in bulk supplies of coolers and fabric, strategies to sell the product through vendors in street stalls downtown, and the profit margin in making handicrafts. The borrower offered to arrange another meeting to teach Cynthia and Ana how to make the decorative beaded sandals that she also sold. The feminized work of financial management comingled with the feminized work of handicrafts as we sat around the table.

This training was a side arrangement negotiated by Ana and Cynthia. It reveals the double bind[36] of credit counselors who had so much in common with their clients that they might actually learn from them while also being tasked with exerting authority over them in their role as financial professionals. This is a double bind in the sense that efforts to manage their loans by establishing distance meant that credit counselors could not draw on the very social resources they relied on for their job. On the other side, efforts to manage their loans by establishing proximity jeopardized their professional superiority and authority when dealing with their clients. This double bind was evident in NGO-led training seminars as well. It was especially visible on the several occasions the regional staff of the Fundadción was summoned to the central office for professional development. In the training seminars run by the microcredit central office in Asunción, the NGO's directors sought to clarify for low-level staff what the organization imagined its mission to be and the place of loan officers and credit counselors in that mission. The general manager of microfinance observed that Paraguay had been getting humanitarian gifts of aid and charity for twenty years, and, laughing ruefully, he observed, "Look where it's gotten us." He countered that microcredit was not humanitarian aid or charity but "developing a tool." To clarify his point, he noted, "Credit is a double-edged sword. If you give too much, you have repercussions, so you [credit counselors] are in charge of figuring that out." Far from being a problem, though, the general manager determined that the dangers of credit were actually part of the solution, part of the task of promoting the spirit of entrepreneurship that differentiated microcredit from gifts or charity. Much like the human development thinking discussed earlier, Fundación Paraguaya's employees were working on a slippery object: not entirely on microcredit clients, or fully a portfolio, but a model of entrepreneurial potential.

The general manager would not let the Fundación employees leave with the impression that the double-edged sword of credit had repercussions only for borrowers. To the credit counselors, he declared that the Fundación was a company that valued its employees: "It didn't run through them 'ta ta ta ta [ticking off a rotation of employees].'" Smiling, he told them:

> We feel a great responsibility towards you. But the only thing that could endanger that is late payment [*morosidad*] in your portfolio. And that really is what we are demanding. And lots of precautions with the loans that you approve. Before, we were knocking on doors to try to round up clients. Now we knock on double the number of doors and reject half of them.

In other words, he outlined two different levels of responsibility. The responsibility that the Fundación felt to its employees was mediated by the ability of those employees to pin responsibility successfully on their own clients. In declaring that preventing default was "really what we are demanding," the Fundación also implicated an important double meaning of the Spanish term *demandar* (demand): (1) a demand that its employees model a certain orientation toward risk and (2) the juridico-legal contractual and legal demands against defaulting debtors that would act out that model.

The slippage around responsibility was felt deeply in the Cisco WebEx Virtual Business Training. Put simply, WebEx was an online platform that instructed users on the fundamentals of running a small business. Martín was linked into trendy international social entrepreneurship circuits as the highly visible face and spokesman of the organization. However, Paraguay's relative obscurity with respect to emerging financial technologies meant that Martín's networking at big microfinance conferences where he was enlisted into Cisco's broader aims of entrepreneurship were only translated with difficulty down the line to his staff. Since Internet training reduced costs (something Cisco advertises on its website), the virtual training meant that tools like cash flow reports, financing options, and marketing strategies were presented in online modules, and the user was tested on her mastery of the concepts before moving on to the next level, all remotely, via the Web portal.

WebEx was not only remarkable for its perceptible mismatch between the sums lent to Committees of Women Entrepreneurs—starting at $65, repaid over three months—and the suggested business strategies recommended by the training module. Like the capacitación training that was supposed to go along with credit access, the Cisco business training program was clearly pitched at a different model of enterprise from the microenterprises funded through solidarity loans, businesses like taking in laundry and selling decorative thermoses. Fundación Paraguaya's group-based loans were unlikely to provide viable financing for businesses that made use of, for instance, square-footage calculations to determine the size of a storefront when the business was run out of the borrower's living room. Beyond the technical side of the training, the program was also remarkable for training the NGO's *employees* in small business management and entrepreneurship. And perhaps most important, only a subset of the Fundación's functionaries was required to complete the training. The program was mandatory for the credit counselors who oversaw Committees of Women Entrepreneurs but not for the loan officers whose clients were already small business owners and might have found the training helpful. Why would the Fundación require credit counselors to complete the Cisco Entrepreneurship course?

Cynthia and her fellow credit counselors stayed late at the office for almost two weeks to complete their Cisco training, clicking through the online course and answering questions about business capitalization, optimal levels of insurance for a small business, advertising strategies, accounting, accessing a line of credit, evaluating market share, and so on. Many of these questions were difficult and highly technical, especially for the group of us, with almost no business experience, huddled around the computer terminal. The Cisco Website advertises the following: "Virtual training also helped attendees feel more connected to one another in unexpected ways. When you're in a session with people from Dubai and South Africa and Chile, you really feel like you're part of a virtual UN of entrepreneurial learning."[37] As we hunched together around the computer screen, we felt a great deal of camaraderie but with one another rather than with a virtual network extending around the globe. Unexpectedly, the WebEx training worked to provincialize and particularize our experience of entrepreneurship rather than widen and connect it. The credit counselors talked about the Cisco training as a valuable capacitación opportunity, much like the rhetoric about individual capabilities that was constantly employed in reference to the development mission of the NGO. Since credit counselors did not run businesses themselves but rather gave loans to women who putatively ran businesses, the training did not put them in contact with a large and vital human network of fellow entrepreneurs. Instead, it figured as a personal credentialing opportunity.

The importance of entrepreneurship from top to bottom in the organization was something taken so much for granted that it could go without saying that credit counselors would benefit from an online tutorial on small business management. Credit counselors were called on to model the risks of credit through their own workaday precariousness and also to act out that model through the management of their portfolios. Entrepreneurialism became the organizing principle of both their object of management (Committees of Women Entrepreneurs and their loans) and their own professional identities. Finally, their upward mobility toward a managerial identity was through the path of entrepreneurship, laid out by the WebEx business training platform.

MANAGING ENTREPRENEURIAL SPIRIT, FEMINIZING LABOR

I want to highlight the importance of social collateral in the working out of an entrepreneurial managerial identity. Looking at this from another perspective, the imbrication of credit counselors and their clients by the WebEx training program puts in relief the economic interdependencies that regulate and sustain both managers and their clients. Importantly, entrepreneurialism creates a double bind for credit counselors who might fail to differentiate themselves sufficiently from their clients. The dynamic of entrepreneurialism laid out by the Fundación's general manager suggested that it was entrepreneurship all the way down: the organizing principle of the employment conditions of credit counselors, the financial tools that they administered, and the borrowing of Committees of Women Entrepreneurs as clients. This meant that credit counselors had to strain to cement their identities as professionals in contrast to their clients, since neither entrepreneurship nor capacity building on its own served as criteria for differentiation.

The category of client as an object of management, however, itself was not straightforward, because credit counselors were always faced with the dilemma of managing microcredit social collateral as a financial object. The Cisco WebEx training exemplified the complex ways borrowers' businesses were absorbed into social collateral. The Fundación's credit counselors expressed high hopes for their Cisco training; they talked about it in terms of professional credentialing and a path to success within the office and the organization. In practice, however, the Cisco capacity building workshop began and ended with the training. Since the credit counselors did not themselves run businesses, there was nothing to manage beyond demonstrating entrepreneurial capacity via the online tutorial, which disappeared into the mysterious depths of the Internet once it was completed successfully.

Within the Fundación's development mission, *Ikatú* highlighted the tension between individual entrepreneurs figured as green women and entrepreneurship brought to bear by women like Claudelina who drew together women who lived in the same communities and borrowed together as a group. This same tension appears in social collateral—the mutual obligations and distributed liabilities that create relationships that go beyond any particular microentrepreneur. And again, this tension was evident in the Fundación's entrepreneurialization of its staff. Credit counselors often expressed frustration bordering on exasperation when their clients chronically called them in to negotiate and administer the cross-cutting social and business ties that shot through their committees. However, they also thought of their clients' business networks as a resource they could learn from. Their feminized labor and hypersociality mirrored the social bonds that anchored microcredit social collateral. In fact, the Cisco WebEx training placed credit counselors in the thick of that social collateral as they tried to step in to advise on and direct the businesses of their clients. If a Fundación Paraguaya employee were to assist Claudelina in collecting unpaid microfinance payments, and thus help her group stay solvent, then the line between lender and borrower in social collateral would seem quite tenuous indeed. Or if the client who made tereré thermoses enlisted the credit counselors as saleswomen for her products the boundary of professional difference might disappear altogether.

Of the several credit counselors in the office, Cynthia was the only one who stabilized an entrepreneurial identity and also successfully avoided mirroring the qualities of social collateral through her professional labor. She managed this feat by carving out an unusual space for herself within the feminized hierarchy of labor within the NGO. Cynthia's financial practices—especially their gender dimensions—were both as disruptive and as innovative as Martín's in his realm. Her colleagues often grumbled that she was too hard on her clients and that she was imperious and exacting in her interactions with borrowing groups. She was also the target of unceasing office gossip, since she would accept the offers of moto or car rides from male loan officers in order to expedite her field visits to clients rather than take the bus or ride with Lourdes, the only female loan officer, and keep her company during her daily excursions. In other words, Cynthia's professional work sat uneasily with the appropriate femininity of credit counselors. Her success in the office—culminating in her promotion to loan officer only a year and a half after beginning work with the Fundación—reveals the glass ceiling for credit counselors marked by their labor on and through gendered sociality. Cynthia, like the green women, performed an entrepreneurial identity that was not overdetermined by gender or culture. She exemplified Martín's positive deviants.

As entrepreneurship linked the project of microfinance from borrowers all the way up to CEOs, the *managers* were the central office team that defined the mission of the Fundación—entrepreneurship—and then used it as a tool to manage people and things at all levels of the organizational hierarchy (credit counselors, credit, clients, social collateral). The work of managing their employees was to make them into managers as a social category through Cisco and other professional training, but since this too was organized around the concept of entrepreneurship, it threatened to collapse back into the general project and cross-cutting social ties of development, as it has been effectively entrepreneurialized. It is not incidental, I think, that the point of tension in this story is the Committee of Women Entrepreneurs within the development framework of the Fundación. Martín was never in danger of being mistaken as the object of development interventions. Rather, entrepreneurship had been stratified into management, on the one hand, and pink-collar financial services, on the other.

As a consequence of the crediting of gender in microfinance, the risks and rewards of entrepreneurship were asymmetrically distributed across the development framework of the Fundación. Further, crafting credit counselors as entrepreneurs through their labor conditions and through the vicarious management training of the Cisco WebEx modules enabled the NGO to reproduce itself as an institution with entrepreneurship as its central mission. The gendering of class—especially the feminization of capabilities and capacity building—was key to the Fundación's vision of growth and innovation. Credit counselors and their clients in women's committees were both thought to develop through capabilities training, while Martín's entrepreneurialism was located outside of the development framework entirely. This should alert us to the fact that the forms of difference crystallized in the workplace proliferate a multiplicity of feminine subject positions. However, the overarching model of entrepreneurship collapsed those multiple feminine subject positions and reiterated the dominant framing of women's choices and freedoms as the target for development. Upwardly mobile pink-collar professionals and microcredit borrowers came to resemble each other too closely, unless an entrepreneurial independence was drawn into relief by maintaining a line of sight on entrepreneurs as active agents. Put another way, the entrepreneurial spirit animating the NGO reproduced the gendered dimensions of class difference across microcredit as a regulatory field, from clients to staff to organization leadership to global development thinking.

CHAPTER 2

Liability

As Easter Holy Week approached, time seemed to be running out for several of the Committees of Women Entrepreneurs with loans from Fundación Paraguaya. I was talking over the impending holiday break with Letizia—or Leti, as colleagues and clients knew her—one of the junior credit counselors. We were riding the rickety city bus out to visit groups that she referred to as "problem committees." This one was based in the adjoining city of Puerto Franco. This committee was facing a difficult loan renewal, and Leti had arranged a meeting in their neighborhood to discuss the issues facing the group. It took over an hour for the bus to make its way through the nine kilometers of congested streets to the semirural neighborhood perched on the lip of the Monday River. As we rode the bus, Leti emphasized that it was a hectic time at the microcredit office; many groups were trying to pay down their current loans and borrow for another cycle right before the Easter festivals. For her this meant long days traveling throughout the city and meeting with clients. As she renewed dozens of microcredit loans in her portfolio Leti seemed willing to think the best of her groups' entrepreneurialism, commenting that women wanted money to stock their small stores and buy ingredients to prepare traditional Paraguayan biscuits to sell during the holiday. She also conceded that many people simply wanted money in their pockets during Easter. The small loans from Fundación Paraguaya were well suited to that aim also.

This chapter is about conditions of liability at the heart of micro-credit social collateral. Being liable is, broadly speaking, about being bound and obliged.[1] Being bound and being freed by debt were two interlinked forms of economic agency produced by these group loans.[2] This section tracks the ways entrepreneurship and liability came to cohere as linked regulatory forms that create both independence and interdependence. On the banks of the Monday River, in a context where financialization of economic life has deep roots and a long history, it is instructive to think about entrepreneurship and liability not simply as processes that homogenize women's experience of the market. I begin with the story of one of Letizia's problem committees because their loan exemplifies both the possibilities and perils of mutual indebtedness, especially as it takes shape in formal financial arrangements like micro-finance. Importantly, I turn to liability here because it is an extension of the conditions of entrepreneurship that are so central to Fundación Paraguaya's lending program. The urgency of Letizia's committee, so eager to renew their loan before the Easter holiday, points to the ways entrepreneurship and liability are brought together in women's group-based microcredit lending and its particular economy of gender. Successful commercial ventures, which were the daily focus of almost everyone in the tri-border area, entailed seeking and managing debt. Together, entrepreneurship and liability went to the heart of value production in Ciudad del Este. I tell the story of liability by illustrating how the process of crediting gender through social collateral regulates the boundaries of debt but also and importantly the temptation to convert debt relationships into something else entirely.

The loans overseen by Leti did not simply replicate inequalities of rank and socioeconomic class that preexisted the collective debt borne by women in Puerto Franco. In many instances, joint liability offered an opportunity to debate anew the justice of this distributional order. The tensions between (1) lateral liability (among neighbors, kin, lender, and borrowers), especially as it was collectivized, and (2) vertical mobility (as business savvy and entrepreneurial success) also offered a vocabulary to talk about the social and economic inequalities that rippled through the communities touched by Fundación Paraguaya's solidarity lending. Focusing on troubles that beset the borrowing group on the eve of completing their payments shows us the inescapable reality that even these collective debts hardly advantage everyone, and not with equal effects.

Letizia's group in the Puerto Franco neighborhood was attempting to close out the current loan cycle and start a new one even though they were still one payment behind and were also mending rifts within the group. Eight of the existing members wanted to pay off their final installments, leave the group, and walk away from the committee. As we arrived at the meeting, Leti noted that it was unclear whether the group would have the compulsory ten existing members from the previous round of borrowing, and which would be necessary to keep the committee together in the next cycle. In practice, the fluid movement of women in and out of the group meant that the borrowing committee was rarely identical from one cycle to the next, though it retained the same name—Kuña Amistad, which means "Women's Friendship" in Paraguayan Jopará[3]—and accrued a personal borrowing history with the Fundación over the cycles of uninterrupted payment. The constant flux of borrowers helped me understand why, given the widespread availability of small loans in Ciudad del Este's commercial economy, women would participate in these microcredit projects. Women's enthusiasm for the loans was especially puzzling in light of the fact that the administrative burden of social collateral was far more onerous than comparable borrowing at finance companies, even if the terms of credit were broadly similar. Regular meetings interrupted women's daily routines, gossip and rumors picked apart the relationships that women had built with their neighbors, and group decisions added a further level of difficulty to already stressful financial decisions. However, moments like the loan renewal for Kuña Amistad dramatize the way many types of loans—and not just microcredit—cohere and fall apart over and over again. Around Easter time people were scrambling to initiate, renew, and call in a whole constellation of debts, of which Fundación Paraguaya's financing was a part.[4] Just as borrowers valued movement in the commercial economy of Ciudad del Este, so too did they bicycle their debts. In broader terms, the movement of credit in Ciudad del Este are continuous with the circulatory metaphors of financial liquidity that, as Kath Weston (2013) has argued, have become a master trope in discussions of markets. By tracking the historical roots of circulation in Western political economy, Weston explores how "a politics of blood can underwrite a diagnostic regime that is dedicated to ensuring an economy's 'health,' in ways that end up promoting certain economic policies and interventions over others" (S28). In Ciudad del Este, movement certainly operates as a barometer of wealth, measuring everything from opportunities for profits in the clandestine circulation of smuggling and petty arbitrage to the patterned movements of money in and out of personal pocketbooks. By looking at liability—binding and obligating claims from the past that shoulder their way into the present—we can see the objects and relations that are held fixed and immobile in order to set others free to circulate, a miniaturized instance of Annette Weiner's (1992) classic study of inalienable wealth.[5] The movements of people and debts in and out of groups like Kuña Amistad can show us how the fixity of liability also, surprisingly, creates value through mobility. Like the credit bicycle, mobility was often talked about as turnover and cadence as the pedals went around and around, which for microcredit groups banking on social collateral meant spinning to stay still.

Kuña Amistad had gathered together many of the women who lived in a cluster of houses in the quiet street of hard-packed red clay, a few dozen meters away from the main road bisecting Puerto Franco. As we sat on the patio in front of the small house belonging to the president of the women's committee, Leti fielded questions from the group members, attempting to untangle the intentions, conflicts, and anxieties of the fifteen women who had borrowed a loan together. The president of the group was the most vocal about her interest in keeping the group together. She repeated several times that she really enjoyed working in these sorts of community organizations and was involved in other neighborhood associations as well. "I want to work, I want to commit myself," she said, looking around at her fellow group members. Her expression of liability[6] was the organizing principle of the meeting. But despite her profession of friendship and group solidarity, which was the committee's namesake after all, Kuña Amistad's continuing existence was in serious doubt. The major issue, as the president explained it to her group, was that many of the women who were leaving the committee had decided to use their savings from the collective account to pay off some of their last weekly installment quotas, though many still owed additional money for late payments as well. The savings of the group were almost entirely depleted. In normal circumstances this would be alarming but not catastrophic, since the Fundación's requirement that the committee produce an account statement certifying that they had accumulated 10 percent of their loan amount in savings over the course of the cycle was met with all sorts of pragmatic work-arounds to demonstrate the financial solvency of the group. But with so many old members leaving and new members joining with no savings at all, even those well-honed practices of creative accounting might not prove sufficient to meet the 10 percent savings requirement.

Setting aside the savings question for the moment, Leti turned the attention of the assembled women to the records of the previous cycle; the group was also plagued by lateness, or *atraso,* in their weekly loan payments. The binding ties of liability were not simply about being stuck. They also implied a backsliding mobility of sinking farther and father behind. The term *atraso* is a technical accounting phrase meaning "arrears" but is also commonly used to describe delays, being held up, or falling behind. Our delayed arrival after waiting for the Puerto Franco bus was colloquially described as "atraso" as well. The Fundación had a strict policy with respect to punctual payment, and if the committee was even a day late in any of their fourteen weekly installments, the line of credit in the next cycle would be kept at the same level rather than scaled up. Groups strained to coordinate their financial lives so as to complete their collective payments on time. Leti complained to these women that she still did not have even a single borrowing group in her lending port-folio that had scaled up to borrow $200 because of late payments. All of these groups, Leti suggested, were losing the cycle, since they were stuck at the same amount without advancing. The president of Kuña Amistad assured her credit counselor that they wanted to advance, but Leti brushed aside her good intentions and stated peremptorily, "Payday is important." Frowning slightly at the women bunched together on the patio, she told the group that if they were really investing in something productive and starting their own business then they should not have any trouble making the weekly payments. Tacitly attributing the atraso to unproductive spending, she scolded the group: "The money is to work, it's not to pay off your bills. But since that did not happen, the group responded with the savings." In her framing, the two issues were linked, as they both pointed to the group's disregard for the future of Kuña Amistad. Neither the atraso nor the indifference to the savings require-ments would have immediate financial consequences, but both put doubt on the medium-term future viability of the group as it confronted impor-tant life cycle events like the end of a borrowing cycle.

As Leti teased apart the payment issues of the group, it increasingly became clear that the atraso was not incidental but related to tensions within the committee; those tensions in turn directly affected the day-to-day solvency of Kuña Amistad as well as the recurring payday issue. One reason the group was keen to undertake another round of borrow-ing was that the president and treasurer wanted to treat the new loan cycle as a sort of reset button for the relational space of the committee. Even if they were stuck at the same amount, the new cycle—conceived in technical financial terms as a loan renewal—could advance in another sense, as the new loan offered the opportunity for interpersonal renewal, leaving behind the past cycle. As the president put it, "What is done is done" (*Lo pasó ya pasó*). The weight of past cycles and past troubles encumbered the group, where one of debt's remainders across transactions[7] was the cumulative affective burden of being stuck and losing cycles through atraso. And that past was not easy to leave behind, since it was bound up with the financial past tense of being in arrears and made itself felt with the lateness of managing the accounting quandaries.

After Leti diagnosed the group's issues, the conversation lulled. Taking advantage of the assembly of neighbors, the gathered women shared gossip about one particularly loathsome neighbor. The woman, rumor had it, had reneged on her payment and then left the neighborhood altogether, abruptly moving to another city in Paraguay. At the same time, the president of the committee ducked inside her house and returned with a heaping platter of empanadas and sandwiches, announcing that she had made from her "little business" and wanted to contribute them to Kuña Amistad. Apparently, investing in the group took many different forms. Given the toxic interpersonal relations within the group, the empanadas seemed to me like a necessary expenditure for maintaining the social collateral that underlies liability's cohesion of entrepreneurship. Moving around the gathering and passing out the steaming empanadas, she told Leti that the group meetings had become less and less frequent because of the constant fighting with the woman who had defaulted and left and that there came a point when nobody wanted to have anything to do with anybody else because of issues with the collective money. Mistrust about the collective management of the group's payments, including covering the outstanding payments of the woman who had fled the neighborhood, meant that many women were reluctant to leave their money in the group savings account, which further attenuated the guarantees that were supposed to hold the group together and make it solvent. Leti reminded the president that if nobody came to meetings, then nobody knew what was happening with the group, implying that they could not make judgments about its solvency or continuing financial viability. Taking a seat with her own empanada, the president retorted that their meetings were pointless: "All I heard was that the money was short, and that's where the dispute started."

As the meeting wrapped up and women began to walk to their nearby homes, a consensus emerged around the idea that they would pay their last installment at the beginning of the coming week and determine where to go from there. They would probably not be able to start a new cycle of borrowing before the Easter bank holiday. They even floated the idea of dissolving Kuña Amistad and assembling an entirely new group, quite literally starting over from scratch. Several weeks later I found the president and treasurer at the office conferring with Letizia. The renewal of their committee had indeed meant putting an end to the existing group and seeking a fresh start with new membership and a new name. The issue of being in arrears was resolved by refinancing the loan and coming all the way back to the beginning. The group savings, which had served as a powerful unifying force within the group, was spent to pay off the arrears. Intractable atraso meant that Kuña Amistad not only remained stuck at the same loan ceiling and did not advance to a new cycle but also lost the accumulated social bonds of social collateral cultivated over iterated rounds of collective borrowing. However, coming back to the beginning would allow the group to shed the unpleasant remainders of past debts, especially the disagreements and mistrust that plagued the group.

One striking feature of the renewal was the way Kuña Amistad held together liability and forgiveness in the same frame as it grappled with the challenges of renewing its loan. Renewing the loan for another round of collective borrowing meant treating the past as "what is done is done." If debt is seen by economic anthropologists a "commitment to the remainder as an agent of ongoing relationality rather than an object for appropriation and alienation through exchange,"(Chu 2010: 168), then some remainders, it would seem, jeopardized future debt *and* relationships as the basis for value production. With these remainders in mind, and taking my lead from the women entangled in long-term collective borrowing, I read liability against the grain of the presumed calendar time and the abstractions of debt.[8] For groups like Kuña Amistad, the intrusion of time, including atraso, was not an exception to the rule of orderly repayment. The argument that quantification and abstraction are important—and exploitative—features of financial debt builds out of the insight that debt disciplines time, and hence people's lives, through regular quantified repayment (Graeber 2011). What is so strikingly apparent from the difficult renewal for Kuña Amistad is that debt service routinely came into step and fell out of step with the day of payment. Importantly, it was not as though other nonmarket relationships intruded on the structured repayment of their financialized and abstracted debt-based liability. Aspects of the debt itself—the affective weight of atraso, the intrusion of past cycles into the present, the evaporation of collective savings—intervened in the calendar time of debt service.

DEBT IN MODERN TIMES, PARAGUAYAN MODERNS

From the intimate debts of Kuña Amistad, it is tempting to locate the politics of joint liability in the small-time financial practices of micro-credit economies. And since Leti's story was populated entirely by women, it is also tempting to equate intimacy with the feminized spaces of domestic economies. One might imagine that the challenges of coming into and out of synch with payment regimes are issues that plague relations among neighbors and all the thick ties they entail. From the cluster of houses on the banks of the Monday River, the affective weight of atraso felt especially debilitating when everybody had a personal relationship with the neighbor who had reneged on her share of the loan and disappeared from the neighborhood, and enjoyed the committee president's homemade empanadas. Joint liability was hypervisible in Kuña Amistad: it was materialized in the footpaths that connected people's houses, the single bus line linking the neighborhood to the city's commercial downtown, and the circle of lawn chairs drawn together to host group meetings. It is instructive, then, to track very similar processes at work in organizations and institutions beyond Fundación Paraguaya and the neighborhoods where it placed its loans. Here I tell the story of joint liability in Paraguay as it emerged during the first moments of economic liberalization in the late nineteenth century. The politics of collective debt at that juncture set the stage for a series of experiments with unencumbered trade and export-oriented development that continue to echo in Paraguay today, including in microcredit development projects. The politics of debt goes to the heart of the conditions of Paraguayan modernity.

Rather than think of microcredit as a new player on the financial scene—a narrative that international development holds great stake in—I suggest that there are important connections to broader regimes of liability in Paraguay and globally. Sovereign debt was one such regime of collective liability. The first time I heard the story of Paraguay's entanglement with sovereign debt was as a student of Eduardo Galeano's widely influential treatise that became a central intellectual pillar of the Latin American political left, *Open Veins of Latin America* (1973). His account—which has been a touchstone for activists and political thinkers in the hemisphere since its publication—equated debt with imperialism and exploitation. Foreign capital markets quite literally opened the economic veins of Latin America and bled the continent of resources and wealth, and ultimately undermined self-determination. Paraguay's despoliation at the hands of British finance capital was Galeano's most emphatic example.[9] However, excavating the liabilities created by Paraguay's sovereign borrowing can take us well beyond simply casting debt as exploitation, in much the same way as the borrowing by Kuña Amistad created liabilities that went beyond turning women's relational value into financial value. Looking through the lens of collective debt, we can gain new insights into the politics of interdependency encoded even in seemingly abstract and homogenized international capital markets: interdependencies that Galeano eclipsed in his polemic against foreign capital. The dilemmas surrounding fixity and mobility debated by Kuña Amistad—and which ultimately led to the dissolution of the group—resonate strongly with Paraguay's struggle to build collectivity through debt-based liabilities. The stakes of that project could not have been higher, since debt was undertaken in order to buttress particular national futures at a moment when those futures were in crisis.

The story of Paraguay's first encounter with international capital markets came, as so many political and economic processes in Paraguay did, in the aftermath of the devastating War of the Triple Alliance (1864–70).[10] Reeling from the defeat of the Lopez political dynasty, which had governed Paraguay for much of the postindependence decades (1844–70), the last remnants of the Paraguayan military surrendered unconditionally to the allied forces of Brazil, Argentina, and Uruguay. The conflict's toll on Paraguay was staggering. Historical demographers estimate that 60 to 69 percent of the prewar population perished by the time an emergency census was conducted by the Provisional Government in 1871.[11] What is more, women came to outnumber men four to one, with far-reaching consequences for the distribution of labor, land, and wealth, as well as social reproduction and political identity of Paraguayans in the aftermath of the conflict.

In November 1871, just eighteen months after the war, Paraguay once again made an almost improbable return in foreign affairs. At the same moment that the Provisional Government was desperately trying to take stock of the survivors and negotiating the terms of surrender with Brazilian occupying forces, a loan prospectus circulated half a world away within England's financial community. The prospectus, like countless other subscription notices ranging from loans sought by the Austro-Hungarian Empire to the state of Mississippi, circulated in

London's financial scene and advertised shares of an 8 percent Public Works Loan of the Republic of Paraguay. The prospectus noted that Paraguay was unable to raise the desired £1 million on domestic capital markets in the wake of the War of the Triple Alliance and subsequent peace negotiations. Paraguayan officials (unspecified in the advertisement for the loan) contracted the venerable London financial firm of Messrs Robinson, Fleming & Co. to seek subscriptions for the bonds on the Exchange, the center of gravity for such financial operations in the nineteenth century. The following year, Messrs Robinson, Fleming & Co. placed an additional Paraguayan loan on the London Exchange. Since independence from Spanish colonial rule in 1811, this was Paraguay's first sovereign borrowing on international markets, since all other state projects had been undertaken with domestic borrowing. In fact, that edenic economic narrative of a land untainted by foreign capital was key to Galeano's story of Paraguay's fall from financial grace. Combined, the loans accounted for the entirety of Paraguay's foreign debt.

After negotiating the terms of borrowing and placing the bonds with the British financial public, Paraguay began making quarterly payments to bondholders in London. In an era when, as the historian Mary Poovey has described, the financial system of Victorian England was hypersystematic but only diffusely institutional, the news of Paraguay's quarterly debt service was advertised in newspapers like the *Financier* of London. These notices would invite investors with bonds whose serial numbers matched those that had been drawn for payment to present their coupons to Paraguay's representatives in London. Poovey, in her research on the forms of knowledge that emerged in Europe during the Enlightenment, emphasizes the systematicity of nineteenth-century British finance. She observes, "At the institutional level, nineteenth-century finance functioned as a *system*. By this I mean that no single institution or group of institutions worked in isolation from others. Taken as a whole, the purpose of the system was to make capital available for purchasing goods, pursuing trade, or otherwise developing economic opportunities" (Poovey 2003: 1–2). The systematic debt service for Paraguay's Public Works Loans of 1871–72 hinged on the contingent alignment of certain institutions within that system, from Messrs Robinson, Fleming & Co. to the *Financier* to the boatload of specie traversing the Atlantic Ocean.

All was well for about two years, until in 1874 there was an abrupt break in the list of coupon payments published in the *Financier*. This was not uncommon at the time, especially considering that the 1870s marked an especially turbulent period for the global economy, and not just in Paraguay or even Latin America. Many such loans entered into default or were even repudiated entirely by debtor nations.[12] For the Paraguayan loan, a short article notifying readers that Paraguay had not sent the necessary funds to its financial representatives in London to make its May 1874 coupon payment accompanied the break in coupon payments listed in London. The *Financier* characterized the situation as "disastrous but not unexpected."[13] In the outpouring of newspaper coverage on Paraguay's default in the spring of 1874, the broad consensus among investors was that, like all defaulting nations, Paraguay's failure to meet financial obligations pointed to moral blights, spendthrift habits, and wanton laziness.[14] Indeed, as noted by an article in the *Financier* in December 1874, shortly after the notice of default, "What Paraguay is now doing, is drawing her closer and closer to that class of past borrowers whose financial career has become synonymous with all that is financially disreputable."[15] Within Britain's financial community, the notices chronicling successful debt service recalled a series of financial decisions that could categorize a country as either a solvent and fiscally responsible "class of past borrowers" or a scurrilous class of "financially disreputable" defaulters. With a failure to service its sovereign debt, the moral reputation of Paraguay as a nation was called into question. Importantly, the question of what counted as economic news was inextricably linked to whom, precisely, counted as the borrowers of the Paraguayan loans of 1871–72. To what extent did collective political goals have bearing on collective economic responsibilities? Broadly speaking, coupon payments that recorded debt service—and were readily identifiable as financial instruments—were immediately recognizable to bondholders in Britain. By contrast, the political conditions that made debt service possible—including a ruinous war, reconstruction efforts, widespread disease and famine after the war, and the redrawing of territorial boundaries—remained largely invisible and did not register as events in the financial chronicle. Those political conditions were broadly excluded from the abstracted system of financial interconnection that was coalescing in London and spiraling outward to commercial centers around the world.

The political grounds for financial decisions were particularly important in the context of the credit politics of sovereign borrowing. At stake in Paraguay's default was the process of accounting for whom, exactly, was obligated to service the national debts. The question is not spurious, since financial reporting at the time cast doubt on precisely this question. For example, an article in the *Daily Recorder* that appeared during settlement negotiations in 1874 suggested:

> There is no Paraguay as a nation. The men, even the horses, are all dead. They fell fighting for a shadow, the independence of their country, as represented by Lopez, a cruel tyrant, their President. But they died bravely, and left the lands fertile, cultivated, and harvest-bearing to any one who would come and occupy them. That is what the Paraguayan Loan was raised for, and it was raised and paid over to the Government, but what has been done with it? That is the question this Commissioner and this Minister Plenipotentiary [as representative of Paraguay's Interim Government] have to answer to the British public.[16]

The reporting in the British financial media discussed the political situation of Paraguay as though it were entirely incidental to its economic prospects in the future. If the country had been depopulated by a hugely traumatic war that left only the resources afforded by the landscape, then that absence, according to this line of reasoning, posed no particular obstacle to economic development per se. Indeed, the forms of continuity and rupture envisioned by this account emphasized a continuity of economic obligation precisely because of discontinuities in political obligation. The article imagined a continuity of economic resources— fecund land that might be "fertile, cultivated, and harvest-bearing"— even in the absence of human effort: it pictured a country reduced to its stock of commodified resources. While the Paraguayan minister plenipotentiary had been invested with the full power to represent his government, it would seem as though, by this account at least, he spoke for a nation of ghosts. Indeed, this economic imperialism supports dependency theory accounts of English capital as it "deformed" Paraguay,[17] as popularized in Galeano's account of Latin America's open veins.

However, this narrative also throws up a series of questions about the political conditions of borrowing and repayment, beyond a straightforward account of British financial hegemony. If there were indeed no Paraguay as a nation as reported in the *Daily Recorder,* to whom was the Paraguayan loan paid? Who could have possibly authorized a Public Works loan for such sizable sums? And who is called to account to answer to the British public? The forms of accountability encoded in the British financial media emphasized the contractual debts drawn up between Paraguayan officials (via their representatives in London) as tangible proof of economic liability while simultaneously concealing the political obligations and commitments that made those contracts possible in the first place and the role of British bondholders in facilitating that—strictly financial—accounting. But the accountability of Paraguay for the Public Works loan also calls to mind the cyclicality of debt, which is palpable in the small scales of microcredit economies like Kuña Amistad but can recede from view in the wider financial world. In addition to abstracting an icon of Paraguay, and extracting value from it on the international bond market, the Public Works loan, like collective debt elsewhere, materialized an economic community. The seemingly apolitical—and certainly exploitative—financial machinations of Messrs Robinson, Fleming & Co. also created contexts where Paraguayan national unity could be staged. This could not have been more important, since Paraguayan territory was at the same time being dismantled and claimed by Argentina and Brazil.

Tellingly, the next prospectus that appeared in the London financial scene exemplified a full accounting of Paraguay's economic obligations and profit-making opportunities while also following a parallel logic to that of Kuña Amistad, "what is done is done." The prospectus advertised shares in "The River Plate Land and Trading Company, Limited." The company sought to raise £500,000 with the purpose "Of purchasing and Working the extensive Estates, with the properties thereon and therein, lately belonging to Lopez, the deceased President of Paraguay, with all concessions, privileges, and rights belonging thereto."[18] This was not sovereign debt contracted by Paraguay, like the Public Works loan of 1871–72. Instead, this was a venture organized by British capitalists seeking investment opportunities abroad. The nature of the venture itself only hinted obliquely at the way in which the opportunity to purchase these extensive estates arose. The prospectus noted, "The conclusion of the war with the fall of the Lopez Dynasty has now for the first time opened this country to foreign enterprise; and its enormous internal resources which enabled it to maintain entire commercial independence, (its exports being double its imports) and sustain long and ruinous wars, present to the Capitalist rare prospects and advantages seldom equaled and certainly never surpassed by those of any other country."[19]

The capacity to wage war figured as a sign of the "enormous internal resources" at Paraguay's disposal but without an analysis of the violent expropriation that brought those lands into the investment portfolio of a capitalist willing to take advantage of the "rare prospects." Indeed, the prospectus did not name the vendors of the estate;[20] although the documents noted that the Lopez dynasty had fallen, the political status of Paraguayan authority over those lands was not submitted to rigorous investigation. While the prospectus might be viewed as an event in the economic time line of Paraguay's financial obligations, the political history—especially questions of sovereignty and territorial integrity—of Paraguay did not undergo the same rigorous accounting.[21] Thus the economic chronology brackets questions of national sovereignty and territorial integrity in favor of a capacious account of financial transactions. Resolving the default meant that in practice multiple cross-cutting liabilities were being debated simultaneously on the British financial scene.

In 1875, just four years after the first Public Works loan had been floated and subsequently defaulted on by Paraguay, a British parliamentary commission was charged with investigating loans issued under suspicious circumstances, including the Paraguayan debt. The cunning of financial reckoning revealed by the Parliamentary Commission was that the completeness of accounting at work in regimenting Paraguay's debt service (or lack thereof) was entirely at odds with the fluctuations and disjuncture that structured London's lending market. Collective obligation and individual gain framed even the seemingly technical accounting practices of the London Exchange. The British parliamentary investigation revealed that much of the problem with these loans—boondoggles for British investors and now regarded as worthless paper—was that trades on the Exchange were not squared until special settling days on which all accounts were reconciled and gains and losses tallied and compared. The *Financier* of London published a full transcript of the hearings on bond trading. In direct questioning, Mr. Fleming (of Messrs Robinson, Fleming & Co) admitted, "It is impossible to tell until the day of the settlement what the result of the 'bear' [seller] operations will be."[22] These settlement days invariably revealed massive speculation, insolvency, and patent misinformation disseminated by a variety of interested parties (banking houses, investors, etc.). The full accounting and accountability that structured Paraguayan financial liability was emphatically *not* how debt was managed in and on the Exchange.

Mr. Fleming continued his explication of the Paraguayan loan, noting that his firm bought back a great deal of the stock "to counteract the operations of the 'bears' [sellers]—to prevent the loan being depreciated by lax speculative sales." When asked if "in short, the buying back was to inspire the public with the same confidence that you yourselves entertained," Mr. Fleming replied, "Not exactly no. It was done to counteract the influences of speculative sales. We should not have issued the loan had we not had confidence in it. The difference between 64 and the issue price [85] was to cover expenses." Put another way, "the difference between 64 and the issue price of 85" was the difference between the price at which Mr. Fleming's firm bought the junk bonds and the original issue price that the public paid. Cover expenses or generate staggering profits? Here the continuous and uninterrupted contractual obligations that figured so centrally in Paraguay's financial woes provided room for short-term speculative sales, colloquially known as stock-jobbing. By playing on the erratic rhythm of the market, Messrs Robinson, Fleming & Co. exploited the gap between competing ways of reckoning liability, which provided a space for massive profits and a hefty commission at the expense of the debtor nation and the bondholding public. Mr. Fleming reported that the firm issued the bonds at a price of £85 but bought them back at £64 themselves, and in turn Paraguay was responsible for amortizing the face value of £100 when the bonds were drawn for debt service. In other words, the profits of Messrs Robinson, Fleming & Co. derived from their capacity to identify spaces where obligation was unclear or asymmetrical. Indeed, Mr. Fleming was decidedly vague on the level of confidence the Paraguayan loan inspired in his firm, discussing it instead in terms of the financial techniques deployed by his firm. Their profits emerged, in other words, from the private appropriation and alienation of collective obligation.

However, Paraguay's entanglement with the Public Works loan of 1871–72 did not end with the parliamentary investigation revealing pervasive fraud, profiteering, and inveterate speculation. Despite widespread condemnation of Messrs Robinson, Fleming & Co. and their fellow financial firms for their handling of these and similar loans, there was a general consensus that the bonds still should be regarded as valid and valuable. The obligation persisted, and Paraguay was barred from further borrowing on British capital markets until the debt was resolved.[23] Provisional resolutions for debt restructuring were discussed in the late 1870s, most of which centered on consolidating and refinancing the existing loans in tandem with ceding land in Paraguay to British bondholders to indemnify them for unpaid interest. The final deal, undertaken through a Paraguay Conversion Loan, was issued on the London Exchange in 1885. The debt conversion featured large land transfers to British interests in conjunction with sovereign debt restructuring, as the 1871 loan was reissued as new 1885 bonds with accompanying land titles.[24] Through the conversion loan, Paraguayan economic ministers paved the way for future borrowing on international capital markets.

One keen irony of these land warrants was that Messrs Robinson, Fleming & Co. had initially advertised the 1871 bonds with greatly exaggerated—and by most accounts falsified—notices of colonization schemes by groups of Lincolnshire farmers, who had taken their modern British farming techniques to settle in remote Paraguay.[25] These bonds were a disaster not only for Paraguay but also for the settlers who enlisted in this scheme and set sail for Asunción. In truth, rather than agricultural experts from prosperous and modern Lincolnshire farms, the unhappy settlers were drawn from the urban poor of industrial England with the promise of an easy life in the bountiful Paraguayan countryside. When seeking recompense for their misfortune—in the end, the colonists perished in droves from disease, exposure, and hunger—the so-called Lincolnshire Farmers found no help forthcoming from the financial companies in London that had popularized the settlement schemes. When they actually set out to occupy the land they had been issued through these exotic financial instruments, they came to ruin. Paraguayan financial history is a surprising vantage point, then, from which to observe the contingent ways collective obligation was asymmetrically distributed throughout the financial system, bringing high-flying bondholders in London together with the urban poor of Manchester through their investment in Paraguayan land warrants. This came about precisely because the bonds had been written in such a way as to avoid being subject to Paraguayan authority. In fact, the Paraguay Land Company, Limited, which was formed in 1889, noted that the "debenture stock" was secured by trustees of the company "but not registered in Paraguay in such a way as to interfere with the sales of Land by the Company" (fig. 5).[26]

The pragmatic result of the debt restructuring was that vast tracks of Paraguayan territory—already diminished by Argentine and Brazilian claims after the war—became the property of British financial speculators.[27] Most of these land warrants were later resold on Argentine commodities markets, since, after the disastrous Lincolnshire venture, the land titles were of little material value to British bondholders. Thus after negotiations on conversion of the Public Works debt were finalized, the *South American Journal,* a publication on Latin American affairs, concluded, "The Paraguayans received no benefit whatever from this loan, but consented to pay it off because their credit was pledged. Unfortunately more than one country is in the code of not having benefited by loans contracted for them."[28] Credit, in other words, generated forms of liability that were reckoned on the field of international relations; meanwhile, the financial accounting practices of the British Exchange excluded politics even when they relied precisely on those

PARAGUAY LAND COMPANY,

LIMITED

Incorporated under the Companies Acts, 1862 to 1886.

Capital £120,000, in 24,000 Shares of £5 each.

To be issued in Exchange for Land Warrants of the Government of Paraguay, at the rate of
2 fully-paid Shares for each £100 Warrant, or 10 fully-paid Shares per £500 Warrant.

5 per cent. Debenture Stock, £60,000, issued at 90 ,

IS NOW OFFERED FOR PUBLIC SUBSCRIPTION, PAYABLE AS FOLLOWS:

On Application :	£10	per £100 Debenture Stock
On Allotment :	£20	"	"
On 1st January, 1889 :	£30	"	"
On 1st July, 1890 :	£30	"	"
	£90	"	"

Applications will be received for Stock in sums of £5 and multiples thereof. Instalments may be
paid up in full on Allotment, or on the 1st January, 1889, and will carry Interest from dates of
payment. The return to the Investor on the issue price is £5 11s. per cent. per annum.
The Debenture Stock will be secured by Debentures or other Securities in favour of Trustees,
having a floating charge over the whole of the property and undertaking of the Company, but not
registered in Paraguay in such a way as to interfere with the sales of Land by the Company, and will
be redeemable at par by drawings or otherwise, and in whole or part, at the option of the Company, on
six months' notice at any time in or after the year 1908. Interest payable half-yearly on 1st January
and 1st July, in each year; first payment 1st January, 1889. Power is reserved to increase the amount
of Debenture Stock ranking with the present issue up to a maximum sum equal to One Shilling and
Sixpence per acre of the whole of the Company's lands.

Trustees for Debenture Stockholders.

THE RIGHT HON. EDWARD PLEYDELL BOUVERIE
THE RIGHT HON. SIR EDWARD THORNTON, G.C.B.

Directors.

THE RIGHT HON. SIR EDWARD THORNTON, G.C.B., Eaton Square, S.W., *Chairman.*
CHRISTOPHER JAMES, ESQ., Consul-General for Paraguay.
LIEUT.-GEN. SIR J. LUTHER VAUGHAN, K.C.B. } *Members of the Paraguay*
E. ZUCCANI, ESQ. } *Land Warrant Committee.*
C. P. OGILVIE, ESQ., Director of the CENTRAL ARGENTINE LAND COMPANY, LIMITED.

Consulting Engineer.

HENRY V. F. VALPY, ESQ., M.I.C.E., Special Commissioner for Designation of the Lands Allotted.

Solicitors.

MESSRS. TRAVERS SMITH & BRAITHWAITE, 25, Throgmorton Street, E.C.

Bankers.

MESSRS. ROBARTS, LUBBOCK & COMPANY, 15, Lombard Street, E.C.

Secretary (*pro tem.*) & Temporary Offices.

H. L. WHITE, ESQ., 17, Moorgate Street, London, E.C.

FIGURE 5. Paraguay Land Company, Limited 1889; To be issued for Land Warrants of
the Government of Paraguay, at the rate of 2 fully-paid Shares for each £100 Warrant.

political processes—that is, the expropriation of Lopez's land, the exploitation of Britain's urban poor, the impunity of Messrs Robinson, Fleming & Co—to generate financial value. However, paying the loan in any case signaled that Paraguay honored its pledges, even if it ultimately received no benefit. Indeed, a statement from the *Buenos Ayres Standard* perhaps best captures the asymmetrical forms of accounting underwriting Paraguay's credit politics:

> The theory that a bond never dies has been fully borne out by the notice [of payment] which we [publish with this article], and the history of the Paraguayan debt which is too long for us now to repeat. Suffice it to say that these Paraguayan bonds which but a few years ago were hardly worth the paper on which they were printed, are now a quotable security on the London stock exchange, and as appears by the notice referred to which we cut from the Times, the coupon which fell due on the first of the present year has been paid, and land warrants for the back interest handed to the bondholders.[29]

"The theory that a bond never dies" was borne out by the continuities in seemingly apolitical financial obligation, which relied on and reproduced credit politics as a power-laden field with frankly unfair and disastrous results for those such as Paraguayan public officials dealing with the London financial community.

One consequence of Paraguay's complex history of debt and repayment in the nineteenth century was that vast areas of the nation came to be controlled by foreign interests as indemnification for the interest arrears on Paraguay's late nineteenth-century borrowing. This was a core argument of Galeano and the basis for dependency theories of development that became a key intellectual movement in the hemisphere.[30] The observation that a bond never dies was all too true, especially when these were converted to other instruments, with even longer shelf lives. However, those longer shelf lives, I suggest, are precisely what trouble the story of imperialism that has become a cornerstone of antidebt movements that take Paraguay as a poster child. The association representing the bondholders who received land warrants as compensation for overdue interest ultimately, in 1888, incorporated into the Paraguay Land Company. They charged the board of the company with overseeing and administering the land in faraway Paraguay in the name of British financial speculators with little interest in developing the territories that they now putatively owned.[31] By looking through the lens of collective liability, we can see that the trend to economic liberalization that the Paraguayan political scientist Diego Abente

Brun (1989: 86) has called "the wholesale dilapidation of the national patrimony in the 1880s" actually moved in tandem with the centrality of a reinvigorated Paraguayan state in negotiating, converting, refinancing, and administering its foreign debts during this same time. In other words, the presence of the Paraguayan nation on the London Exchange as a member of a morally reputable class of sovereign borrowers was linked to the contingent result of ceding political control over large areas of its national territory. Sovereign borrowing internationally and foreign control of Paraguayan socioeconomic conditions domestically actually worked hand-in-glove. But like Kuña Amistad, which sought to renew a cycle of borrowing in order to shed its troubled past as "what is done is done," Paraguay's debt refinancing hinged on one crucial thing: Paraguay too could move on while maintaining the collective bonds and cross-guarantees of its national social collateral.

Casting our view forward over a century, we can still appreciate how the boundaries of collective politics continue to grip Paraguayan borrowing to this day. On June 22, 2012, Paraguay's first opposition party president, Fernando Lugo, was impeached in an extremely controversial congressional political judgment (*juicio político*). By December of that year, the interim president, Federico Franco, had brokered a deal to place $500 million in Paraguayan sovereign bonds on the New York Stock Exchange. President Franco had risen to power through Paraguay's free-market-oriented Liberal Party and had been part of a coalition that brought the more left-leaning Lugo, a former bishop in the Catholic Church and longtime social activist, to the presidency in 2008. When asked about the new sovereign debt by Paraguay's leading national newspaper, Franco commented, "This demonstrates that Paraguay is serious."[32] These serious bonds came on the heels of prior borrowing that was dogged by controversy. The most recent foreign debt was contracted in 1999 in the wake of a massive banking sector failure in Paraguay. The issue of bonds, which totaled $400 million, was intended to indemnify Paraguayans who had savings accounts that were wiped out by bank failures, widely linked to clandestine bank ledgers even in the country's largest financial institutions. The foreign debt came to be called Chinese Credit (*crédito chino*) in the Paraguayan press because a conglomerate of Taiwanese banks largely held the Paraguayan treasury bonds. However, the Chinese Credit ended in scandal, since the $400 million was funneled off by state officials before ever reaching the individual account holders affected by the financial crisis.[33] By contrast, the serious bonds contracted by the interim government of

Franco can be thought of on two levels. First, they are a counterpoint to the Chinese Credit and even the Paraguayan Public Works loan of 1871–72, which combined collective liability with private appropriation of national resources. Second, they are serious in the way that microcredit joint liability is serious about regenerating economic collectivities and refinancing loans beyond scandals ranging from political impeachment, to stock-jobbing, to troubles with atraso.

LIABILITY AND THEFT

The peculiarities of Victorian finance might seem quite distinct from the conditions of indebtedness experienced by microcredit borrowers today. However, Paraguay's entanglement with Messrs Robinson, Fleming, & Co. should alert us to the fact that liability is a regulatory form with complex effects. I return to those effects here. In fact, the delicate work of synch up collective payments for groups like Kuña Amistad—and the risk those payments might go sideways if a member absconds, somebody gets sick, or the neighborhood floods—has clear parallels with the syncopated payment rhythms of stock jobbers and speculators that organized debt on the London Exchange. The enabling consequences of keeping it together—renewing the microcredit group and renewing the Paraguayan Public Works loan—also show us that liability tells a nuanced story of economic agency by offering the opportunity for movement as well as fixity.

It was not merely the risk that group relationships might break down that threatened the repayment of loans for microcredit committees borrowing from Fundación Paraguaya today. One economic process that was subtended in Kuña Amistad's difficult loan renewal was the financial liability built into a whole host of economic instruments beyond the microcredit loan itself. Collective savings were one of the contractual requirements for borrowing, and Kuña Amistad was certainly not the only microcredit group pushed and pulled in multiple directions by overlapping claims to those resources. So much so, in fact, that the group had to dissolve and reintegrate in order to reconcile those financial obligations. These ancillary requirements were only tenuously related to the contractual relation of credit and repayment: written in the contract but not related to structured debt service. Like fees charged for financial services—recalling the fees charged by London financial firms to handle bond subscriptions—loan requirements like group savings as collateral live in an ambiguous relation to putatively self-animating and efficient markets.[34] For instance, Maurer traces the overlooked place of bank fees back to Adam Smith's *Wealth of Nations*:

> Interchange has no place in classic or critical accounts of modern political economy. In the *Wealth of Nations*, Adam Smith briefly mentions fees charged by the city of Amsterdam at Amsterdam banks for opening accounts, transferring funds and other services. He noted that the amounts collected through such fees had become considerable, but that this was essentially an "accidental" revenue stream which, though profitable, was incidental to the main operations of the bank itself. The levying of such fees, he wrote, was supposed to serve the interests of "public utility," to help facilitate clearance and settlement for the bankers. This was, we note, revenue that accrued to the public coffer, not the bank. (2012: 27)

As Maurer deftly shows, the revenue streams from these regulatory infrastructures are no longer incidental. They are an important part of what makes markets work in day-to-day practice, as well as a very lucrative profit-making engine for those who control them. For group loans in Paraguay, the "accidental" value created by economic interchanges that seem to simply facilitate normal day-to-day bank labor intersects in surprising ways with the liabilities produced by indebtedness. As I track here, these "accidental revenue streams" were caught up in the very lending processes that cemented joint liability. What is more, focusing on the specific liabilities that took shape through social collateral can shed light on the gendered dimensions of that "accidental revenue."

It had been three years since I had last seen Letizia. In follow-up fieldwork I found that she was no longer working as a credit counselor at Fundación Paraguaya, and I had contacted her in an effort to learn about the lives and loans of her clients, especially groups like Kuña Amistad that I had grown to know well over the course of my long-term fieldwork in Ciudad del Este. Leti pulled up in a diminutive Toyota hatchback, smiling widely and talking excitedly as she dragged me quickly inside the pastry shop where we had agreed to meet. But as we tackled our pieces of cake, her smile faded. She looked around nervously and leaned in close, dropping her voice as we spoke. The story she was about to tell me was a sad one, full of loneliness, regret, and bitter recriminations. I am going to spend a moment with Leti's narrative here since it lays bare some of the accidental value at the heart of microcredit liability, to recall Maurer's framing. What is more, those accidental revenues were actually patterned on putatively nonfinancial relations—especially relations of kinship—but reconfigured in powerful ways by microfinance liabilities. While social collateral has been thought to extract value from the social relationships of borrowers, Leti's story shows us how debt-based liability becomes complicit in the processes of kinning,[35] as well as de-kinning. In other words, social collateral actively reshapes how women create and sustain family ties. Also, social collateral spotlights how their families call on them to channel and redistribute their money within a broader political economy of sexual systems (Rubin 1975).[36] As with borrowers in Kuña Amistad, credit counselors like Letizia found themselves implicated in the shifting collective liabilities of social collateral.

Since Letizia worked for Fundación Paraguaya as a credit counselor her story shows not only how microfinance banks on the neighborly and familial obligations of the poor as subjects of development. As she told it, the trouble began when she started working closely with Graciela, one of her colleagues at Fundación Paraguaya, where they both had been employed for about four years. Graciela had been a credit counselor at a different office of Fundación Paraguaya and had been promoted to loan officer. She had moved to Ciudad del Este to oversee commercial loans for individual clients. Her new position offered bigger commissions from bigger loans. In Letizia's framing, Graciela had cooked up a scheme to appropriate money from Leti's clients, women who borrowed group-based loans and were understood to be beneficiaries of antipoverty development aid. Letizia had not only agreed, but in fact had taken an active hand in organizing the fraud.

Leti and Graciela's scheme turned on a peculiarity of Paraguayan banking law, which prohibited nonprofit organizations from holding their clients' money as savings or collateral. The women's microcredit loans presented a conundrum, since the NGO had built in a savings requirement as part of its mission of financial literacy and women's empowerment. And perhaps more pragmatically, the savings were a sort of de facto collateral that could be seized by women in the borrowing group if any one member were to fall behind in her payments. Thus while Fundación Paraguaya had no official collateral requirements and washed its hands of having to deal with the messy task of seizing assets from defaulting clients, the joint savings account created a very useful context (i.e., a pot of collective money) for women to undertake that task themselves. If anybody were to fall behind, the president or treasurer of the group could simply garnish her savings in order to make the collective loan installment payment. This was less successful when a member absconded, as in the case of Kuña Amistad, where the balance of the member's savings was less than the amount owed on the loan. But to deal with day-to-day lateness and avoid falling behind, the group savings routinely came to the rescue.

In order to comply with the savings requirement most groups opened up an account at one of the myriad small finance companies in Paraguay and presented an account statement to their credit counselor as proof of their collective savings. A photocopy of the account statement was filed in the thick three-ring binders that tracked the life cycle of the group from one round of borrowing to the next. In essence, this was a parallel process to the fees charged by the City of Amsterdam to open a bank account but where private parties (rather than the state) alienated the revenue streams: (1) the finance companies, which profited from fees on the savings accounts and (2) Fundación Paraguaya, which offloaded the financial risk of uncollateralized loans onto these ancillary borrowing requirements. Leti and Graciela disingenuously proposed to take care of this service on the group's behalf, offering to act as the informal bank, as it were, for collective savings. Their borrowers readily agreed since, unlike finance companies in Ciudad del Este, their homegrown savings program did not charge for use of the interchange. What the pair really did, though, was deposit the women's money in an account at a finance company, print an account statement, immediately withdraw the money, and keep it. They were found out when several groups went to them at once to withdraw their savings and eventually complained about the missing funds to the Ciudad del Este branch director. It was a run on the (fictive) bank. For their part, Graciela and Leti thought that they would be able to keep the scheme going indefinitely since the very turnover of loans that animates Fundación Paraguaya's microcredit lending would also fuel rapid turnover in groups' savings. Should any one group come to them to withdraw their money, Leti and Graciela would be able to dip into the savings of a different borrowing group to meet the immediate demand, much like the Ponzi schemes that flourished in the interstices of informal banking systems. Their ability to exploit the quality of fungibility of money[37]—the exchangeability of any one unit of currency for another—was directly linked to the highly regular and regulated cyclicality of borrowing and paying at Fundación Paraguaya.

Leti and Graciela's fake bank resonates with the occult economies described by Comaroff and Comaroff (1999: 281), who point to precisely these sorts of pyramid schemes as diagnosing a particular cultural-economic conjuncture: "scams and stratagems . . . that flow from a promiscuous mix of scarcity and deregulation". And casting a look back at the postwar 1870s, there was certainly a florescence of financial maneuvers at the intersection of Paraguayan political crisis and global economic turmoil. However, one reason for prefacing Leti and Graciela's story with an account of Paraguay's induction into foreign debt is to highlight what is old about these financial practices rather than what is emergent or new. Both the stock-jobbers of the London Exchange and Fundación Paraguaya's microcredit staff created value by exploiting liability-in-motion, be it in the periods between settling days for Victorian capital markets or between credit cycles for women's borrowing groups. Indeed, perhaps Paraguay's distinctive brand of antiregulatory political economy can offer a preview of the shape liability might take in ever more unfettered markets. What is especially notable about Leti and Graciela's savings scheme, however, is that it does not rely on fast capitalism and the increasing speed at which financial instruments circulate in order to generate value. These women were definitely not high-speed traders. Instead, the success of their specific venture hinged on the humdrum and methodical movement of credit cycles: the banality of joint liability.[38]

Letizia was remarkably composed as she laid out the details of her fake bank, even as she told me about being fired from her job at Fundación Paraguaya, worried that state attorneys would impound and auction her car, and described the implosion of her long-term romantic relationship from the stress of the situation. However, she grew more and more angry as she described her fraught relationship with Graciela as the savings scam was falling apart. "It was all about her brother, that was all she thought about, she left me to deal with everything! She abandoned me!" Letizia shook with frustration, her lips pressed tightly together as she lowered her head in theatrical shock. Piecing together Leti's account from what I had known of Graciela's story during my fieldwork, Graciela's brother has been incarcerated in their home city, and she had long described her own efforts to save enough money to pay the bail (or perhaps the bribe) to get him out. Over the course of my time with the Ciudad del Este office we had all grown accustomed to Graciela's frequent travel to visit her mother and siblings, and many in the office sympathized with her dilemma of balancing work obligations at the office with family ties back home. Letizia wasn't sure what eventually happened to Graciela or her family; all efforts to contact her—especially when her attorney wanted a deposition from her partner in the scam—went unanswered. Leti was particularly angry that Graciela's flight had left her to shoulder the burden of confronting the aftermath of broken trust and stolen money. She commented that several times women in the borrowing groups that she had diverted funds from had publicly confronted her, sometimes descending on her as a large and threatening group. Since Leti lived in a small apartment with her sister near the city wholesale market and worked at informal jobs downtown, much like the women who were enrolled in the microcredit program, it was impossible to hide away while the scandal passed. Her economic world was too enmeshed with the women who borrowed from her to avoid them. Leti concluded her story by telling me that she feared for her safety as she found herself utterly alone, abandoned by Graciela, facing the repercussions of their theft. However, the ambiguous and emergent circumstances of theft and fraud, just like the flexible contexts of being liable, show that Leti and Graciela's scheme was not at all unusual, as I show below.

BORROWING, SAVING, AND "EATING THE MONEY"

An important part of Letizia's story about stealing her clients' money is that the scheme drew directly on borrowers' own efforts to fit their unpredictable financial lives into the strictures of Fundación Paraguaya's lending program. It was not uncommon for the treasurer of a women's borrowing group to deposit the group's savings, print an account statement, and immediately withdraw the money, just as Letizia and Graciela had done. The pair had probably thought of the scheme because they had gently scolded many borrowers for doing it on countless occasions. However, unlike the scam conceived by Leti and Graciela, within borrowing groups this creative accounting was only occasionally about misappropriation. Usually it was done with the full knowledge of the rest of the group. Indeed, it was a common strategy because women who borrowed preferred to have that money in their pockets over locking it up in a savings account. Kuña Amistad demonstrated just how dangerous it was to leave savings in the hands of strangers, even if those strangers were bound by social collateral. One microcredit treasurer commented that her group agreed to hold fund-raisers in order to cover the $20 fee charged by the bank for failing to maintain a minimum balance, since it was deemed so important to have the cash on hand rather than in savings. Although Fundación Paraguaya's credit counselors routinely emphasized in their meetings that the savings could save the groups, many women weighed the micro crises of daily budgeting against the macro crises that would require accumulated savings. More often than not, they felt the former more acutely than the latter. And although showing the account statement was a key part of the ritual of getting credit, that statement was more of a snapshot of a particular moment rather than a fixed reality. It dramatized the collective effort to produce at least the semblance of financial solvency on paper. The microcredit organization thought of it in this way too, knowing full well that reality is more complicated than a printed statement but taking comfort in the fact that those economic resources (dispersed as they were) could be called in as collateral if the loan were to go awry.

As Letizia's story so vividly demonstrates, however, the ebb and flow of resources became a scandal and a crisis when it was permanently diverted and hence was framed as theft rather than debt. This was often talked about as "eating the money" (*comiendo la plata*), a common phrase in Paraguay used to describe situations as diverse as political corruption, bribe taking, mismanagement, and legal cases over theft. Unsurprisingly, it was often the treasurer and the president of the borrowing groups—women who were elected by their fellow members to manage the accounts of the collectivity—who were most often accused by their own members of eating the money. Being president or treasurer was often a highly sensitive and complicated job, for authorized and licit diversions—say, to pay a late loan installment using the group savings, or investment of part of the savings for a group fund-raising activity—often made the account books treacherous, even for the most organized and amicable groups (fig. 6).

For many borrowing groups the slow dissipation of funds from collective savings was a feature of exactly its intended function as collateral for the loan. In practice, those collective moneys were routinely seized to cover late payments and avert atraso for the group. For instance, during one troubleshooting field trip with Maria Elena, another credit counselor at the Fundación, I began to really appreciate the push and pull of claims on the group savings. The group, which went by the name Mujeres Progresando, or Women's Progress, had asked for help from their credit counselor because they found a shortfall in their savings account. When the president had printed the latest account statement at the finance company, the balanced showed just $160, even though according to the group's internal ledgers there was supposed to be well over $250. The shortfall of nearly $100 was a significant concern to everybody, including Maria Elena. First, it meant that money was bleeding out of the account, and second, it meant that

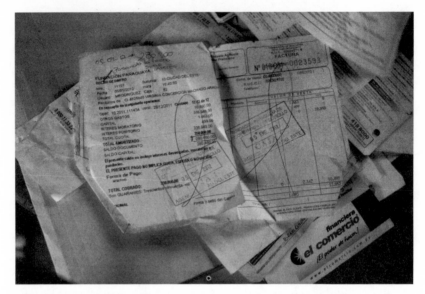

FIGURE 6. Collection of payment receipts and account books from a Committee of Women Entrepreneurs.

the missing funds would jeopardize the group's loan renewal in the next cycle. According to the president of the Mujeres Progresando committee, the group's treasurer, who was her counterpart in managing the collective finances, had been doing a poor job of collecting money from group members for the joint savings account. Collecting this money usually happened in tandem with collecting loan installments, which were taken together each week to meet the installment payments for Mujeres Progresando as a financial entity. As the president told it, she had decided to step in to help out with coordinating the savings deposits of her fellow group members since the treasurer was proving unreliable. Since the treasurer was not present at the meeting nobody in the group heard her side of the story. The president, in turn, said that when there was a shortfall she would go to the treasurer to get the remainder of the money but that the woman never told her if she had collected it from members of the group or, perhaps more important, if there were any additional funds beyond the immediate deficit that she hadn't handed over. At each loan installment the president lamented that three or four group members did not pay their share, so each time she would have to dip into the savings to make the payment. Consequently, the floating funds between the treasurer and president were stretched thinner and thinner over the course of the cycle. The problem, she said, was paying "in two parts" to two different people, which added to the strain of keeping an account of the collective payments.

As Maria Elena, the officiating credit counselor, pulled out her cell phone to use as an impromptu calculator and asked how many women were missing payments so that she could calculate the deficit, she mused aloud that perhaps the group was too spread out in the neighborhood. She speculated out loud that "maybe they [members of Mujeres Progresando] don't have the motivation to come all the way here to pay," which was why they were paying "in two parts." And more pointedly, Maria Elena insinuated that if the president were stealing from the savings fund, then others in the group would surely find out and spread the gossip. The implication was that despite the distance that made coordinating payment difficult, that space would ultimately not be able to protect her from the intimacy of joint liability if she were in fact misappropriating the money. The president responded angrily. She said, "I don't owe them [the group] an explanation because there is always a shortfall." Tellingly, the phrase that she used to refuse "owing" the group an explanation—"*no les debo una explicación*"—was the same one Maria Elena routinely used to describe borrowers who were "owing" late payments. In the context of collective liability, explanations and information, it would seem, were part of what was owed on a debt. As they discussed the shortfalls the president kept repeating that she had carefully written down all of her transactions. Despite her efforts she told Maria Elena, "I don't even know how to manage it," since the money was always short. The gap in reconciling what was owed, though, was not an easy one to square.

PINNING DOWN NEIGHBORS, KIN, AND COLLEAGUES

The Mujeres Progresando president's effort to assure her fellow borrowers that she was not eating the money depended on giving a clear account of the accounts. By recourse to the technical features of atraso and lateness, she sought to protect herself from rumors that she had misappropriated the collective funds. Time and again, when I accompanied credit counselors to meetings with borrowing groups that were in trouble, the issue came down to the group's collective savings and the worry that somebody was eating them. And usually, as with the scam perpetrated by Leti and Graciela, the borrowing groups marshaled evidence of kinship relatedness as evidence of fraud. In one case, women sat in a circle with arms crossed in anger as members described the opulent baptism that their president had hosted while the group's savings had (inexplicably) disappeared. In several instances, treasurers or presidents would face down the group and their credit counselor to explain the family crisis that had necessitated the diversion of funds, ranging from paying medical expenses for a sick child to sponsoring the migration of a family member to Spain or Argentina for work. The idiom of kinship obligations was a powerful explanation for accusations as well as justifications. Just as Letizia had pointed to Graciela's brother, languishing in a Paraguayan prison while his sister worked to free him, resources were expected to flow along the channels of familial relatedness. The relationship seemed to run the other direction, too, which helps explain Letizia's shock at being abandoned by Graciela even though they were bound like family by the financial flows.

Liability is rooted in a repertoire of financial practices rather than simply an accounting logic or a feature of double-entry bookkeeping that records crediting and debiting. And importantly, creating liability hinges on successfully defining debt *as a debt,* as opposed to some other type of financial connection. The common charge of "eating the money" relied on the consensus of the group that there was an appropriate distributional order for that money and that somebody had violated it. That consensus, as with Paraguay's sovereign borrowing, was actually quite tenuous. This was especially the case with collective debts that were reckoned within the neighborhoods blanketed by Fundación Paraguaya's microfinance loans. The coincidence of multiple, overlapping debts meant that the microcredit borrowers thought of their group solidarity in much the same way that they felt connected to certain categories of neighbors, especially shopkeepers who managed credit for their neighbors, family, and friends. One such shopkeeper in Ciudad Jardín, a young woman named Viki, was quite emphatic about the central place financial debt held in her life. She had participated in a microcredit borrowing group similar to the one managed by Letizia and Maria Elena but also had lines of credit at small-scale finance companies throughout Ciudad del Este. However, despite her framing of debt as enabling, indeed, as a crucial lifeline, Viki also had a long and troubled legacy of the debilitating consequences of serving as creditor to her neighbors via her corner grocery shop. When I asked her about her shop she said bitterly, "It celebrated a year in April 2010; and celebrating a year, I closed it down." The problem, as she narrated them, was twofold. First, there were lots of shops on her block, so "there was very little money that came in every day, and if no money comes in you don't have enough to replace the stock that you used up today for tomorrow." All of the shops sold nearly identical merchandise. Household consumer goods featured prominently, including common items like rice, tinned tomatoes, small packets of shampoo, cigarettes, and lightbulbs. Second, and related to that, she sold the majority of her goods on credit, using an account book to note down what people owed. Credit built loyalty among her customer base. However, Viki lamented that with so much sold on credit she never was able to collect full payments. When I asked her who her clients were she told me:

> From the neighborhood. They are all from the neighborhood. It's not that they don't want to pay. I would, for example, set up accounts for every eight days or every fifteen [i.e., weekly or biweekly payments], come two weeks and you don't even collect half of what is owed. And that other half [that you didn't collect] is the half that you might use to buy new merchandise, to renew the stock a bit, well, it just didn't work out. And that's how it was. Two, three times, I had to quit my shop. And I would fill the shelves again— loans of $650, $215, $130, another $215[39]—I filled and filled the shelves. And it never progressed.

Viki linked her economic troubles to a general feeling of distress—many women in Ciudad del Este linked various types of stress to nerves— stemming from the "frustrating puzzle" of the shop's progress.[40] She continued: "It was really hard, a puzzle really, to collect every eight or fifteen [days]. Saturday would come around, and I would have such hope that they would come and pay their bill. And they didn't come. And another two weeks would pass, and they wouldn't pay again. Really a headache. And I was so nervous, while I was pregnant, and I had an attack of nerves." Her self-diagnosis offered a nuanced picture of exactly the sort of internal motivation and personal drives that the *Ikatú* project of interiority and entrepreneurial spirit was trying to map. However, Viki's story of her business troubles offers an important counterpoint to the Fundación's presumption that internal states could be neatly matched to external outcomes. Instead, Viki's "frustrating puzzles" suggest much more back-and-forth between outside and inside worlds. As Viki explained the life course of the loan, first she waited for borrowers to come to pay her, which caused her boredom and nervousness. At the same time, more debt led her to hope the business would succeed. In fact, that hope allowed her to restock her store and fill her shelves again, which further tangled her finances with credit to her neighbors. And once again she found herself nervous about collecting money she was owed. As Viki's story transitioned between internal states and somatic ones, I had the distinct impression that her effort to be *activa*—to be an active and busy entrepreneur—was perpetually disappointed. In her words, "it never progressed." One of the reasons it never progressed is that Viki was never able to make a successful case that the endless deferrals from her neighbors were akin to the sorts of diversions that were framed as eating the money by microcredit groups. Both types of loans relied on social collateral to generate liability. However, Viki's passive frustration as she waited and hoped for a brighter economic future highlights her powerlessness to enact liability as a sociality of action.

As a counterpoint to Viki's unfulfilled efforts to exert neighborliness—and collect her debts—the group of financial professionals at the Fundación found effective ways to come together at work but also outside of their professional lives. The forms of connectedness that drew Fundación Paraguaya's staff together—including Leti and Graciela—were differentiated from the familial idioms that often were the site of intense anxiety over eating the money. During my fieldwork with the branch office I found that I was quickly recruited into a whole host of personal obligations that spilled outside of the workplace and brought staff members together in surprisingly intimate settings. The colloquial term for a colleague in Paraguay, *compañero* or *compañera*, blurred the line with family, since a range of close relationships, from teammate to schoolmate to romantic partner, could all be described in the same terms. For an inner circle of staff members, especially those whose own family ties were strained by long distances like Graciela and also the branch manager, Don Edgar, the affection felt for compañeros/as took on many of the relational qualities of family life and extended kinship circles. Leti was one of several staff members who had close connections with her family in Ciudad del Este but was always eager and willing to participate in after-hours gatherings with her compañeras. In fact, on many occasions the office parties held to celebrate the birthday of a colleague were drawn out of the workplace to evening festivals at the person's home, which was a ritual usually reserved for close family and schoolmates. My fieldnotes are peppered with stories of friendly nighttime gatherings that featured traditional BBQ and stretched late into the evening. As with the customary family events, liters of Brahma beer were shared by passing around a single small glass among the group. The constant refills assured that the beer stayed bracingly cold even in the summer heat. The shared relational space of Fundación Paraguaya, which extended to private homes and personal connections, offers a hint as to why Letizia might have been persuaded to join with Graciela to divert and appropriate the savings of her borrowers. On workdays, both women took an active hand in enlisting the extended relational networks of their borrowers into the liabilities of microcredit debt. Once the workday was done, they found themselves further entangled in one another's lives as intimate colleagues. In other words, Fundación Paraguaya created the very kinned subjects that it purported to find and enroll in its lending program, and not just among borrowers. These dense ties of joint liability were in marked contrast to Viki's disappointed efforts to claim neighborliness among the people who owed her money.

These accounts of fraud and theft—and the unexpected ways in which they tracked family and neighborly ties—cannot be told without an interwoven story about crediting gender. Microcredit loans have long framed kinship ties as a productive force in the collateralization of women's loans. Borrowers were expected to draw on family resources in order to pay their loan installments, and the benefits of microfinance are expected to lift up the whole household. Women were expected to be always already hyperobligated, and those obligations were expected to be felt most strongly toward family members. What Letizia's story tells us is that the microcredit program was an active participant in *creating* the contexts—indeed, the highly gendered contexts—that make both fraud and familial relatedness possible. It came down to the seemingly accidental revenue streams of collateral, especially through group savings. Family ties came into being and were claimed around assertions of mutual obligation: the stranded brother, the baptism, the migration to Spain, the neighborhood store selling on credit. The particular way women had access to large funds in microcredit meant that they were called on as socially dense beings to care for family members through financial support and were mobilized in broader reproductive systems within neighborhoods and family networks. Put differently, women became ipso facto suspects of fraud, of eating the money. This, precisely because the contexts—large pots of collective money—were brought into being and justified in terms of loans to women because they were considered especially obligated and caring. The accidental value, to borrow Adam Smith's classic framing, was actually patterned in highly gendered and unequal ways. As a consequence, and what is surprising here, is that women *became* kinship, and kinship is restricted to women. And this of course was not the case beyond the world of microfinance, where all sorts of categories of people are called on to enact relationships of care in and through financial support, from the commensality of tiny glasses of cold beer among compañeros to household obligations between spouses. Indeed, the boundaries of social collateral were felt especially acutely by people like Viki, whose efforts to create relations of liability were to no avail. In other words, women certainly are not the only agents of kinship in Paraguayan formations of familial relations. What the temptation of fraud shows us is that in tandem with the move to expand the ties of economic obligation outward into borrowers' families, there is, I argue, a countermove, a radical narrowing—and gendering—of the categories of people who enact liability.

ACCIDENTAL VALUE

This account of the institutional and administrative side of microcredit takes place in what Julia Elyachar has remarked as the era of Microfinance 2.0. As microfinance has ceased being a visionary call for pro-poor financial inclusion and is being transformed into a mainstay of both global development and global finance, it is crucial to understand the inner workings of these loans on their own terms. In a moment when collective debt is at the root of important public debates, including the regulation of financial markets, austerity programs, and sovereign debt crises, microcredit social collateral can contribute a critical vocabulary to the politics of interdependency in and across collectivities that do not readily correspond with big banks or with national political actors. And as the politics of interdependency moved from Paraguay's sovereign borrowing and debt refinancing, we can see social collateral in surprising places in the wider world of Latin American economic experimentation and development policy. Indeed, Paraguay's forced borrowing on international capital markets in the late nineteenth century and subsequent default and economic restructuring interwove the political conditions of nationhood and self-determination via the economic instruments put in the service of national development. This historical alliance between debt, development, and nationhood lays out the conceptual and political stakes of collective debt, which still resonates today.

This chapter has offered an alternative framing to the common perception of liability as a condition—something that happens to people through the machinations of creditocracy.[41] I have considered liability a set of practices or economic agencies that unfold unpredictably through collective indebtedness. And rather than dwell on the sentimental or enabling facets of interdependency,[42] I have focused on how those binding ties—which go to the heart of microcredit liability—were both created and undone in the context of social collateral. When the regular and highly regulated repayment of Kuña Amistad gave way to the grinding problems and frequent fights about lateness, I was not convinced that debt homogenized women's experience of financial markets. Nor was the impersonal double-entry bookkeeping of the Mujeres Progresando committee sufficient to inoculate the group's leadership from charges of eating the money. Rather than invite borrowers and lenders to conceptualize their relationship in terms of payment schedules bound to the calendar, social collateral created an intimate temporality for intimate debts.

I have refocused on the economy of gender—especially the gendering of kinship—in the broader discussion of the socioeconomic inequalities that have been the central concern of critical studies of microcredit. Letizia never did say why she stole her clients' savings. But her bitter anger at Graciela offers a hint. During the two years that I was involved in the microfinance office, Letizia had been very close to her credit counselor colleagues. From her telling, Leti's shock at what she saw as Graciela's abandonment had to do in part with her own sense of being de-kinned on her expulsion from the NGO: this was a violent breaking of intimate ties that she had cultivated through years of shared affection, both inside and beyond the workplace. She seemed heartbroken by the cold treatment she received from people she thought of as compañeras and compañeros.

Indeed, Leti gave an especially sour account of her treatment by the branch manager, Don Edgar, who had summarily fired her when the scheme was exposed. She had known him for years and spent many evenings with him and other colleagues during celebrations and festivities. As Leti related the story of being dismissed by Don Edgar, she made a point of commenting that some months later another functionary at the branch office of Fundación Paraguaya had told her that if the decision had been up to him he would have offered her a loan through the microfinance program to pay off what she owed her clients. This compassion—overlaid on financial obligation—was evidently closer to what Leti expected from her close relationship to her colleagues at the NGO.

When she told me about her fake bank, I could not help but be surprised by her outrage. Why, I thought, would Leti expect that her manager would save her with a loan? Why would she think that he would consent to ongoing relationality when prudence would suggest terminating the relationship? Leti's story, though, reveals just how close she was to the microfinance world of social collateral. The compassion she expected from her manager slipped easily into the world of poor women's entrepreneurship. It is important to keep in view the fact that Letizia's narrative arc—from microcredit counselor to seeker of microcredit—is not all that unusual in the cyclical movement of liability and its perspectival accounting of obligations. And it shows how closely linked entrepreneurship and liability are, especially in the collective debts of Fundación Paraguaya's microfinance. In fact, Leti and Graciela's predicament at first struck me as a limit case of entrepreneurship, since credit counselors took the financial innovations of groups like Kuña Amistad and Mujeres Progresando to heart and turned them into an engine of profit. However, Leti's story ended with a plea to liability. She wanted nothing more than to be bound anew to her compañeros and to her clients through another cycle of borrowing. Being bound and being freed by debt were *both* enfolded into the interdependencies of social collateral.

PART TWO

Life Cycles of Loans

CHAPTER 3

Creditworthiness

The staff of the Ciudad del Este branch of Fundación Paraguaya must have known from the start that they would never be able to provide enough chairs in their waiting room to seat all of their clients. In the mornings when I visited the office, located on the bustling downtown commercial artery Avenida Bernardino Caballero, I had to squeeze carefully through a huge crowd of women that pushed through the glass doors of the office, spilled down the hallway and the front steps, and coalesced into the hot, smoggy commotion of the street. Sometimes over 150 women, surrounded by eddies of small children, gathered at the office in the early hours as they waited for their loan disbursals. The half-dozen-odd office chairs were intended for intimate conversations between loan officers and clients inquiring about their debt; they were not intended to accommodate the crowd waiting patiently to present their ID cards, sign the forms, and receive their next loan installment. Occasionally staff members from the Fundación would organize a committee to take a group photograph and record the occasion. These quarterly rituals provide documentary evidence of the lending process of Kiva.org, one of the Fundación's powerful financial backers.[1] But aside from briefly structuring these moments of administrative formality, Fundación Paraguaya's credit counselors seemed nonplussed by the congregation of borrowers and dealt with the situation by choosing, for the most part, to ignore it.[2]

The women who came to the microcredit office to initiate their next cycle of borrowing attempted to accelerate the process by arriving promptly, often waiting outside the locked office door before the Fundación opened at 7:30 a.m. This sparked a sort of early morning race between committees as they arrived earlier and earlier in an effort secure a spot at the head of the queue, sometimes leaving their homes as early as 4:30 a.m. This race to get ahead in the goings-on of business in Ciudad del Este was thought of as similar to the rhythms of smuggling, arbitrage, and commercial sales that moved the import/export economy of the city center. Visitors to Ciudad del Este have long remarked on its early morning bustle, and it is uncanny to find the streets practically deserted by midafternoon.[3] However, efforts of women's committees to beat the market, as it were, were often foiled by the administrative requirements of the Fundación. Every member of the group needed to be present in order to produce the necessary loan documents and sign the official forms recognizing joint liability. If a group member arrived late, the committee inevitably got bumped in the queue as credit counselors rushed ahead with the loan documents of the next group in line. Many cell phone minutes were inevitably spent urging tardy members on to the office as borrowers juggled morning domestic duties, work schedules, and the capricious bus system. Some groups partially resolved the problem by traveling together on the same bus. But this strategy posed its own problems. It was often an uncomfortable and treacherous endeavor; Ciudad del Este's buses were notoriously rickety and dusty, and the women far outnumbered the available seats. The better part of a full day, then, was inevitably consumed with the uncomfortable and burdensome administrative process of initiating or renewing a group-based microloan.

The huge morning crowds outside the Fundación Paraguaya microcredit office—especially when five or six borrowing committees had the same loan disbursal date—were an inconvenient corollary of the joint responsibility of social collateral. It was what made Committees of Women Entrepreneurs creditworthy in the first place. Every member of the committee was required to be present for the purposes of signing the *pagaré* IOU contract before the lump sum could be paid out to the group treasurer and allocated to each woman. The administrative requirements that publicly and repeatedly made visible the social collateral of Committees of Women Entrepreneurs were an ongoing reminder of personal ties that entangled the economic lives of its members and bound them to their creditor. The bureaucratic ritual of loan authorization and disbursal dramatized borrowers' access to credit as a group by convening the Committees of Women Entrepreneurs even though this unit was cumbersome, inconvenient, and in many cases unnecessary for both lender and borrower. What, then, was being staged in these moments of group unity? What sort of solidarity was being produced in practice through the long bus ride together to the office, the hours of waiting together in the crowd without a proper place to sit, and finally the ritual cosigning of the contract of joint indebtedness?

Looking at the crowd at Fundación Paraguaya's branch office in Ciudad del Este, one might assume that the organization lent only to women. Indeed, acquaintances with only a passing familiarity with the NGO routinely mistook it for a women's rights organization. As I came to learn over the course of my fieldwork, this impression did not accurately capture the underlying business model of the microcredit nonprofit. In fact, less than a quarter of the total capital in Fundación Paraguaya's lending portfolio went to women, a fact that seemed at odds with the NGO's public—and visibly gendered—face. Since the organization opened its first branch in Asunción in 1985, Fundación Paraguaya has pioneered pro-poor small business financing and support, with loans nearly evenly distributed to men and women borrowers.[4] What is more, beginning in 2008 the NGO experimented with lending specifically to groups of men as a counterpoint to its enormously successful Committees of Women Entrepreneurs program, which had been instituted just two years earlier. By 2010 the men's committees program was being dismantled after disappointing results in its pilot program. The visible feminization of microcredit in Paraguay, then, invites an analysis of the bureaucratic and administrative side of lending in order to understand the gendered logics of creditworthiness animating the NGO's development mission.

Women's often frustrating efforts to manage creditworthiness were not restricted to the administrative spaces of Fundación Paraguaya's microcredit office. Credit suffused daily life for many people living and working in Ciudad del Este. For instance, Viki, a microcredit borrower who intermittently ran a small grocery shop in her neighborhood, reflected on the challenges of sustaining multiple payment regimes and her own credit access. Her frustrated attempts to collect on the bills her neighbors owed her, described in the previous chapter, helped me understand the moving connections and disconnections of liability. Importantly, in addition to being a borrower from Fundación Paraguaya, Viki was a lender as many of her neighbors made purchases at her store on credit. Viki's husband had a steady job at a parking garage in the city center, but she still relied heavily on credit as an economic lifeline.

Describing her financial obligations, she quickly ticked off a list of her monthly bills (*cuentas*):

> [My husband's] income went up a bit to $360, but from that $360 I owe my washing machine, I owe the moto, I owe the loan at the cooperative [savings and loan], I owe the microcredit, I owe my wardrobe, I owe the television, and from there it's already over half of the salary. There's nothing to spare. They say, "Your husband makes good money," but the truth is that it isn't much. . . . That money [the largest bill in Paraguayan currency], once you make change into smaller bills [*sensillás*], it's gone in an instant. And that, together we owe a great deal . . .

When I interviewed Viki she was twenty-one and in charge of the finances of a household that included her husband, infant daughter, and five-year-old son. At the time, I took note of her striking features and keen sense of feminine fashion as she made a side-note of her passion for jewelry and cosmetics, which she hoped someday to turn into a small business in her home. For now, however, she framed her economic pursuits as well as her sense of personal fulfillment in terms of her young family. Laughing wryly that she used to feel trapped at home and took every opportunity to get out and about, now her economic and emotional center of gravity pulled her back to her neighborhood and her small house in the periurban settlement.[5] She and her husband moved to their current home three years earlier, and she already felt overwhelmed by the debts she owed for the things that solidified and sustained her household. Pausing for a moment after enumerating the multiple debts she owed, Viki told me, "The thing is, if you owe, you also *have*." Inclusion in the forms of consumption offered by commercial trade in the dynamic import/export economy of Ciudad del Este meant stretching out and deferring payments for as long as possible. In other words, debt was the condition of *having*.

This chapter considers the relationships that were stitched together and then unraveled by creditworthiness, a crucial moment in the life cycle of a loan. The everyday credit worlds of borrowers like Viki revolved around decisions about installment payments for a moto-bike and managing household bills. These quotidian financial obligations were tied to the offices and teller windows of credit institutions in surprising and powerful ways. Every day both microcredit staff members and borrowers were engaged in the work of turning the tangle of financial obligations into loan contracts. In addition to the material effects of lending and borrowing, I analyze the *social unit of debt* at the heart of credit access and repayment in order to understand the stakes of bundling some obligations and holding others apart in the process of administering the financial tool of microcredit.

A key aspect of the global microcredit model is the pervasive assumption that women are more responsible borrowers and also that they are more likely to pass along their gains to their children and families.[6] Indeed, the uplifting stories of individual women who borrow are an important part of the authorizing discourse that has made microfinance so appealing within international development frameworks. However, considering the broader implications of microfinance beyond feminized borrowers per se can let us see "woman" as a fragmented category refracted through the terms of credit. As I argue, the tightly interlocked credit/debt dyad (Peebles 2010)[7]—or the seemingly self-evident financial terms binding borrower and lender[8]—puts us at risk of taking the unity and stability of the social unit of debt for granted. While economic anthropology has long shown how even the most abstruse and high-flying forms of finance are deeply social, here I trace the regulatory forms by which credit and debt in development—and beyond—produce gendered sociality in and through the lending practices themselves.[9] I suggest that the social collateral of Committes of Women Entrepreneurs hinges on a crediting of gender in a double sense. Gender difference serves as the basis for entrepreneurialism and creditworthiness for the hundreds of women who enrolled in the Committees of Women Entrepreneurs program, but gender is simultaneously framed by borrowers and lenders alike as a force and is credited with certain effects including a repertoire of economic practices at the heart of social collateral. Following loans as they unfold in the credit worlds of borrowers and lenders goes beyond positing a formation of gendered economic sociality that preexisted and was transformed by microfinance. It also goes beyond theorizing how microcredit assumes and banks on women's solidarity. By focusing on collective indebtedness where it seems most natural, I trace how the seemingly obvious embeddedness of women is produced and its consequences.

I compare Fundación Paraguaya's administration of individual and group-based microloans, credit counselors' selective use of credit scores, and finally the institutional post mortem of the short-lived men's borrowing committees, to examine the regulation of gender and credit in daily financial practice. In each case, Fundación Paraguaya's staff read creditworthiness through the economic relationships of an unruly (and unstable) social unit. What I am calling the social unit of debt—be it the microcredit client, household, guarantor, or borrowing group—always threatened to exceed the contractual terms of debt and repayment because of shifting obligations to fellow group members but also families, neighbors, and business partners, which all anchored the repayment possibilities of financial debts. The gendering of creditworthiness was a crucial mechanism for producing and defining that social unit in daily administrative practice.

DILEMMAS OF INCLUSION: ECONOMIES OF GENDER IN PARAGUAY

Microcredit's purchase in development circles has in large part been due to its promise of correcting a gender injustice, namely, that men had physical collateral and women did not. Of course, as feminist scholars have long pointed out, inequalities in economic access are not merely questions of inclusion. Women's empowerment through economic independence has been a flashpoint in feminist debates about gendered inequalities, as many have argued that the emancipatory ideals of second wave feminism have been co-opted and appropriated by the very ideological apparatuses that they sought to free women from in the first place. Nancy Fraser (2009) has noted that the very language of empowerment and independence voiced by feminists in the postwar era now feels uncomfortably close to neoliberal ideals of women's economic self-help through the freedom of market participation.[10] In the world of development NGOs in Latin America, the surprising conjuncture of neoliberal economic reforms and women's empowerment had the pragmatic effect of reshaping the institutional structures and mission goals articulated by feminist organizations.[11] Sonia Alvarez (2009) has tracked what she terms NGO-ization in Latin America in a study of feminist advocacy groups across the region. As she argues, the regulation of the NGO sector reshaped the debate about gender justice by promoting "technically capable and politically trustworthy [organizations] to assist the task of 'social adjustment'" under Washington Consensus economic restructuring (176).

Paraguay's tri-border area typifies many of the asymmetries in women's wages and remuneration that go to the heart of microcredit's calls for more inclusive forms of credit. The tectonic shifts in economic policy in the hemisphere raise a further set of questions about gender and labor in Paraguay: why were these forms of gender division valued over possible others? Founded in 1957 as one of the inaugural policies of the Stroessner administration, Puerto Presidente Stroessner quickly became the epicenter of a population boom on the triple frontier between Paraguay, Brazil, and Argentina as migrants sought work opportunities in the city's vibrant cross-border trade and later as laborers on the nearby Itaipú Dam construction site. In keeping with labor discipline in company towns elsewhere,[12] John Howard White's history of masculine labor and feminized domestic life in the Itaipú era found that "while male dam workers were being transformed into industrial laborers and skilled professionals at the dam site, female spouses were instructed as how best to be housewives, to scientifically manage the home and raise children, and to fill the 'free hours' of the day with productive activities" (2010: 160). This distinction perdures to the present day, as the Itaipú facility continues to pay for a daily shuttle service for dam employees to go home and enjoy a midday meal prepared by their wives. I would often see the sleek air-conditioned Santania buses contracted by Itaipú as they made their daily rounds through the city. They were a striking visual contrast to the patched-together private city buses that bumped and bounced their way out to the neighborhoods of Fundación Paraguaya's Committees of Women Entrepreneurs. Unlike the hermetically sealed Santania transports, the ramshackle vehicles usually had a damp towel available to passengers so that they could clear the dust before sitting down.

This division was not solely a feature of wage labor, in contrast to self-employment. In commercial life, too, masculine trades were licensed and recognized through syndical federations, the most dynamic being the taxi drivers' union, which was central to cross-border transportation, and the street-stall vendors' federation, which controlled access to semiformal commerce downtown.[13] The development of the city, then, crystallized distinctions between masculinized vocational labor and feminized domestic life, even though the latter was expected to be productive as well. Ciudad del Este's history raises important questions about the cultural politics and contexts of gendered economic life that bear explicitly on women's collective borrowing in microcredit programs. The fact that women's economic networks would later be recruited into microcredit social collateral in order to guarantee loans, then, is in keeping with a wider history of how women came to be highly obligated subjects in Paraguay and through changing work and consumption patterns more broadly.

As Paraguay's economy liberalized further in the twentieth century, and especially in the two decades after the formation of the Mercosur regional trade bloc in 1991, the gendered division of work and domestic responsibilities shifted very little. Paraguayan labor sociologists conclude, "The observable data shows that the Paraguayan labor market is highly segmented by sex. The roles and 'responsibilities' culturally designated to women are different from men, and this has repercussions for their work opportunities" (Geoghegan 2008: 79). Echoing orthodox theories of labor economists that emphasize women's flexibility, sociological studies of the Paraguayan labor market suggest that the difference in income between men and women is much lower in the formal sector (10 percent) than in the informal sector (25 percent), since women are much more likely to take nonwage positions.[14] Thus economic analysts figure women's work in informal microenterprises as doubly disadvantaged. They suggest that women receive lower wages in informal businesses because of unequal income structures compared to men. Further, this difference is attributed to unequal allocation of unpaid household responsibilities.[15]

This explanation and justification for women's disadvantaged share of wage labor protections is part of a much bigger story about flexibility and self-employment in management theories and policies drawing on neoclassical microeconomics. This line of analysis is one of the primary justifications for microfinance and its focus on women's social collateral. Women, Paraguayan labor economists conclude, work predominantly in these low-paying positions in small and microenterprises because of their "flexibility" (flexibilidad), a term they used to gloss both flexible entry and exit from the market and flexible hours.[16] According to this line of reasoning, flexibility allows women to fulfill family obligations as well as work for income but also means that they must settle for jobs with a high degree of precariousness and limited social security and pension access.[17] But the recourse to "flexibility" in labor theories, as feminist economists like Drucilla Barker have pointedly argued,[18] is bundled up with a broader value judgment about women's work, and its invisibility. As Barker (2005: 2189) suggests, "Gender analyses highlight the asymmetric effects of economic theories and policies that are hidden by conventional theorizing." It is my aim to undertake such an analysis of flexibility within microcredit social collateral.

This is not to say that women do not widely work in nonwage positions, which of course they do. The informality of women's work is particularly acute in the border city of Ciudad del Este, where women have long participated in small-scale smuggling (contrabando de hormigas)[19] that sustained commercial society in the tri-border area even before the city was officially named a special customs zone in 1971.

Flexible labor of all sorts—from Viki's neighborhood grocery shop to cross-border contraband—is not a last resort for women. Both informal labor and informal credit are indispensable to what Viki called the conditions of having. However, I emphasize that when women's work is glossed as flexibility more generally, it also means that women as economic subjects in Paraguay are understood to be always already obligated and interdependent, which serves as both the explanation and the justification for income difference, particularly in the informal sector. If Paraguayan women are figured as especially bound by a whole repertoire of duties—to the family, and by extension to the nation—then this has important implications for microfinance collateralized through personal ties and mutual indebtedness.

The feminist anthropologist Carla Freeman has highlighted the important cultural-historical processes that can fade from view when examining an analytic object that feels deeply familiar. Her study of entrepreneurialism—and especially its affective and embodied modalities of self-fashioning and interior growth—is a provocation to retheorize neoliberal flexibility. Rather than a uniform principle that is "the essence of neo-liberalism,"[20] paraphrasing Pierre Bourdieu, Freeman shows how flexibility in Barbados is scaffolded by particular configurations of sociological categories like gender, class, kinship, labor, and production but also affective modes of desire, belonging, love, and aspiration. Beneath the apparent ubiquity of "flexibility" as a feature of neoliberalism—a sense of familiarity heightened by our increasingly flexible universities, from unpaid student internships to competitive research funding regimes—there are important differences. While economists might point to Paraguayan women's flexibility as a general feature of the labor market, at the same time flexibility is a specific set of financial practices at the NGO and a key to commercial trade in Ciudad del Este. As I argue throughout this book, there is a constant knitting and raveling of independence and interdependence at work in social collateral and its reconfiguration of women's flexibility.

The relationships among woman microentrepreneurs and the market are not straightforward at Fundación Paraguaya, or in Ciudad del Este's commercial economy more generally. Women's traditional support networks—especially familial and neighborly ties—made up only a portion of the social collateral that secured collective indebtedness. More to the point, Fundación Paraguaya took an active hand in shaping the priorities and proximities of its borrowers by asking relative strangers to rely on one another for credit access and repayment. Many women talked about their fellow group members using the impersonal term for business affiliates, or socias, even when those groups included kin and close friends. Borrowers' efforts to maintain distance had dramatic consequences when groups had to settle internal disputes or even come together to pay the loan installments of a socia who had died. Since Fundación Paraguaya was founded and run by a prominent member of the Liberal Party political opposition with strong commitments to Paraguay's legacy of market-led development, and not by First World activists, the origins story of the feminist principles animating women's social collateral is not easy to untangle. Turning women into socias is neither entirely about creating neoliberal individuated agents nor wholly an exercise in feminist consciousness raising. At stake is a politics of debt that is not reducible to the moral valences of creditors and debtors,[21] since the transactors themselves—their boundaries and qualities, inclusions and exclusions, component parts and unified whole—were themselves up for grabs in the process of lending and borrowing.

INDIVIDUAL AND GROUP-BASED MICROLOANS

In 2006 Fundación Paraguaya expanded its lending program to include group-based lending to Committees of Women Entrepreneurs, the center of my story of social collateral so far. However, since it was founded in 1985 the NGO had extended microloans on an individual basis as small-scale business and consumer credit, with its clients nearly evenly distributed by gender.[22] Despite its thoroughly local provenance, Fundación Paraguaya had long been in conversation with international organizations shaping the global microcredit project, including a long-standing partnership with Acción International. One reason for the sudden shift in policy to include the Committees of Women Entrepreneurs program had to do with the renewed visibility of social collateral after the Grameen Bank group was awarded the Nobel Peace Prize in 2006 for its work on "village banking." Fundación Paraguaya embraced the classic—many might say outmoded—social collateral model even as commercial microfinance was eclipsing the nonprofit model in Latin America and globally.[23] Suddenly women became the face of Fundación Paraguaya. The Committees of Women Entrepreneurs program extended credit to groups of women who jointly borrowed and were jointly responsible for loan repayment. In a practical sense this meant that the group paid its loan installments as a unit, and the NGO tracked the borrowing history of the whole group rather than its individual members. In effect, one woman could owe her group money, but if the committee managed to come together to cover her share the NGO would never know. Conversely, a borrower might be paid up with her committee but be considered in default if the treasurer of her group turned in the collective payment late.

In the office senior loan officers managed the loans for individual small business and consumer credit. Junior credit counselors worked entirely with women, since they oversaw the group-based loan program. This division of labor meant that loan officers managed credit generally and discussed their work in terms of an unmarked client; credit counselors managed the credit of groups,[24] which often required the additional oversight of individual women who made up the membership of the group.[25] I would often shadow both loan officers and credit counselors on their daily field visits and that way gained a sense of the patterns that structured Fundación Paraguaya's lending and administrative practices.

In many ways, the working categories of individual loan and group loan relied on by Fundación Paraguaya to structure and manage its lending programs were serious misnomers. In practice, individual loans were not individual at all. As with most loans in the Paraguayan formal banking system, individual microcredits required a guarantor, who had a separate assessment process for fitness to underwrite the loan. Thus individual loans were legible as contractually binding on a singular client but also included a host of other social connections, which in practice made them quite similar to group loans, even if not in name. Those economic relationships usually took the form of official paperwork certifying the claims that the prospective borrower was creditworthy, that is, had sufficient assets, inventory, credit lines, savings, income, and collateral. Many documents were required to authorize individual borrowing, and the same documents were required of the guarantor, including proof of income and residence (usually a paid utility bill), a copy of the title to some property (land, vehicle registration, business inventory), and a credit check. A family member, most often a spouse, served as guarantor for the vast majority of Fundación Paraguaya's individual microloans, though grown children were also common cosignatories. Having a spouse or other household member as guarantor often eased the burden of collecting documents. If borrower and guarantor owned joint property, some of the documents sufficed for both parties. And quite often the loan was not destined for the exclusive use of the individual who signed as the primary borrower but rather was subsequently divided between the cosignatories for their own purposes.

This inappropriate designation—individual loan—was consequential because it marked the relationships and forms of interdependency (or lack thereof) that were expected to underwrite these different types of microfinancing. Two longtime affiliates of the Fundación were typical examples of individual borrowing. Their loan officer, Josefina, spent her afternoons making house visits to her clients to initiate lending to new borrowers, as well as approve further borrowing from her existing clients; she brought the necessary documents to their homes in order to verify their addresses and assess their merit for further borrowing from the Fundación. Josefina's use of the plural *clientes* was key, since it already signaled the slippages in the social unit of debt; although only one of the pair—in this case, the husband—was the contractually liable borrower, both husband and wife were glossed as clients with equal standing at the Fundación. Josefina's clients were a married couple in their early fifties. The pair had grown children and lived alone in a modest house in an outlying neighborhood of Ciudad del Este. The woman was an Avon representative and sold other cosmetics to her neighbors and extended family; her husband was a wholesaler and owned a vehicle that he used to make deliveries. As with many of Josefina's visits to establish creditworthiness and approve a loan, I hoped for an in-depth account of who her clients were, how they saw their livelihood, and what they thought of their loan. However, the brief and highly structured meetings had a utilitarian purpose for both Josefina and her clients. Together they were focused on establishing the financial footing of the family and completing successfully the necessary loan documents. Both the clients and their loan officer dismissed my queries about the wider context of the loan in their lives. Instead, they focused on how their line of credit at the Fundación had increased over several years of borrowing, and now they were automatically approved for about $520 (with 33 percent annual interest) to be repaid in twelve monthly payments. The loan amounted to about double the monthly minimum wage for salaried positions in Paraguay (a wage that was considered adequate income for a working-class family). For an average borrower this loan might represent a quarter or more of his or her annual income. The aim of Josefina's visit was to confirm that nothing dramatic had changed since the previous loan cycle that might affect the couple's creditworthiness.

When Josefina asked how they planned to use their loan, they said that part of the loan was earmarked to pay for repairs on his truck so that he could continue making deliveries. His wife also wanted to pay some of her cosmetics suppliers and make purchases for the household.

The loan essentially functioned much like a joint credit card, allowing the couple to make purchases for big-ticket items and then make smaller monthly payments to cancel the outstanding debt. Individual loans were most often for families and were usually destined for a combination of consumer credit, bills, and investment in self-employed business ventures. In other words, Josefina's clients were a dual-income family with assets distributed across multiple economic relationships: suppliers and loyal customers for both businesses and a jointly owned house are just a few of the economic relationships at work here. There is certainly a class dimension to their designation as individual clients and participation in the small business credit program. However, as Viki's laundry list of credits attests, women who borrowed group-based loans often were individual clients elsewhere: in Viki's case, a Paraguayan finance company and various forms of consumer credit. For Josefina's clients at Fundación Paraguaya, many relationships anchored the creditworthiness of the loan applicants, who, despite these manifold interdependencies, fell under the administrative category of an individual loan.

I suggest that the individual was very much a product of his or her encounter with the lending structure of the microloan since this loan might equally be described as a group-based loan or a household loan, especially in light of the fact that if it went to collection *both* the borrower and guarantor would be liable. The individual borrower stood in for the heteronormative household and was brought into focus through the lending process itself. The individual social unit of debt gained coherence despite the fact that the loan was effectually distributed across a variety of persons and was carried by the intimacies of family, work relationships, and household obligations. Tellingly, the family was thought of as a feature of the unmarked client, since clients' relations were considered personal attributes or qualities of the individual borrower. The individual creditworthy borrower as the social unit of debt stood in for and subsumed those modes of interdependency.

DILEMMAS OF GROUP MEMBERSHIP: SOLIDARITY AS JOINT RESPONSIBILITY

In contrast to the NGO's individual loans, group-based loans did not recognize social relations as personal attributes that could be concretized in documents. The only requirement for group-based borrowing was a photocopy of each woman's national identity card and a credit check performed at the office by the credit counselor. The most important marker of creditworthiness was membership in the borrowing group. Indeed, joint liability was conceived in response to women's lack of documented assets and income; women's unequal access to physical collateral, after all, is one of the primary justifications for microcredit loans. In the administration of loans for Committees of Women Entrepreneurs, relationships were recognized as structural bonds that grounded the social whole and encompassed various individuated parts. On the one hand, individual loans spun off all sorts of other social effluvia, including manila folders stuffed with merchandise contracts, land titles, and wage and salary contracts, all of which supported the creditworthiness of the Fundación's individual clients. On the other hand, for group-based loans the social unit of debt was the committee, to which women were related as members of a group rather than personally creditworthy individuals.

As with labor economists studying the informal economy, for the Fundación, women's "flexibility" made them ideal candidates for group-based microcredit borrowing. However, this also highlighted the precariousness of women's claims on income; when flexibility was read as instability it could jeopardize their loan repayments. In the absence of documents that concretized financial relationships, credit counselors administered the creditworthiness of committees' group-based loans by managing the shifting intimacies and connections that held the borrowing groups together. In contrast to individual microloans, where the identification of client(s) was thought of as flexible, and often based on the contextual parameters of the business, family, and guarantor relationships, the membership of Committees of Women Entrepreneurs was seemingly clear-cut in administrative practice. However, in everyday administrative contexts, the credit counselors who administered these loans were fully aware that women relied on a whole host of social and economic obligations that extended beyond the boundaries of joint liability anchoring the microcredit group. Fundación Paraguaya's relationship with one of its financial backers, Kiva.org,[26] underscored some of the dilemmas that arose regarding the terms and extent of membership in a borrowing group. If women were thought to be especially good candidates for group-based loans because of their already hypersocial economic lives, for the purposes of determining creditworthiness, where was the boundary around the social unit of debt to be drawn? Which relationships counted for social collateral, and which fell outside the bounds of credit?

For borrowing groups that received loans through Kiva.org, the group as such was dramatized in several administrative rituals, in addition to the daily work of Fundación Paraguaya and the prosaic management of credit. A photo of the group of borrowers was published on the organization's website, accompanied by the names of each member. Fundación Paraguaya's credit counselors were tasked with reporting the progress of the group—labor they talked about as "working my Kiva"—in elaborate computer spreadsheets that were forwarded to the head office in Asunción and from there to Kiva.org's headquarters in San Francisco, California. In practice, there was more bureaucratic give in the system than the claims to total transparency and accountability might suggest. As scholars have noted, the credit cycles often overlapped unevenly with the information and reporting cycles that underpinned the fund-raising drives on the Kiva.org website,[27] such that American donors were encouraged to offer a loan to a group that was already midway through its credit cycle. However, from Fundación Paraguaya's perspective, Kiva loans differed only slightly from group loans administered through other funding streams, the major difference being that group membership was visible through more bureaucratic moments than loans that were handled entirely in-house. In fact, Fundación Paraguaya's own policies in many ways anticipated some of Kiva.org's requirements and were if anything more rigorous about defining and convening the group, from long bus rides for women to make periodic appearances at the headquarters to detailed maps drawn by credit counselors locating each of the borrowers in a neighborhood. The relationship between Kiva and Fundación Paraguaya upended many of my expectations about the power relations between international development organizations and their local partners.

The importance of fully accounting for group membership, then, was a central concern at the Ciudad del Este branch office when a group of Kiva.org interns traveled to Ciudad del Este to interview Fundación Paraguaya's clients. The credit counselors at the branch office hurriedly arranged meetings with their clients, calling several committees to arrange midafternoon field visits in the neighborhoods of several of their borrowing groups. These sorts of home visits were not unusual for NGO staff, as both loan officers and credit counselors spent about half of the workday traveling throughout the city to initiate, oversee, and renew the loans of their borrowers. Maria Elena, one of the young credit counselors at the NGO, arranged a meeting for the afternoon, and I followed her and the Kiva interns out to meet with the committee. This particular borrowing group was located in a middle-income neighborhood not far from the city center. The modest houses were quite similar to the dwellings of Josefina's individual clients. Considering the proximity to Ciudad del Este's commercial downtown, it was unsurprising when only fifteen of the twenty members were present at the meeting. Many women in the group had full-time work in the bustling commercial trade and had not been able to leave their jobs to attend the hastily arranged meeting.

Many of the absent group members worked as cleaners, cooks, domestic workers, and street vendors downtown, which meant that they used their microcredit loans for consumer credit rather than as capital for a business. Their labor was both semiformal, with few wage protections, no licensing, and no documentation, and highly *inflexible*. They thus did not enjoy the flexibility of self-employment presumed by the entrepreneurialism of the NGO's Committees of Women Entrepreneurs program. As a consequence, the same sort of wage labor that could be converted successfully into loan documentation for Fundación Paraguaya's individual clients actually served for many women as an impediment to meeting the basic terms of the putatively more inclusive group-based lending and social collateral.

Maria Elena speculated aloud that fifteen women might be sufficient to hold the meeting. After checking her Kiva.org handbook, however, she found that the organization required that for a group of twenty borrowers, at least seventeen members had to be present for the purposes of photos and other documentation for the organization. Neither of the Kiva.org interns seemed particularly inclined to press the point and cancel the meeting, but Maria Elena took the guidelines seriously and suggested that they try to arrange for another time to visit. The borrowing group, clearly annoyed that they had left their homes and work for the meeting, quickly set about making arrangements to fulfill the seventeen-person requirement so that they could hold the meeting as planned. When Maria Elena attempted to reschedule, the president and treasurer of the group insisted that they could "complete" (*completar*) the group for the purposes of the photo. One woman was dispatched to find her teenage daughter, who was at home, and another woman enlisted the neighbor she employed to help with cleaning and cooking to stand in for another group member. These "recruits" were considered part of the group anyway, as they routinely participated in the economic livelihoods of the borrowing group. Their ease in asking other neighbors to stand in for absent member was consistent with the dense economic obligations that undergirded the solidarity loan, even if it was only a justification for the use of substitutes in a routine administrative requirement. Their primary concern was to "complete" the group, even if not with the correct women.

The meeting was rescheduled for later in the evening when seventeen members could be present. The group, in the borrowers' view, was anchored in the neighborhood and was not wholly defined by contractual joint obligation for the loan. The credit counselors, the Kiva interns, and the committee all seemed inclined to consider the group "complete," but the institutional imperative of matching money directly with people meant that solidarity stopped at the terminus line of the group. And this was certainly not the only bureaucratic ritual that required the full group membership. As discussed above, the full committee was required to be present at the office in order for a new loan cycle to be initiated. In both cases, the arithmetic of solidarity emphasized the sum total of membership of the group.

In these diverse ways the Fundación operated under a sort of Goldilocks rule of solidarity. Too much, and the group ran the risk of having their economic lives so entangled that they would not be able to generate income independently in order to repay their loans. Too little, and the connection forged through contractual joint liability would not be sufficient to hold the committee together. Within the broader administration of microcredit group-based lending, establishing and regulating the social unit of debt was hard work for both lenders and borrowers. Crucially, all of these modes of interdependency relied on external ties to sustain and stabilize the group: a social reality underscored by the Kiva.org incident, which showed that women managed all sorts of obligations, many of which were conceptualized and carried out in economic terms. Conversations with Fundación Paraguaya credit counselors revealed that it was precisely the flexibility of women's economic livelihoods that made them so eager to incorporate members with external claims on sources of wealth and support. As exemplified by the Kiva.org meeting, however, the convertibility of women's work into creditworthiness had a gendered cultural politics, since it was precisely a steady job that prevented women from complying with the institutional and administrative requirements—of both Kiva.org and Fundación Paraguaya—that were the basis of social collateral. Credit counselors expressed relief when they found that a prospective women's committee borrower had a husband or mother-in-law or daughter with a stable salaried job, like Viki's husband who worked at a parking garage downtown. If the borrower ran into difficulty making her weekly loan installments, the credit counselors reasoned that the borrower could probably enlist the financial help of a relative to make up the shortfall rather than impose that burden on fellow committee members.

Credit counselors like Maria Elena managed their clients based on their sense that women's unstable employment in the informal economy meant that each borrower on her own probably would not have the income to consistently pay back her microcredit loan while also tacitly acknowledging that the loan was rarely for a borrower's personal entrepreneurial venture.

If the individual microloan brings into relief the individual borrower through his or her encounter with the loan contract, so too does the solidarity loan bring into relief the committee, particularly as a unity based primarily on joint liability. In other words, Fundación Paraguaya's two-tiered lending structure not only managed a sizable loan portfolio; it also managed the individuality and groupness of its clients. Social collateral shaped what it meant to be a woman and a borrower. The different loan requirements, documentation procedures, and membership criteria worked to construct different classes of borrowers based on different assumptions about gendered forms of economic joint liability, from the unmarked client/guarantor relationship to the marked microcredit committees. The constellation of documents and relationships marshaled as evidence of creditworthiness for individual and group-based loans produced and reproduced economic subjects with differential capacity to embody or encompass those external relationships. It produced the social unit of debt.

BUYING INTO SOCIAL COLLATERAL

In the absence of documents that concretized financial relationships, credit counselors undertook to administer the creditworthiness of committees' group-based loans by managing the shifting intimacies and connections that held the borrowing groups together. This was particularly important because committees drew together relative strangers. Here I tell the story of one such meeting as an example of the type of administrative work that occupied the vast majority of credit counselors' time and energy. Midway through my fieldwork in Ciudad del Este, I shadowed a credit counselor as she processed the application for a loan renewal with a Committee of Women Entrepreneurs that was beginning its third cycle of borrowing. The concerted discussion about group membership that formed the basis for much of the meeting for a loan renewal by this group was very similar to the dozens of other loan renewals undertaken each month by credit counselors at the Ciudad del Este microcredit branch. In nearly each instance, the shifting membership

of the group posed a significant challenge to both the borrowing committee leadership and their credit counselor. Stabilizing the group and making it cohere from one loan to the next involved the technical labor of
assessing creditworthiness of the group but also evaluating and managing the interpersonal bonds between individual group members. These
bonds of joint responsibility made the committee self-similar from one
cycle to the next and grounded the social whole even as group membership was constantly in flux.

In the case of this loan renewal, the torrential rain made the roads to
the neighborhood impassable, and the local city bus that connected that
neighborhood with downtown Ciudad del Este shortened its normal
route by a full kilometer and a half when the weather was bad. Their
credit counselor from the Fundación, Silvenia, hitched a ride in my
ancient (but usually all-terrain) Volkswagen Beetle, and, carefully navigating the slippery roads, we arrived a full hour late for the meeting. En
route, the credit counselor called the president and treasurer of the committee on her cell phone to see if they had access to a meeting place
along the rock-cobbled roads that connected their neighborhood with
the highway; otherwise, even my trusty VW would not be able to get us
there in the bad weather. A compromise location at a local community
center closer to the highway was agreed upon as the new meeting place,
though it was nearly a twenty-minute walk from the homes of most of
the committee members. The roads and the weather were so treacherous that many of the members of the committee trickled in behind us,
squeezing water from soggy sandals and commenting on the long walk
from the housing settlement through Ciudad del Este's ubiquitous red
clay mud. Fundación Paraguaya's policy that every member had to be at
the meeting to sign the loan documents for the next cycle was in part
because of the serious nature of signatures in the Paraguayan legal system but also because the Fundación wanted to be sure that all members
were fully accounted for and integrated into the group before issuing a
check for the loan. If any one of the women were to back out at the last
minute, the contract, and by extension the check, which the central
office in the capital sent to Ciudad del Este by courier, would be void.
This would represent a loss of institutional labor and investment returns
for the Fundación. It would also pose a serious problem for the committee members, who were required also to be present in person at the
office to pick up the check, and would waste a long bus ride and the fare
to the office. And although many women said that they would be willing to vouch for their neighbors, many of whom were at home caring

for children and did not want to brave the storm, their credit counselor insisted that each woman had to be present to renew the loan.

Because the group had a history of borrowing with the Fundación, in this next cycle the biggest issue to settle was the question of membership in the committee for the upcoming cycle. Some members had left the group, which was a common predicament for committees at the Ciudad del Este branch office. Borrowers often found that the weekly or biweekly payment structure was too onerous, sought out other avenues of credit, or decided that the administrative burden of group membership was difficult to manage in practice. The diminished membership in the next cycle left a few spots open before the group reached its maximum size of fifteen members. The controversy revolved around the contention that if they let one new member join, existing members would be showing preferential treatment if they selected one woman out of the several who wanted to join. Groups have to balance the social pressure from other acquaintances against anxieties that new members might not be a good fit for the group, either because of personality clashes or repayment issues. The stakes were high for these decisions of inclusion and exclusion because the structure of joint liability meant that if one member missed her individual installment, other group members would be forced to cover her share to stave off missing a payment as a group.

Despite the rain, seven nonmember women came to the meeting, hoping to join the group and begin borrowing in the next cycle. As they debated membership in the group, the treasurer, Bernarda, commented that there was one woman who was staying but as a *prestanombre*, which literally means a "name lender," a woman who takes out credit with Fundación Paraguaya and then turns that money over to somebody else, much like serving as a guarantor for individual loans. These arrangements were sometimes overtly commercial, and borrowers would charge a fee or interest for relending. Beyond the potential profits, prestanombres often re-lent money at zero or negative interest to cement ties with family, friends, or work associates.[28] The group and the credit counselor seemed to agree that there was nothing untoward about this arrangement since each member was responsible for how she used her portion of the loan. As long as the prestanombre reliably paid the weekly quota, the other members were unconcerned about the social arrangements that anchored her repayment since they were external to the forms of obligation—the structural bonds between group members—that bound the group together and to the Fundación. Those modes of collective affiliation were also external to the Fundación's development mission, which centered on the progress of the group through consecutive borrowing cycles, even with its shifting membership. This was made clear by the Fundación's lack of institutional measures regarding group members' business relationships. In fact, all of those relationships were subsumed by the group as the social unit of debt.

It was important for the group to maintain itself because the loan ceiling increased with every cycle and because the wage and commission structure for credit counselors prioritized the number of renewals they made every month. Both lender and borrowers were committed to maintaining the committee. Because it was the start of this group's third cycle, Silvenia advised that it would be best if the group membership remained stable (i.e., old members only) as they progressed. She counseled them that there were always problems with women who did not know the system and warned that new members could cause the group to fall behind because they were not fully cognizant of the implications of late payment. And, she noted, the old group had worked together for the past two cycles so they already knew how to make the group function correctly. Raising her hand, one member spoke up and told the group that she wanted to leave and have her daughter replace her. Silvenia contemplated this briefly and responded that it might be acceptable because it simply entailed substituting for a member who was leaving. Unconvinced, other members complained that it was unfair and playing favorites. Silvenia's concern with substitution in the group resonates with the anthropologist Annette Weiner's (1980) suggestion that replacement, in addition to long-standing concerns in economic anthropology about reciprocity, should be considered a central element of exchange relations. Weiner notes that norms of reciprocity must be analyzed as part of a larger system—a reproductive system (71). In other words, replacement leaves the original obligation intact but *expands* it by incorporating the social ties of new participants. The expanding effects of replacement are interesting in the case of microcredit and its social unit of debt, since the daughters replacing mothers still include the relationships between kin within the group and, importantly, the daughter's claims on her mother's income if she ran into payment problems. Simply integrating new nondaughter members would not regenerate the group in the same way. It would exclude the previous social connections— which had already proven to contribute to the group's repayment in the previous cycle—rather than build on them.

Fundación staff were sensitive to the density of connections that crosscut borrowing groups. Indeed, the Fundación had a policy that no more than half of the committee could be members of the same family, but Silvenia encouraged bringing in members who were known to the group and thus was supportive of a daughter replacing her mother. It was not uncommon for all the members of a borrowing group to be related in extended networks of kinship. On a different occasion, another committee nearly ran afoul of the cap on relatives in the group, but after asking for clarification about which relatives counted for the purposes of the Fundación, they realized that they were all related but skirted the rule by virtue of having different last names (it was common for a woman also to take her husband's last name). Their credit counselor was fully aware of the group's tactical portrayal of family ties. She would rather err on the side of too many personal connections than too few. In the case of the daughter who would replace her mother in Bernarda's borrowing group, that credit counselor based her decision about relatedness on her perception of the women's ability to act independently, especially concerning sources of income. When deciding whether a mother and a daughter might join that group together, she asked how old the mother was (fifty-one) in order to determine whether she still might be generating income. From the perspective of the Fundación, the main concern was that the older woman was not relying on her daughter for financial support; if they had different "activities" (businesses) their kinship connection was less alarming. Satisfied that the two women were sufficiently independent, Silvenia seemed to take the *absence* of mutual interdependence and support as a key factor in making her decision about whether the two were too closely related to be in the group together.

As Silvenia contemplated the quandaries of group membership and replacement, she seemed on the one hand to assume that bonds like neighborhood friendships and family ties were part of what brought the Committee of Women Entrepreneurs together. On the other hand, she was nervous about relying too much on the regulatory capabilities of the group and emphasized that familiarity with financial management and the payment system—a regulatory intimacy of organizational practices rather than the intimacies of shared personal connections—was the most important feature in assessing the fitness of a new member to join the committee. This is likely the reason she was willing to accept the daughter as her mother's replacement; being already familiar with the structure of the loan, the new member would replace—and presumably still be able to rely on—the financial know-how of her mother.

As the debate about replacement wound down, Bernarda, the group's treasurer, commented that there were enough new borrowers who wanted to join that they could really just start their own group. She said, "I waited seven months to form my group. I made my group," implying that the new group should thicken their group bonds in the same fashion. One of the women who wanted to join the existing group responded that she worried that the other potential borrowers she found for her group would not be responsible, and asked what would happen if there were twelve members and eight decided not to pay. Silvenia responded that as soon as they figure out the system, they would pay because they would all see that it is necessary for the next loan: "They will want to pay for their next credit [Van a querer pagar para el proximo crédito]." She added that it would never be the case that half the committee would decide not to pay: the Fundación would not permit it it because it's not good business. It is important to reiterate that the Fundación did not track the individual payment records of group members but only kept records of the whole committee's payments. In other words, Silvenia was expressing great confidence in the system to *generate* obligation so that she would not need to intervene in the group at all.

This renewal meeting was very similar to the countless others that I observed. In each instance, consolidating a borrowing group and making it cohere from cycle to cycle felt like an achievement. What I want to call attention to are the ways that the mechanics of group-based lending often worked at cross-purposes to the ideal of group cohesion and solidarity expressed by the NGO. As noted at the beginning of this chapter, many of the rituals of the Fundación sought to dramatize the unity of the group by making sure that the committee performs key formalities as a group. Showing up in person and standing in the Fundación's office together, convening for a meeting in the driving rain even while neighbors and friends would be happy to pass along information to ease the burden of attendance for some of the members, and grumbling from the credit counselor about changing group members—all this served to instantiate the committee as a unit of debt. These were performatives that were physical and embodied. And in the instance where the group observed that "we are all relatives," credit counselors were attentive to the other forms of mutual obligation at work in committees, and which form the basis for successful credit and repayment. However, if the individual microloan brought into relief the individual borrower through his or her encounter with the loan contract, so too did the solidarity loan bring into relief the committee but particularly as a unity based primarily on joint liability. Both the credit counselors and the women who borrowed agreed that personal connections could serve as a good basis for collective liability but were nervous that those dense ties would overburden the group. From the delicate work of forming and maintaining the group, we can appreciate how obligation is produced and managed through the hard relational work of credit counselors and borrowers. It was certainly not an automatic consequence of women's work, as studies of economic "flexibility" would suggest.

CREDIT SCORES AND THE CONSEQUENCES OF DEFAULT

The link between the social unit of debt and external relationships is especially significant in light of the central place of formalized credit as a socially important way for women to manage their own claims and the claims of others on the economic resources of their households, communities, and extended kin networks. Often the strictures of formal financial relationships offered a way for women to protect resources, as borrowers often lamented how "money flies from your pocket." The story of women's creditworthiness did not just unfold in the intimate interpersonal encounters between borrowers and their credit counselor. The gendering of creditworthiness exposed women's committee members to especially debilitating forms of externalized surveillance through Paraguay's private sector credit scoring system. Ciudad del Este's gendered division of labor, however, would not necessarily predict the hierarchy of obligations within and between households. Women often took the lead in managing household finances, including their loans and the wage income from a husband or partner. As Viki's enumeration of credit so vividly demonstrates, monthly debts were a key mechanism through which women managed their household finances. Their credit worlds were made up of a list of anticipated obligations rather than a daily tally of income and expenditures.[29]

The importance of debts, or cuentas, as a hierarchy of obligations could be seen most strikingly in the moment in the loan's life cycle when the installment payment came due. Months after meeting with Bernarda's committee about the contentious loan renewal and membership, the group's leadership was involved in a local neighborhood association with its own financial commitments and also had economic ties within neighborly and kin circles. I had followed up with her group after their loan renewal and spent several months volunteering and participating with their committee and several others in the neighborhood. Both Fabiana and Viki, whose stories of indebtedness I detail elsewhere, lived nearby.

In one example of the broader context of these overlapping obligations, the day before the biweekly loan installment came due, the group members were working on a community fund-raiser and bake sale at the same time that they were collecting the microcredit quota from members. As I was helping with the preparations, a former member of the group, a formidable woman named Doña Modesta, rolled up on a scooter, horn tooting merrily, and waved to us over the wire fence around the home. Calling Bernarda—who was still the treasurer—over from her culinary preparations, Doña Modesta opened her purse and extracted two green bills, each worth about $20 (100,000 guaranis). This was a visually striking payment since these notes were the highest denomination of Paraguayan currency. The money was for the microcredit payment that was due the next day, but Doña Modesta had left the group in the previous cycle and her payment was for her daughter's and her niece's loan installment. Both of the younger women lived in the neighborhood; in fact, Doña Modesta's daughter lived right next door. Bernarda, as treasurer of the microcredit group, would take all the group members' payments to the Fundación's office downtown the following day. But the $40 was not just for the microcredit payment; it also was meant to cover the family's contributions to the neighborhood fund-raiser. Neither Bernarda nor Modesta made clear exactly where the line separating the microcredit payment from the community fund was drawn. Bernarda accepted the money and told her friend that she would get her change later when she had a chance to break the big bills. In practice, this sort of delay in making change often served as an informal credit. Money came in for the microcredit and neighborhood commission. Money was expected to go out for expenses and loan payments. And a floating loan remained in the form of the unreturned change that the treasurer would pay later.

Money bled back and forth between the collective funds for the two different associations, both within and between families. After Doña Modesta left, Bernarda and her neighbor—who was Modesta's daughter—undertook the task of accounting for the upcoming microcredit installment. The fat envelope that held the microcredit installment payment was passed back and forth across the fence between neighbors in order to double check that they had, in their words, "completed" the installment, in the same way that the group of Kiva.org borrowers strove to "complete" the group. Here the word seemed particularly apt. The installment was a fixed amount and loomed large. The women were concerned with filling in whatever little shortfalls there were in order to complete the requisite sum.

FIGURE 7. Bernarda's microcredit group collects payments for its weekly loan installment.

Since Fundación Paraguaya imposed a strict payment schedule on the microcredit group, it was usually considered more important to account for all of the committee money than the neighborhood commission money. The labor that Bernarda put into the activities for the commission also seemed to do some of the work of "completing"—here, making up the difference—for what money might have been shuffled from the neighborhood fund to the microcredit payment. But accounting for her cooking labor was not a straightforward process either. Surveying the ingredients, Bernarda commented that she might even be able to double or triple her investment and perhaps make some money for herself. Puzzled, I asked how she was going to make any money if the investment came from the neighborhood commission; wasn't the profit supposed to go to the association's fund-raiser? Bernarda answered a bit evasively, saying that it was, but she still hoped to make some money if she worked hard. She hoped, it seemed, to have some extra profit once all of the obligations to the neighborhood commission and the microcredit group had been met. Tellingly, the fund-raiser actually had an inbuilt sense of debt organizing the expectations around the money they were hoping to collect.

Both external support and external surveillance on borrowers' finances, then, came from a variety of locations. In the microcredit world, external surveillance had a specific gendered component and mapped differently onto the social unit of debt for the NGO's distinct categories of loans. Whereas Bernarda's borrowing group moved fluidly between individual and collective management of economic obligation—an interplay of neighborhood resources, personal gain, and group membership—the Fundación emphasized collective liability for women's committees. Collective liability was especially visible in how the NGO used credit scores. Borrowers' credit histories were provided by Informconf, the private sector Paraguayan credit scoring service, established in 1963, that offers an annual subscription to its database and collects credit information on all Paraguayan nationals. The credit check system is so far-reaching that even borrowers with few links to the formal financial sector figure in the Informconf database.[30] Informconf has become nearly synonymous with creditworthiness in the world of business, as well as the lived experience of most Paraguayans, similar to the way Fico scores have come to permeate the U.S. consumer credit market.[31]

Informconf credit reports for Committees of Women Entrepreneurs epitomized the collective liability at the root of group-based loans. Each borrower signed a contract for the total amount of the loan and was listed in the Informconf database as indebted for the total sum the group borrowed. This was true for both the borrower and the guarantor in individual loans as well; both were listed on an Informconf credit report. However, the large size of the group and the dearth of other documented financial ties women who borrowed as a committee pushed the implications of that joint responsibility and external surveillance to an extreme. For example, when the twenty members of Maria Elena's group renewed their loan for another cycle, and each borrowed about $200, they would sign a collective loan contract for about $4,000. That sum, which represented more than twice the annual income of many of those borrowers, was then divided up and a portion allocated to each member. If any member of the group were to default on her loan, the group would have to respond to cover her installment or risk being collectively "entered into Informconf" as defaulters (morosas).[32] The arithmetic of joint responsibility would not, however, record the outstanding balance of each member—that is, the $200, which represented one-twentieth of the total—but rather each woman would be listed as owing the full $4,000 of the twenty-member group-based loan. The collective debt of group-based loans meant that the social unit of debt was the committee, and thus group membership made the aggregate sums breathtakingly large for each group member.

The specter of *morosidad,* then, highlights a tension at the heart of these microcredit antipoverty programs. Namely, Fundación Paraguaya's mission of financial inclusion in formal banking and finance is premised on the implicit—though rarely discussed—threat of permanent exclusion. If the loan were not repaid, the staggering debt recorded by Informconf would mean that each borrower would be effectively barred from any formal financial relationships that rely on Informconf data to evaluate creditworthiness, from a cell phone account to an employment contract. Given Informconf's permeation of the Paraguayan market, morosidad was a horrifying prospect. One credit counselor cautioned her group, "Informconf closes doors; it's how people blow it." In fact, when I followed up with Bernarda's group in 2015, five years after we first discussed their group loans, she described payment problems that had led them to "almost be entered into Informconf." The prospect was so alarming that the group collectively covered the payments of defaulting neighbors who could not pay their share, and all of the women left the Committee of Women Entrepreneurs program for good.

While external surveillance in many cases was a way for women to stabilize claims on wage income and household wealth, in order to stave off default, external sources of wealth were tapped to forestall repayment problems and avert morosidad. However, by locating those relationships outside of the financial connections recognized by Fundación Paraguaya, the NGO cemented the borrowing group as the primary administrative unit and target of its development priorities, and recast those other economic relations simply as kin or neighborhood ties, rendering them invisible to the organization and its metrics of creditworthiness. The extended network of economic interdependency that was so palpable in the repayment strategies of Bernarda and her borrowing group and that undergirded and made possible the information that appeared on a credit report, ultimately went unaccounted for in the case of Committees of Women Entrepreneurs because the *only* criterion for membership was a credit check, which reiterated the ties of joint liability of the group. The reified group stood in for those relationships, even as responsibility was affixed on each woman individually through her personal score and accountability for the full loan.

However, groups only in very rare cases imploded; this occurred only a handful of times in the course of my long-term fieldwork, and in those cases because cascading catastrophes had successively torn the group apart. Thus the remarkable thing about the credit score was not simply its punitive measures but also all of the pragmatic work-arounds that it produced in everyday practice. When I expressed alarm about the potential consequences of collective debt, both credit counselors and women borrowers assured me that things never reached that point, and groups always found a way to close out the cycle and then simply walked away, presumably with a clean Informconf record, just as Bernarda's group had done. In twenty months of fieldwork, only a single borrowing group entered into judicial proceedings (*proceso judicial*) for defaulting on collective debt. Both the organization and the borrowers were quite confident about the resiliency of the system of social collateral. While the disciplinary potential of collective debt, which appeared so starkly on the credit score and seemed quite frightening as a thought experiment for me and for credit counselors, what was most significant about the looming horizon of an inflexible credit score was its effectiveness at producing everyday flexibilities: the frantic scramble to close out the cycle, the multiple business activities to pay a quota, and the family resources recruited into payments.

This was in marked contrast to individual clients, who could formalize those ties of mutual obligation in documents that attested to their creditworthiness: guarantor relationships, joint property, business inventory, supplier contracts, and so on, which also showed up on a credit report. For individual microloans those documented relationships figured as durable qualities of persons, in contrast to the contractual ties of joint responsibility that bound women together as flexible members of a collectivity. Gendered tropes of creditworthiness organized and structured the very mechanics of the financial tool—enacting and embodying the social unit of debt—down to the incorporation of seemingly objective and impartial credit scores. While the dense relational ties of women were assumed to be the intrinsic qualities of women borrowers, the borrowing practices themselves actually created meaningful differences through the production and management of the individual and the group as the social unit of debt. The labor of completando illustrates how microcredit lending practices *create* the very flexibilities that are attributed to gendered cultural logics in Paraguay.

REFUSING TO PAY ANOTHER MAN'S BILLS: MEN'S COMMITTEES

Perhaps the most visible site of gender-regulated creditworthiness can be found in Fundación Paraguaya's disappointingly short-lived men's committees (*comités de hombres,* or *kuimba'e aty* in Guarani). Initiated in 2008—two years after the *comités de mujeres,* or women's committees—the program was diagnosed as a complete failure and dismantled after just two cycles of its pilot project. When I began working with the Fundación in 2009, the project had already been judged a disaster by the Ciudad del Este branch, and a single loan officer, Josefina, was overseeing the last handful of participants. Josefina explained to me that the men's committee loans had a structure similar to women's committee loans, except that men's committees offered much more individual autonomy for its members. In her words, "It is a solidarity group except that each one [member] is independent." This was familiar rhetoric from the women's committees and indeed from the broader emphasis on empowerment and self-responsibility that drove the development programming at Fundación Paraguaya. Credit counselors often emphasized both the element of joint liability and the independent allocation of shares of the women's committee loan to each member. However, for women's committees the Fundación did not track the individual payment histories of each of the borrowers in the group; that responsibility was delegated to the group's treasurer. By contrast, in men's committees, each member had his own slim green folder in Josefina's file cabinet, and each borrower was responsible for his own loan. The reason these were deemed committee loans, however, was that the documents needed to establish creditworthiness were minimal and the group progressed together through cycles of borrowing. As with women's committees, there was a real incentive to pay on time, or risk "getting stuck," as they termed it, at a lower credit ceiling. Josefina explained that with men's committees, too, the group as a whole could not fall behind on its payments or they would not get to the next level or cycle of the loan. Also, as with women's committees, the Fundación relied on men's group members to recruit potential borrowers and thus shoulder the risk and surveillance that might otherwise be the responsibility of the lending institution.[33] Fundación Paraguaya envisioned the men's committees as an inroad to potential clients.

However, despite the centrality of social collateral in framing men's committees and their creditworthiness, men's committee borrowers were authorized to act independently of one another and of the group in a few key administrative moments during the life course of the loan. For instance, any one of the men's committee members could bring the whole group's payment on a weekly basis, but Josefina explained that he would also bring the account books (*libretas*) for each member of the group so that each payment could be recorded separately. Women's Committees also relied on payment account books to track the payment histories of group members, but the accounting forms were internal to the committee and held no regulatory or contractual weight with the Fundación. Usually women's committees ran into trouble when a member whose personal payment to the group was up to date, and meticulously recorded in their own account books, complained that her group was considered in default because collectively they were behind in payments. The structure of the men's committees obviated this problem by assigning liability on an individual basis.

Other key differences between the men's and women's committees reflected different assumptions about the flexibility of borrowers as the basis for credit access. For instance, men's committees were not obligated to have a 10 percent savings component. For women's committees the savings requirement served nominally as a cushion for the member's personal or household budget and—perhaps more important—as collateral for the next cycle of lending. One reason the men's committees lacked a savings component was because the Fundación thought men were more financially stable than most members of women's committees. For instance, when asked by their credit counselors to list their vocation on the credit application forms, many women laughed and replied that their work was "a little bit of everything" (todo un poco) to make ends meet. However, the loan applicants for Josefina's men's committee listed their employment by trade. One worked as a mechanic, two worked in construction, one sold bread for a local bakery, and another was a bill collector. In practice men's committees incorporated important aspects of the consumer credit of individual microloans but without the documentation and asset requirements that would be necessary for a personal line of credit, relying instead on self-reported work histories.

Finally, the small list of members is itself noteworthy. While women's committees struggled to coordinate the financial lives of fifteen to twenty-five members, men's committees were permitted to have only five to eight members. This meant that men's committees had an ambiguous relationship to Informconf credit scores and morosidad: the smaller groups meant that the joint liability was somewhat attenuated, but this was offset by the possibility of larger lines of credit. What is more, after giving a brief orientation and fielding questions from the five potential members, Josefina left the organization of the committee almost entirely up to the five men. While the credit counselors for women's committees routinely made several trips to organize new borrowing groups and fill out a veritable mountain of paperwork, Josefina parted company with the five applicants for the men's committee by suggesting that they organize themselves, fill out the paperwork, and have somebody deliver it to the Fundación. Once the documents were in order, she assured them that the loan would be processed within one or two days. Women's committee meetings, on the other hand, would routinely take two or more hours, including a walking tour of the neighborhood to confirm that all of the dozen or more members lived in close proximity. Men's committees were spared much of the monitoring and discipline that was central to the creditworthiness of women's committees, primarily because Josefina was used to dealing with individual clients, for whom creditworthiness figured as a personal quality. And since so much of microcredit social collateral is about the instrumentalization of borrowers' social relationships through mutual surveillance as well as mutual support, the differential treatment of men's committees is especially telling. Josefina tacitly read creditworthiness through the individual qualities of her borrowers, including earning potential and ability to self-organize.

When I asked several NGO staff members at the Ciudad del Este office why the men's committees were so short-lived, the loan officers and credit counselors gave me the same answer: men refused to pay somebody else's bills (*cuenta ajena*). In fact, this was the same language that people used to talk about their discomfort and uneasiness around strangers more generally (*personal ajena*). In other words, they would refuse to recognize their relationships of mutual obligation as collateralizing their loan. While this refusal was naturalized by the microcredit functionaries as an unfortunate but inherent attribute of Paraguayan men— stemming from machismo—in effect, the special configuration of men's committees already worked to undermine the ties that bound the group together. In other words, the loan itself was only partly collateralized by men's relationships, relying more heavily on individual income potential and repayment records of men's committee members, which figured as a feature of borrowers' masculinity. To gloss the failure of the loans as a failure of social ties began with the premise that these were in fact solidarity loans just like the women's committee loans and that men's solidarity failed. However, the regulation of men's committees actually undermined their social collateral, even as bank functionaries lamented its failure. Since men's committees did not rely on documented physical assets as collateral to reify those social connections and attach them to the borrower as a source of creditworthiness, unlike Josefina's other individual clients, it seems as though masculinity was doing much of the work of attributing creditworthiness to the borrower. And the failure of the program suggested that this was not sufficient in and of itself.

In administrative practice, part of the reason staff members were cautious about drawing parallels between men's and women's committees had much to do with the division of labor in the microcredit office itself. Josefina was a loan officer with professional credentialing in financial services, and she had worked on small business credit since the Ciudad del Este branch opened in 2006. Compared to credit counselors, she was much less attuned to the everyday work-arounds that were produced by the peculiar forms of external discipline at work in women's committees, since she thought of herself as a financial professional equipped to evaluate and bank on the creditworthiness of each one of her clients on his or her own terms. At stake, then, were forms of gendered professional knowledge within the office and the tacit acknowledgment of the glass ceiling when it came to banking on women's creditworthiness. Staff members' assessment that men's committee members would refuse to pay another man's bills highlights the corollary taken-for-granted assessment—that women *would* consent to paying another woman's bills. At one level, one could read this statement as an observation about gender relations in Paraguay, rearticulating pervasive views about men as independent breadwinners and women as caring and always already obligated. However, at another level, the Fundación staff members had identified the capacity of their own financial tools to generate different forms of economic joint obligation through the technical, managerial, day-to-day routine of administering the loans. This had important implications for the labor of lending as much as borrowing and paying. The production of creditworthy subjects and the production of financial instruments went hand in hand and worked to reproduce gender ideologies regarding domesticity and economic flexibility in Paraguay.

MARKED GROUPNESS IN THE GENDERING OF SOCIAL COLLATERAL

Returning to the questions of inequality and credit access that have long been the inspiration and justification for microcredit, I argue that it is important to look at how creditworthiness relies on gendered tropes of economic life above and beyond the asymmetrical distribution of physical assets as collateral and even beyond how microcredit capitalizes on the gender differences of its borrowers. Microcredit staff and borrowers understand credit as a mechanism to define, negotiate, and sustain many types of economic interdependency; gender marks and reproduces the link between those forms of joint liability and the "flexibility" of economic life. In pointing to the feminization of the administrative category "women's committees" compared to individual loans and men's committees, I go beyond analyses of microcredit that draw out the implications of instrumentalizing women's economic obligations.[34] Instead, I draw inspiration from Leslie Salzinger's (2003: 2) observation that "understanding that capital makes rather than finds such [feminized] workers, and that gender is implicated in the process, gives us new tools for thinking about how we might challenge the terms under which global production takes place." Salzinger's feminist scholarly commitments are invested in "making visible the connections between the production of subjects and the production of commodities" (2). As with labor in transnational production, credit instruments and development policy, too, are organized around gendered tropes in the management of debt, including the very unit of borrowing.

The presence of the *group* as the social unit of debt was crucial to establishing the creditworthiness of Committees of Women Entrepreneurs and also to instituting the management practices that continually dramatized group cohesion. For committees, the relationships of economic interdependency that undergirded the solvency of the group and its capacity to repay the solidarity loan were always located as external to the group itself, including in the broader context of neighborhood life and kin circles in Ciudad del Este. By contrast, for individual borrowers, relationships of economic interdependency that established creditworthiness were considered attributes or qualities that were attached to borrowers as personal properties of the unmarked client. The failed men's committees show that masculinity was implicated in the link between borrowers and the economic relationships that made them creditworthy. In administrative terms, through the many documents collated to bolster creditworthiness, individual borrowers stood in for and encompassed those modes of interdependency. Membership in a committee was markedly different. Instead of recognizing social relations as personal attributes that could be concretized as assets, for committees social relations were recognized as structural bonds that grounded the social whole and encompassed various individuated parts.

Fundación Paraguaya recognized two features of interdependency at work in creditworthiness: it glossed these as enabling relations of solidarity and punitive relations of joint liability. For individual clients the Fundación valorized both categories of interdependency, whereas for Committees of Women Entrepreneurs it recognized only the latter. This is immensely important, because drawing and stabilizing the line between enabling and debilitating forms of shared economic obligation had material consequences for microcredit borrowers, from credit scores to missing work in order to attend microcredit meetings to completing payments. For committees the group qua group exhibited the only bonds that counted: the bonds of joint responsibility that linked all of the individual members of the group to one another.

Crucially, a crediting of gender is at the heart of social collateral—from a glass ceiling in financial work to men's committees to completing payments—and creates both independence and interdependence. By enlivening and theorizing economic obligation in a context where it seems most natural, I consider the social unit of debt in order to rethink the anthropological project of reembedding commercial capitalism in its social context, as it risks overlooking how the seemingly obvious embeddedness of women is produced and the consequences it has. At stake is a cultural politics of interdependency that binds borrowers and lenders, financial technologies, and Paraguayan development in ways that structure global inequality and opportunity.

CHAPTER 4

Repayment

As Margaret Atwood (2008) has written in her literary work *Payback*, credit and debt are often "twinned" in popular imaginaries as a dyadic unit.[1] And as the anthropologist Chris Gregory elaborates, credit and debt—and hence, creditor and debtor—are a feature of double-entry bookkeeping and its twin columns of numbers that record the balance of crediting and debiting.[2] While it might seem like the simple act of signing a contract, shaking someone's hand, or exchanging money for a promise to repay would cement a person as a creditor or debtor,[3] in Paraguay these identities were often quite complex when people took up these obligations and forged relationships around them in daily economic practice. Meanwhile, the clandestine economy of Ciudad del Este made the clarity and certainty of bookkeeping and audit particularly fraught. By telling the story of the life course of loans, I track the different perspectives that offer slightly divergent accounts of obligations as they unfold over time. I argue that crises of repayment often happen when the loose-fitting nature of those perspectives cannot be held together.[4] In a context where bicycling debt is a common form of economic movement, this usually happens when somebody—either borrower or lender, or sometimes both—can no longer keep the pedals turning.

In Ciudad del Este's world of microcredit lending, the work of regulating this shifting terrain of practices and debates about who owed what to whom, and under what conditions that debt might come due, was evident from the breadth of institutional and colloquial terms deployed to talk about microcredit liability: responsibility (*responsabili-dad*), indebtedness or owing (*debiendo*), obligation (*compromiso, obli-gado*), legal claims for settlement (*demanda/demandado*), various usages of the word *credit* or *lending* (*préstamo, crédito, a fiado, a cuaderno*). In other words, pinning microcredit liability and making it stick in social practice was not as straightforward as signing a legal contract. I find Atwood's metaphor of twinships especially helpful here, as her focus on "payback" emphasizes simultaneity and resemblance rather than zero-sum accountancy.[5] Borrowers often thought in these terms as well, as they often were creditors and debtors simultaneously. I found that there was a great deal of work in the twinning of credit and debt: fixing both terms in the relationship and stabilizing them as a connection of repay-ment. This chapter tells the story of repayment in all its multiplicity and ambiguity. When multiple overlapping credit/debt twinships coincided, I tracked how the priority of one relationship could in effect capture, reorient, or cannibalize other credit/debt twinships—relationships that might not even, on their face, appear to be connected.

In practice, liability was not an abstract concept or form of economic rationality[6] configured around calculations of profit and loss, assets and liabilities. Most people who came into the orbit of Fundación Paraguaya considered liability in concrete and practical terms of repayments. The effort of "completing," or completando, payments was an embodied and affective form of labor that was only tenuously linked to the financial terms of credit. For microcredit group-based loans, repayment was framed by social collateral and the promise not only to recognize each member's credit and ensuing obligation to pay but also the total amount owed by the group. However, despite the practical difficulties of coordinating the economic lives and livelihood possibilities of women who borrowed through group-based lending, in the end Fundación Paraguaya's Commit-tees of Women Entrepreneurs only rarely terminally defaulted on their microcredit loans. In fact, exceptions to this pattern were especially revealing. The rare cases of default and nonpayment exposed the struc-tures of expectation around repayment in Fundación Paraguaya's cycles of borrowing. I start with a story of loans diverted into Ciudad del Este's smuggler economy in order to examine repayment that did not synch with the normal life course of a loan. In this case, Maria Elena had negotiated several loans at the very outset of her employment at the Fundación, and realized that she had made some critical errors in judging the joint liability of the group when those loans seemed intractably in arrears. Try as she might, Maria Elena could not get those committees to repay their debts.

Maria Elena was among the youngest of the credit counselors, just twenty years old, having secured her position at the Fundación on completing her secondary education. All of the qualities that made her especially good at her job—she was an extroverted colleague and also a central node in the office gossip network—also caused her to lean on her personal connections to make judgments about the creditworthiness of her clients. This was especially difficult when she was pitching the program to complete strangers, as she was doing when she sought to establish new committees in neighborhoods where none were enrolled. Maria Elena and her colleagues were encouraged by their manager to seek out and form new groups. In fact, a portion of their monthly commission was linked to the expansion of their lending portfolio. Early on in her tenure at the Fundación she had taken a risk and visited a neighborhood that was outside her normal beat in an effort to gain a foothold for the Committee of Women Entrepreneurs program. Of the several credit counselors, she relied heavily on the counsel of others when making decisions, often making her daily field visits along with one of her colleagues so that she could get a second opinion before making a decision about a particular group. This new group presented a risk for her not just because it was in an unfamiliar part of the city. It also presented a risk because all of her normal channels of information—her personal connections and those of her colleagues at the Fundación—were absent.

For one of those loans, the general manager of the branch office, another credit counselor, and I, went to visit one of the committees that had long been in default and refused to negotiate settlement. From what I could gather from the Fundación staff, disputes had erupted almost immediately within the group, and they had ceased paying their loan after a few installments. Arranging for the meeting in a neighborhood called Remansito already seemed like an achievement as even discussing the loan with the committee's president on the phone was a tense affair. The whole office could hear the conversation squawking through Maria Elena's cellular phone as she tried in vain to negotiate with the women. However, in the end our debt collection visit was—at least from the Fundación's perspective—largely in vain. We drove together to meet with the president and treasurer of the group; Maria Elena seemed relieved to have "backup," as she termed it. After half an hour of debating the loan, the meeting did not change anything from the perspective of Fundación Paraguaya and its financial bottom line. The women we visited were adamant that they had no interest in repaying their loan since the borrowing group no longer existed as such. The money was gone, and the treasurer and the president refused to pressure the other group members to pay. It would be useless, the office manager concluded, to press the liability any further by entering into legal proceedings and arbitrating the debt contract in civil court. In other words, these particular borrowers could not easily be enlisted in the social collateral that organized the usual administrative techniques of the Fundación. We left Remansito, and the loan was written off as unrecoverable.

Back at the office, Maria Elena was clearly disappointed that even with "backup" she had been unable to resolve the issue and worried that the default would continue to reflect poorly on her loan portfolio. Complaining angrily about the women we had just met with, she observed that the women of that neighborhood were "very hard women" (*mujeres muy duras*), and lesson learned, she would never make loans there again. When I asked her what she meant by "hard women," Maria Elena responded that the neighborhood of Remansito, located on the Paraná River, was, she learned through her work in different parts of the city, the central conduit for smuggling and contraband across the river to Brazil and Argentina. She noted that the periurban settlement that we had visited was located close to the crossroads of the triple frontier. Along the shore, skiffs and barges dock at camouflaged ports tucked into the thick foliage of the riverbank, loading and unloading the contraband. I recalled spotting these sorts of watercrafts from the international bridge connecting Ciudad del Este to its sister city in Brazil, Foz do Iguaçu, but I had not made the connection between the skiffs and that neighborhood in Ciudad del Este. Maria Elena reflected that the neighborhood was very insular, run by the *contrabandistas* and traffickers who operated the cross-border commerce in illicit merchandise. As residents in that neighborhood, her microcredit clients would surely be tied into that smuggler economy. I asked how this affected her microloans, speculating that if people made a lot of money from smuggling they would not be interested in the small sums proffered by the development NGO. Shrugging, Maria Elena repeated that the neighborhood made the women hard, adding that they had taken the loan but immediately defaulted. In other words, they had treated the loan as some other financial relationship entirely; in Maria Elena's view, they had brazenly stolen the money.

From the perspective of the creditor, all of the usual techniques for enforcing group-based liability were unavailable in this particular neighborhood because other, unknown sites of authority organized the regulatory field that authorized and sustained the economic claims people had over one another. The priorities of Maria Elena's borrowing committee on the banks of the Paraná, then, were oriented away from Paraguay's credit rating agency, from formal-sector banking services, and from NGO-based microfinance development loans. The punitive arithmetic of the Informconf credit score discussed in the previous chapter was an important reason committees infrequently walked away from their creditor without having settled accounts. Also, in a practical sense, the short amortization cycle of the loan meant that whole groups as well as individual group members could decide every three to four months whether they would continue in the program, so many women had only a brief brush with the Fundación. Unlike most borrowers who were deeply entangled with other semiformalized financial relationships—from installment plans to real estate debts to finance company loans—what set the women from Remansito apart was that they were oriented away from the institutionalized forms of credit that defined economic obligations for most residents in Ciudad del Este.[7] Yet they were not completely separate, as evinced by the fact that Maria Elena could sell the microcredit loan in the first place. The "hardness" of these women, in Maria Elena's view, referred to the impenetrability of these other circuits of economic interdependency in comparison to her financial tools of microfinance joint obligation, which she glossed using the vocabulary of insularity, camouflage, smuggling, and clandestineness. In other words, in this case Maria Elena's professional capacity as a credit counselor left her at a loss to prioritize the microcredit loan and get women she regarded as opaque and hard to recognize it *as* a liability because the usual forms of arbitrating who owed what to whom had neither the same grounds nor consequences as her other loans.

When the microcredit NGO negotiated the repayment of loans, the varied consequences for both staff members and their clients highlighted the economic interdependencies of creditors and debtors, especially when the process of arbitrating those categories effectively refigured and regulated the relationships between NGO staff and their clients. I argue that establishing regular relationships of repayment—as a contract, as a priority, and as a material relation of payment—hinged on twinning creditors and debtors, that is, matching the right borrower with the right lender to clarify, stabilize, and prioritize a relationship as one that is legible as a financial instrument: microcredit.[8] This was not always clear, since financial relationships also simultaneously meant other things: debtors might be family, creditors might be neighbors, or a loan might be made on behalf of an invented person and thus be seen as fraud. Importantly, polemics for and against indebtedness can impose an unwarranted unity on the financial instrument and miss the power effects of liability as they emerged from—instead of being presupposed by—borrowing and repayment. This is especially the case since important mediating relationships—NGO credit counselors and staff as managers of credit if not creditors themselves, leadership in borrowing groups as representatives of other borrowers, and so on—intervened in the conditions of being a creditor or debtor in Paraguayan microfinance.

The microcredit failure of Maria Elena's loan highlights the importance of the *people* who deal with borrowers, as much as unpacking the consequences of microcredit liability for the Fundación's clients.[9] Maria Elena's positioning of the hard women as contrastive debtors to her usual feminized microcredit clients carved out both a professional space for her work of crafting borrowers and her alliance with the category "lender." By focusing on end-users of development programs we often miss the labor of "proxy-creditors," in Sohini Kar's (2013) terms, who create debt through their financial labor and alienate that labor when debts are set free to circulate as financial objects. It is important to understand how the young women who work as credit counselors came to regulate their financial work and were implicated daily in producing and managing the social unit of debt in and among their clients. In this chapter I focus on how microcredit repayment presses on the professional identities and livelihood possibilities of microcredit *lenders* as much as the borrowers. By shifting the focus to microcredit lenders as equally important in understanding the regulatory field of microcredit social collateral, I provide an alternative focus to scholarship giving primacy to microcredit borrowers and the effects of development on their lives, identities, and economic relations, though that is of course an important part of the story. I begin by examining the work of Fundación Paraguaya's permanent staff and their consulting legal adviser, Don Gregorio, who negotiates debts that are long in arrears. I then contextualize Don Gregorio's work by tracing the shifting regulatory landscape of Paraguay's financial sector, which whitewashed Paraguay's assets and liabilities during the mid-1990s financial crisis as a way of stabilizing the banking sector. I return to the professional identities of microcredit lenders, which were particularly apparent in the case of credit counselors caught between their own interdependencies with their clients and their professional self-identification as managers of lending if not creditors themselves. While this broke down for Maria Elena with her hard committee, the daily struggle to stake authority through microcredit liability exposes broader questions about dependency, interdependency, and indebtedness as modes of economic practice.

GESTIONANDO: ADMINISTERING AND NEGOTIATING IN THE WORK OF NGO STAFF

Upon returning to the United States from Paraguay I was reconnected with the staff members of Fundación Paraguaya with reliable consistency: at the end of each month. During my fieldwork, home computing was still a luxury beyond the means of the employees who staffed the administrative ranks of the microfinance NGO. Up until the smart phone boom that seemed to be reaching a crescendo during my most recent fieldwork in 2013, NGO staff had limited access to the Internet, mostly through the computers at work. Without fail, however, on the last day of the month their Facebook status updates erupted in a cascade of sad emoticons, forlorn pleas begging for the workday to end, and then an outpouring of relief celebrating the start of a new fiscal cycle. Even if the last day of the month fell on a Sunday and the credit counselors were not being paid for their overtime work, their virtual comments posted well into the evening hours testified to their long day toiling in the office, overcome with grinding boredom during long stretches between phone calls as they closed the books on their loan portfolios. In this respect Fundación Paraguaya was quite similar to other banks and finance companies in Paraguay. Tellingly, a television commentator reporting on an evening soccer match gave a special shout-out to all the bank functionaries who still were at the office closing the books during a 2015 Copa America semifinal match.

During fieldwork, I found that those long hours at the end of the month were a tense period for the office, as loan officers and credit counselors desperately tried to drag performance numbers from one accounting column to the next—from nonperforming to working capital—and drive down their default rate. It was especially tense because most of the day was spent with bottled-up anxiety and little outlet. A successful close to the fiscal period hinged on staff members' ability to negotiate the reinitiation of repayment on loans that were in arrears. This work of conversion was glossed as *gestionando*: a bureaucratic catchall phrase that can mean negotiating, attempting or endeavoring, and also administering or managing. In a sense, the work of management and the work of negotiation were one and the same. The administration of the loan portfolio had little to do with technical financial tools that assessed returns on investment, risk management, or operational sustainability. Instead, it meant undertaking the hard interpersonal work of convincing borrowers to honor onerous debt contracts.[10]

One reason for this flurry of activity around gestionando loan portfolios was that the portfolio goals of credit counselors and loan officers counted individual defaulting debtors and penalized the NGO staff equally for each loan in arrears. The work of negotiating repayment was equally concerted for even the smallest loans, and even when these were long in default. Further, nonperformance of loans had a direct effect on the monthly income of Fundación Paraguaya staff. The technical work of administering interest rates, loan disbursals, and risk assessment was often eclipsed by the less technical work of negotiating relationships of repayment, which often came down to begging, pleading, and cajoling borrowers to restart loan payments. Staff members lamented the fact that they were not given bonuses for exceeding their portfolio goals but were routinely penalized for coming up short. Failure to administer loans and negotiate repayment properly was met with a cruel blow to the slim paychecks of credit counselors, who were themselves living on the razor edge of financial solvency.

For the Ciudad del Este microcredit branch office of Fundación Paraguaya, a key measure of portfolio performance was centered on the default rate for the office (*taza de morosidad*). The workspace of the branch manager, Don Edgar, was a glass box at the entrance of the office. His desk was positioned so that he could observe the day-to-day goings-on in the microcredit branch without being interrupted by the near-constant commotion of morning loan disbursals, which was particularly intense when several Committees of Women Entrepreneurs had the same date of loan renewal. The politics of supervision at the office were crystallized in the high glass wall that made visible the director at his desk. Sitting in front of his laptop, he was framed by a large whiteboard that recorded the precise details of the portfolio performance and number of defaulting clients of each one of the loan officers and credit counselors. Those individual performance goals were aggregated and tallied to report the total percentage of nonperforming loans for the office. The board was visible to everybody in the office, and often served as an excuse for employees to compare intimate details about wages and commissions. The board drew attention to itself particularly when cells in the matrix were circled or underlined in red or blue to underscore subpar performance. Importantly, while the director and the board were visible to everybody in the office, his computer screen was positioned to maintain his privacy. Other staff members were not so fortunate. Their computer monitors were turned so that their home screens were visible to the entire office. This meant that loan officers and credit counselors only surreptitiously carried on conversations on MSN Messenger or updated their Facebook statuses while diligently filling out loan information in the automated approval system that linked staff portfolios with the branch manager and the branch manager with the head office of Fundación Paraguaya in Asunción. The professional identities of staff members were secured through that link of credit and successful repayment. In a startlingly visible fashion, the liabilities of borrowers came to frame how the Fundación's staff understood and perceived themselves and one another.

Information, then, flowed first in a single direction up the administrative hierarchy at the NGO, beginning with the Fundación Paraguaya staff, which translated information about prospective clients into standardized loan documents, and then passed that data upward for final approval by the head office. Before the global financial crash in 2008, regional offices had a considerable degree of autonomy, but supervision had increased as default rates crept upward as a result of the economic slowdown. By 2009 a core team of account specialists based in Asunción oversaw the rollout of a new computerized database that gave the central office the ability to monitor the individual loan decisions of regional officers. During normal business days, credit counselors and loan officers scrambled to upload their applications to the system so that account specialists in the main office in Asunción could approve them during the afternoon. A check would be drawn for loan disbursal the next day. That routinized information was aggregated monthly and subsequently reflected back to local staff in the form of the portfolio performance board, which distilled their many loan approval requests into numerical performance measures and lined them up on the whiteboard with the professional accomplishments of other staff members (fig. 8). Further, those performance measures were not merely comparable to the other loan officers and credit counselors at the Ciudad del Este office. They also stood side-by-side with a depiction of the ideal version of themselves based on portfolio goals determined by the accounting algorithms at the head office. However, despite the clear attribution of success and failure to each individual staff member, the only data pulled out of the chart to summarize the performance of the Ciudad del Este branch office were the aggregate default rate,[11] located on a separate line below the default rate for the entire office. The Fundación staff was thus

FIGURE 8. Loan portfolio performance board in the manager's office.

constantly made aware of the potential for credit to turn into debt through the specter of morosidad.

Although the anthropological literature has long pointed to the fact that credit is a relationship, it is commonly assumed to be an asymmetrical one.[12] Creditors are thought to wield authority by dint of their power to lend, and borrowers find themselves dependent on and are captivated by powerful interests to which they are beholden. The rhetorical power of the office default board to frame and reassign managerial expertise in the back office of the NGO invites a reconceptualization of the asymmetries of credit and debt as a twinship. When managerial identities seam together with flows of money loaned through credit, it is difficult to disambiguate professional subjects and the financial technologies on and through which they work.[13] Credit counselors, of course, are not actually creditors. What, then, is their role in the conditions of being a lender and borrower?

The portfolio board at Fundación Paraguaya hints at the volatility of the staff members' relationship to the flows of money that they channeled every day, particularly when loans slid into arrears. In practice, Fundación staff constantly displaced that volatility onto the borrower and his or her economic logics and incentive structures. For example, at the bottom of the automatically generated payment receipt that recorded each loan installment there was a notice that read, "Dear client: The Prompt Payment of your installments allows you to receive your next credit the same day that you cancel [pay off] your current one, and remember that with your punctual payment YOU APPROVE YOUR NEXT CREDIT YOURSELF."[14] The managerial work of Fundación staff in administering and negotiating (gestionando) the loan went unspoken in this image of hyperagentive borrowers. However, the importance of the portfolio board in the office pointed back at the fact that liability was, instead, a two-way street. Both lender and borrower were on the hook for the financial commitment of credit/debt.

One of the consequences of negotiating each and every defaulting loan was that this mode of accounting for liabilities turned the orthodox logic of risk assessment on its head. In the most basic measures of portfolio risk and return, the salient mathematical operations are rates and ratios, not brute quantities. The number of clients in arrears (1, 5, 35, 100, etc.) is meaningless without the total number of clients to render it a percentage: the default rate (2 percent, 5 percent, 13 percent, etc.). At the Fundación, tallying morosidad—lateness—was a complicated accounting process of managing and assessing default. Since lateness was not figured as a rate but rather as a list of delinquent clients, from the perspective of the Fundación morosidad signaled a quality of its borrowers rather than a quality of its portfolio, which would be captured better by a percentage of defaulting loans managed by the office. Counterintuitively, this meant that each and every client figured as a dangerous potentiality that Fundación staff worked to manage and contain at the end of each month. The quality of the quantities on the performance board hints at a further level of displacement.[15] The microcredit division at the head office of Fundación Paraguaya in Asunción, staffed by a team of economists and accountants who calculated the figures into rates and percentages, systematically reported the performance data of the Fundación's microlending operation to its financial backers: Kiva.org, the Inter-American Development Bank, and commercial lenders including HSBC and Citigroup. The Ciudad del Este branch office fit awkwardly between the microcredit organization, in its capacity as a self-sustaining (though not profit-oriented) financial entity, and the daily reality of administering loans, since the stakes of loan nonperformance were different across the institutional hierarchy. For the head office in Asunción, their working capital and returns on investment were at stake. For administrative staff in the branch office, their wages and commissions were tethered to managing other people's money.

Discussing repayment by focusing on each and every borrower led staff members to describe and envision the contents of their loan portfolios in surprising ways. One loan officer explained to me that she didn't have any morosidad in her portfolio because she got rid of "everybody who was owing [*todos los que estan debiendo*]." She continued, "I got rid of everybody who was owing; the debtors don't enter any more." In a sense, her whole portfolio comprises clients who are repaying their loans. However, from her perspective, when borrowers pay on time they are clients or committees rather than debtors.

The recurrent theme of lateness in discussions of financial work underscores the centrality of microcredit's role in producing identities and persons as much as producing financial outcomes. Indeed, a sign on the office wall, posted adjacent to the teller window, declared, "Dear client, please allow us to continue to trust you. Pay your loan on time," signaling the other values—trust, responsibility, hope—that were endorsed along with the promissory note. A similar sign read, "Credit is an opportunity for business, don't lose it." The inspirational posters declaring credit an opportunity as well as a site of loss were located just feet from the portfolio board, which, too, figured credit as a site of danger. Repayment, then, was a moment in the life course of a loan that generated deep anxiety for the Fundación. Despite this volatility, credit counselors and clients alike nearly always talked about borrowing in terms of opportunity by speaking of credit rather than debt: taking out a credit, paying a credit, canceling a credit, and renewing a credit. Very rarely in my many months at the microcredit organization did I hear anybody use the term *deuda*, or debt, directly.[16] However, it is important to note that debt most often figured in terms of the quality of lateness rather than terminal default. It was the moment when credit became a burden, a concern, and a liability for both borrower and the Fundación staff. But aside from the exceptional cases like the neighborhood that figured as impenetrable to the Fundación, late payment did not abruptly end the creditor-debtor relationship because the liability continued as the link that twinned lenders and their clients. This link was constantly dramatized by the anxious task of closing the books at the end of the month and related efforts to start a new cycle of borrowing.

COLLECTING DEBTS, REACTIVATING CREDITS

Although the hard work every month of gestionando fell to the staff at the Ciudad del Este branch office, the Fundación contracted an in-house attorney, Gregorio—referred to by staff and borrowers as *el doctor*—to deal with the cases that obstinately resisted conversion from debt to credit. He was the last recourse for the Fundación as it attempted to manage the repayment or lateness of microcredit clients. In the moment of collection, relationships of liability forged through mutual obligation were most apparent. Morosidad was an instance when the relationships that under normal circumstances ensured repayment were recast as a site of danger or failed altogether. For Gregorio the unfixed and movable nature of different perspectives on obligation made morosidad a puzzle. In fact, the puzzle of collecting debts threw up abundant—and sometimes competing—solutions.

Gregorio was a prototypical Paraguayan midlevel professional. Clad in a business suit even in the subtropical summer heat of Ciudad del Este, in his fifties, el doctor had thickened slightly around the middle from years of eating greasy street food for lunch while running between meetings on field visits. His sensible rubber-soled loafers indicated a professional life not so much spent in an office chair as on his feet, knocking on doors, mediating between his employer and its clients. His university degree in engineering had not generated a stable salaried position, so he returned to law school and found his consultancy with Fundación Paraguaya much more lucrative than a career as a government technocrat. Like most staff at the Fundación, commissions based on arbitrating debt collection for nonperforming loans augmented Gregorio's salary. However, unlike the loan officers, who did not have the same level of education, Gregorio's professional degree solidified his status as a Paraguayan professional, with all the accompanying class aspirations. This meant that his salary was sufficient to assure an adequate livelihood on its own. Indeed, the honorific "the doctor" was recognition of his professional training, and is a common form of address for lawyers generally. Gregorio's role at the Fundación was closer to professional consultant than permanent staff. Rather than being attached to a particular branch office, as was true for most of Fundación Paraguaya's employees, Gregorio lived in Asunción and made one- or two-day trips to regional offices in order to serve collection notices to clients in arrears. He often took the overnight bus from the capital city and worked a full day, rushing to board the 4:00 p.m. bus back to his home and family. His professional identity was caught up with his mobility and role as troubleshooter.

In April 2009 el doctor arrived in Ciudad del Este to serve collection notices to clients with outstanding debts to the Fundación. Some of these were long overdue. Many were in the portfolios of loan officers and credit counselors who no longer worked there. In those cases, there was nobody else in-house to negotiate those particular loan settlements. The notices drafted by Gregorio combined intimidating legal language with a printed notice of the amount of the outstanding debt (though it was not clear if that figure included late fees, back interest, etc.) and the time frame, in bold print—48 hours—in which payment in full was demanded. Gregorio confided that these papers did not really initiate legal action but rather were a tactic to scare delinquent clients into canceling their outstanding debts. In fact, the forty-eight-hour time frame was flexible, underscoring the regulatory rather than statutory character of these demands: it could begin at the end of the business day, tomorrow, the end of the week, or from the start of the next fiscal period, depending on when the client said he or she could repay their debt. Gregorio noted that he had to tread a fine line between causing clients to despair and give up on paying altogether and making them understand that the Fundación was serious about repayment, even if the debt was long overdue, some by over a year.

As we went from house to house, for the most part the people being served were not at home, so the notices were left with neighbors and kin. Gregorio said that this was the moment when people really got serious about paying their debts. He observed that in the instances when neighbors or family members found out that they owed money, clients paid up in order to keep up appearances. Indeed, a good deal of his work was as a shrewd negotiator. Gregorio gave an example to illustrate how the process of collection worked. He told me, "You have to know how to press. And suddenly the client will say, 'Sure I'll pay, it's just that I don't want so-and-so to know about it.'" With a satisfied nod, he concluded, "And right there you know that either so-and-so has already paid the client [that it was a joint business venture and the money was already supposed to have been paid to the creditor] and the money went elsewhere, or that so-and-so didn't know that the client had taken out the credit, and either way it was going to land the client in hot water. It's a question of psychology."

Echoing the *Ikatú* project, which was part of the strategic mission of the organization, Gregorio's psychology of repayment hinged on accounting not just for the financial footing of defaulting clients but also for their internal motivations. The most important part of his job was not bringing the Paraguayan legal system to bear on debtors or arbitrating legal claims around debt settlement and property repossession. Rather, it was a matter of assessing the personal qualities that would cause a person to be disposed (or not) to pay his or her debts. Gregorio worked at determining people's commitments and connections, which forms of attachment and belonging were a source of danger and anxiety, and tapping into the relationships that give people claims over wealth. In other words, the work of Fundación Paraguaya's attorney was to reassemble the social unit of debt. Moreover, he not only reckoned the relationships that anchored economic liability, but also had to activate them. His success as a debt collector had real personal and material consequences for all involved in creating and maintaining social collateral.

Gregorio's tactics were finely attuned to the complicated interplay of the shame of default, the exigencies of running a business, and the dense interpersonal dramas that cross-cut his collection demands.[17] He was always cautious not to tip his hand too early to signal that he was there in the capacity of an attorney, instead attempting to obliquely triangulate the whereabouts of clients. He would usually begin near the last known address of the client, which is one reason the loan officer or credit counselor had to accompany him, in order to interpret the abstracted data compiled in their loan portfolios and translate it into the vocabulary of neighborly or kin relations and of local place. For example, even central neighborhoods of Ciudad del Este did not have street names or house numbers, so finding anything or anybody in the city entailed locating them in a social landscape rather than on a map or grid. The Spanish term *ubicar*—to find or locate—was often used in conjunction with visiting microcredit clients on field outings. Both credit counselors and loan officers would carefully draw a sketch that located the client or committee in a neighborhood on a hand-drawn map. The map charted the neighborhood using local landmarks and depicted the homes of borrowers vis-à-vis those landmarks. One reason credit counselors and loan officers preferred to call clients on the phone when they were *moroso* was because they were already friendly with many borrowers and their neighbors and family members. Their terse phone calls were sharply different from the phatic labor—to borrow Julia Elyachar's term for this infrastructure of connectivity and sociability[18]—that conditioned their normal administrative routines.

Since el doctor was an outsider, other staff members at the Fundación had to accompany him in order to decipher the sketched map that located the defaulting borrower. For credit counselors and loan officers, workaday administrative practices demanded that they be familiar with the social terrain over which their loans were layered. In fact, their failure to understand that terrain led to crises like Maria Elena's loans in the neighborhood of *contrabandistas* and smugglers on the banks of the Paraná. Gregorio's presence underscored the everyday reality of entanglements between NGO staff and their clients, perhaps even more vividly than the harrowing whiteboard at the office that recorded and made visible morosidad. It was precisely his objective distance from the interdependencies of economic liability that gave him a privileged view of the credit relationships. His work as a collection agent relied on the mutual entanglements of NGO staff and their carefully sketched social maps of their clients' social worlds to interpret and activate those relationships.

It did not take too much sleight-of-hand to serve default notices, because it was just as likely that loan officers or credit counselors would need to locate the borrower for the purpose of extending credit as collecting debt. Thus it was not uncommon for strangers representing a finance company to ask around for the whereabouts of somebody in the neighborhood. Bill collectors also crisscrossed the city on motos to facilitate regular payments for services ranging from installment plans for a refrigerator to an encyclopedia set purchased for school-age children. In a sense, credit was one of a handful of important connections that people made to extend themselves beyond the neighborhood.[19] As such, Fundación staff members found that they were investing substantial time and care in getting to know the neighborhood affiliations that anchored and sustained their credit relations. Importantly, the long-term relationships of credit produced neighborhood-based economic interdependencies that unexpectedly worked to capture the NGO staff and include them in the web of liabilities.[20]

After I inquired about what sort of work he did for the Fundación, Gregorio offered to let me accompany the team on their excursions to negotiate outstanding debts. We all piled into Josefina's car, a minuscule Chevy Corsa, and visited clients in order of geographic proximity to the Fundación headquarters. One of the most interesting cases arbitrated by Gregorio was an individual microloan in an urban barrio close to the

Fundación headquarters in the market district. In this case, the whole family owed one another, but some of those debts were more legible to the Fundación than others. Indeed, the only debt that was written as a formal contract was the loan to the family matriarch from Fundación Paraguaya. When Gregorio questioned her, it came to light that one of her sons owed her the sizable sum of $840 and also owed his brother money. He was not present for the discussion; those present in the small shop were the son who had lent to his brother, his mother (the Fundación's client), her husband, and a younger daughter or granddaughter. They all accused the absent son of malfeasance. The son who was present told Gregorio that he would get his brother to pay him so that he could pay off his mother's debt of about $160 to the Fundación. The situation grew more complicated when he admitted that the $840 loan to his brother had been to buy a house, and the land title from that property was the guarantee for his mother's loan at Fundación Paraguaya. What is more, the matriarch's husband had dengue fever. During most of the interview he was propped in a chair on the front stoop, wrapped in blankets, following the conversation with difficulty. His inability to participate in the negotiations meant that his wife was left to negotiate with her son and with her debt collector without the support of other family members. Her delinquent son, on the other hand, was apparently supported in his decision to break family obligations by his wife, who was disliked by the whole family. It was a complicated financial context to say the very least. We all stood clustered on the front stoop, listening as the matriarch and her son took turns explaining the situation.

Despondent, the matriarch told her loan officer that she had always paid her debts on time and that she was deeply embarrassed to be in this situation, so she proposed giving the Fundación the freezer she had purchased with her loan. It was the capital improvement that she had made to her little store and which allowed her to stockpile more inventory and sell high-turnover items such as ice. The Fundación, Gregorio agreed, would be able to auction it at the price that she set and would keep the amount that she owed, giving her the balance. Her son, however, would hear none of it. He reasoned that asking his brother to make good on his debt was the best solution. So Gregorio got on the phone with the absent brother to discuss the land title that was the guarantee for his mother's loan at the Fundación. Listening in to one side of the conversation, we could hear him emphasize that the title was the collateral for the loan and that attorneys for the Fundación would come to repossess the land. After a brief exchange, Gregorio hung up the phone and reported to the matriarch that her son had refused to recognize his obligation. In fact, he told Gregorio that on Tuesday (when the forty-eight-hour notification period ran out), he would have his own attorney waiting, as the land had been legally transferred to him and his mother had no further claims on it. On the verge of tears, the mother once again pleaded with Gregorio to simply take the freezer; the loss of her business capital was of secondary concern to repairing the bonds between her sons. Gregorio nodded, responding that they had better get the situation in hand because it was a family matter, and he had intervened as much as he could.

We left without the freezer, without payment for the loan, and with a great deal of uncertainty about how the family would resolve the issue. In the car en route to the next debtor, Josefina grumbled that the matriarch's husband probably did not even have dengue and that he was dissimulating in order to garner sympathy. In the end the woman managed to scrape together enough cash to restart payments on her loan, and the Fundación never found out whether she had sold her freezer or repaired her family relations. From the perspective of the loan officer charged with negotiating the loan in arrears, the one relationship that counted most—reactivating the tie between the Fundación and its client—had been mended. In fact, repayment had also reaffirmed the matriarch as a "client" and thus as the individual social unit of debt. The rest of the relational drama was, from el doctor's perspective, beside the point.

In a similar case, which had become rather infamous in the Ciudad del Este branch office, a loan officer for Fundación Paraguaya had embezzled thousands of dollars by taking advantage of precisely these sorts of cross-cutting relationships of debt and guarantee within families. Luis, fired shortly before I arrived for fieldwork, had apparently masterminded a complex scheme to boost his portfolio ratings by negotiating dubious loans and making loans to fictitious clients and pocketing the money. In other words, he profited from the commissions he charged for initiating loans that did not comply with the Fundación's basic lending rules and also outright stole money by inventing loans to fake clients. Months later, Gregorio was still trying (apparently to no avail) to recover Luis's bad loans.

A particularly troublesome case involved a series of loans to a family whose members were simultaneously business partners, loan guarantors, and clients of the Fundación. The business venture apparently had been pitched as a small shop to sell office supplies in the city market. Luis's genius had been to issue a loan to the husband with the wife as guarantor, a separate loan to their grown son with the husband as guarantor, and a third loan to the wife with the son as guarantor: three loans, mutually guaranteed between three borrowers, and all to capitalize the same business. Gregorio noted that this should have seemed suspicious; no office supply shop would need over $1,500 for inventory to get the business off the ground.

It was unsurprising, then, when the business went bust—if, indeed, there had ever been a business to begin with. Perhaps more important, there was also no stance outside of the network of debt and obligation from which Gregorio could press (apretar), to recall his strategy for knowing how to apply pressure to clients. As a consequence, there was no way to compel the family to prioritize repaying the Fundación and reorganize the many cross-cutting economic interdependencies into individual social units of debt. Like the hard women of the smugglers' neighborhood, their credit priorities were oriented elsewhere. Further, unlike the unhappy family debating whether to sell the freezer, where the single contractual debt between the Fundación and the matriarch took precedence over competing claims around family obligation, Luis's scam meant that the circuit of debt within the family and the Fundación were isomorphic, and el doctor had no leverage to draw the microcredit debt into relief. There was no brother or son outside of the contractual obligations who could be called on to recognize a liability and thus renew the financial solvency of the Fundación's clients. In the eighteen months of fieldwork that I conducted with the Ciudad del Este branch office, Gregorio visited half a dozen times to try to resolve Luis's bad loans.

The scam loans from Luis to families in a self-contained circuit that all guaranteed one another were ultimately written off as unrecoverable debts and taken off the books of the Ciudad del Este branch office. These loans short-circuited repayment since they were tantamount to credit with no debt, no twinship, in fact, at all. And thinking with classic studies of kinship, relatedness, and exchange, the scam loans might in some ways fulfill Lévi-Strauss's fantasy of social independence that closes his classic work, *Elementary Structures of Kinship*. He ends with the dream of taking without giving, or as he put it, "the joys, eternally denied to social man, of a world in which one might *keep to oneself*" (Lévi-Strauss 1969: 497).

This situation was not unique to individual borrowers who had outstanding debts with Fundación Paraguaya. As noted earlier, Committees of Women Entrepreneurs occasionally entered into terminal default on their loans. Most committees, however, did not break ties with their creditor while there was a pending obligation. Instead, most of the work related to morosidad had to do with late payments that were not grave enough to necessitate the regulatory intervention of Gregorio. This is important because it often implicated the ties of joint responsibility within the group as the crucial site, from the perspective of Fundación staff, for reactivating repayment. Similar to the dilemmas faced by the family beset by competing obligations, the troubles of committees that had late payments usually hinged on the debts that were not recognized by the terms of the debt contract itself but which undergirded the wealth transfers regulated by microcredit loans.

However, as I underscored in the previous chapter on creditworthiness, the Fundación lent to Committees of Women Entrepreneurs precisely *because* they were under contractual obligation to pay other people's bills. Each borrower's individual payment or nonpayment was incidental to the group's obligation to the Fundación. Groups like Maria Elena's committee that as a group refused to pay, were an exception. Indeed, I want to highlight the fundamental *similarity* between the social worlds that entangled individual borrowers and Committees of Women Entrepreneurs but the fundamentally *different* liabilities at stake when the microcredit financial technologies captured and instrumentalized those interdependencies in relationships of repayment. In other words, the conditions of being a debtor in Paraguay always seemed to spill over the boundaries of contractual obligation. However, microcredit group-based borrowing was set up such that the boundaries of contractual obligation always worked to incorporate and domesticate those social relationships, which meant that although borrowing was inevitably anchored in dense social connections, in practice very different liabilities were at stake for loans secured through social collateral.

When staff members from the Fundación negotiated late payments for group-based loans, they responded with logic identical to Gregorio's: it was a family matter, or more aptly, it was an internal matter. But in the case of the Committees of Women Entrepreneurs, they had not intervened as far as they could. The ties that bound the group together were not merely relational but contractual and legal as well, since committees signed a joint IOU contract, a document taken very seriously by just about everybody I met in Paraguay. The joint liability of women's committees, then, was open to intervention and regulation by the Fundación. Or so it seemed if they adopted the perspective of el doctor. Gregorio was very adept at drawing one contractual obligation into relief—the liability the Fundación claimed against the committee—and enforcing its priority. The success of his consultancy hinged on ensuring that those relationships could serve the function of legal action. Debt collection involved managing collective wealth and arbitrating claims on and about it. Gregorio's work serving notices of default centered on the emplacement and displacement of obligation in these dense configurations of shared responsibility and mutual support.

In all these instances of debt collection, Gregorio's position was secure and obvious to all involved. He arrived in the neighborhood as an outsider and functionary of the Fundación in order to enforce legal claims against defaulting debtors. Gregorio was only interested in the modes of interdependency that he so astutely tracked insofar as they could be instrumentalized to reactivate debt service. His presence on the scene was itself an argument for a dyadic, juridico-legal liability between Fundación Paraguaya as lender and a client as borrower. The credit/debt twinship was obvious to the point of cloaking Gregorio's mediation. In practice, the complicated conditions of indebtedness made the priority of the microloan far from clear and its social unit of debt far from stable. In fact, the multiple valences of debts implicated various people who might or might not even have realized that they were part of the same circuit of repayment. The wayward son might not have been aware of his mother's debt until the attorney came knocking, neighbors might not have perceived that their delayed repayment of a local obligation also jeopardized the payment of a borrowing committee, and Maria Elena did not at first see the dense web of obligations that hijacked her loan in the neighborhood of contrabandistas. In the midst of that complexity, the only position that was certain was Gregorio's authority to negotiate liability and insist on the priority of the Fundación's claims.

CRISIS AND REFORM: DEBT IN
THE WHITEWASHING LAW

From this account of legal demands and el doctor's work to prioritize the contractual debts to the Fundación, it might be tempting to read his efforts as a response to the challenges of enforcing repayment in the context of economic informality. Indeed, the impression of economic difference or separate spheres of exchange[21] might seem to be supported by the debts that the Fundación wrote off as unrecoverable. Theft or fraud—at least from the perspective of a legal contract or repayment—

might be interpreted as emblematic of the inconvertibility between the market sphere and local spheres of exchange or moral economy. A related argument might be made about the difficulty of enforcing debt contracts as one additional barrier faced by businesses operating below the regulatory purview of Paraguayan financial laws, in the vein of the economist Hernando De Soto's (2002) studies of the "price" of informality. This is particularly the case in an economic context where few companies were registered with the municipality, many did not comply with licensing rules or make social security and pension contributions, and most were cross-cut with illicit circuits of commerce and credit. I develop a different set of arguments here. I suggest instead that the multiple perspectives on the debts negotiated by Gregorio were not merely a by-product of the informality of those businesses or separate spheres of market exchange and local values. I contextualize the interworking of morosidad and debt collection in microfinance in a wider exploration of repayment in the Paraguayan financial system and thus in global credit markets generally.

Paraguayan banking regulations illustrate the broader point that in the formal financial system, debts become legible insofar as one looks at them from a particular, situated direction (i.e., as a depositor, as a lender, as a borrower, as an accountant, etc.). The hard work undertaken by the Fundación to stabilize and reactivate a repayment relationship is instructive in both formal and informal finance. To show that, I lay out a brief history of financial reform in Paraguay to underscore what I take to be the perspectival nature of liability. Paraguay's banking reform resonates with Maria Elena's experience on the banks of the Paraná. As she attempted to collect on the loan in Remansito it became clear that while liability might appear to be a uniform contractual relationship, in practice liability is *not* the same everywhere and in all contexts. Working through the macroanalysis of Paraguayan finance sheds light on the modes of authority that produce and reproduce the conditions of being a lender and a borrower. In my effort to look at broader financial processes beyond face-to-face interactions of microfinance, I suggest that credit in Paraguay, and in institutionalized banking more generally, is bundled with claims about the priority of repayment in some financial relationships, often at the expense of obscuring or ignoring others. Beyond this specific case, I think that the concept of priority may be useful to think with in other analyses of credit and repayment, especially as policy makers debate anew the moral, ethical, and social consequences of default in the wake of the 2008 global financial crisis.

I highlight the vocabulary of whitewashing at particular moments of national economic crisis[22]—crises that are replicated at a microlevel when specific microfinance loans go bust—as a way to start thinking about the power effects of credit/debt twinships. When the uneven fit of alternative perspectives could no longer be held together, various forms of persuasion—some quite chilling—were brought to bear.

With the halting expansion of democratic politics and greater civic freedoms after 1989, Paraguay's economy also moved markedly in the direction of greater openness, including such reforms as loosening of interest rate ceilings, a floating exchange rate, and greater competition among financial institutions. José Aníbal Insfrán Pelozo, an economist at the Central Bank of Paraguay (BCP), has written extensively on the Paraguayan financial sector, particularly the policies of economic liberalization undertaken in the 1990s. In response to the incremental deregulation of finance, the number of registered financial entities in Paraguay nearly doubled in seven years: from 88 in 1988 to 147 in 1995.[23] However, Insfrán Pelozo suggests that the apparent vitality of the booming financial sector in the early 1990s masked deep underlying problems with capitalization and risk assessment. His research chronicles the devastating financial-sector crisis that gripped Paraguay's banking system from 1995 to 1998. During the crisis, more than half of Paraguay's banks and financial entities required some degree of state intervention, and nearly all of those were ultimately liquidated owing to the "vast quantities of capital required to stabilize them," costs that Insfrán Pelozo estimates ranged from 7 percent to 12 percent of Paraguay's GDP.[24]

A key factor that contributed to the 1995 crisis was the high degree of so-called informality at the heart of Paraguay's formal financial sector. The IMF Fund—an institution particularly vested in the management and assessment (i.e., the formalization)[25] of the economy—attributed Paraguay's informality problem to the overly conservative regulatory framework that set a high reserve requirement for private banks.[26] Reserve requirements, which are intended precisely to guard against the capitalization problems experienced by Paraguay's banking system in the mid-1990s, were labeled by the IMF as having distortionary effects since they "contributed to the fast development of the informal financial sector, including off-balance-sheet operations and the offshore banking system" (García-Herrero 1997: 16). In other words, banks accepted deposits off the books in order to have liquidity to extend loans that would otherwise run afoul of the high reserve requirements, which would have prohibited that lending. Perhaps unsurprisingly, causality was attributed to the incentive structures put in place by the regulatory regime and not to the unrepentant profit seeking and illegal lending of Paraguayan banks and their foreign counterparts. Indeed, the Banco do Brasil office in Paraguay was widely known to have taken advantage of the multiple ledgers that were accommodated by the off-sheet operations common at the time. What goes unsaid in the IMF's critique of Paraguay's regulatory framework was the fact that President Stroessner had long relied on precisely that rampant rent seeking of the financial sector as the "price of peace"[27] to maintain his political coalition. Those practices were partly responsible for attracting many important international banks to Paraguay in the 1970s and 1980s and were enthusiastically endorsed by the IMF in earlier iterations of its policy recommendations.

The orthodox macroeconomic reforms[28] undertaken in the wake of Stroessner's ouster in 1989 ultimately resulted in increased deposits in private sector banks, especially as public pension plans were privatized, but many of those were recorded in parallel account books off the normal, or "white," balance sheets of banks as "*depósitos en negro*," or black deposits. In other words, IMF policy was caught up in producing the very liquidity problems implicated in the distortionary effects of high reserve requirements. Reports on the crisis described two types of off–balance sheet holdings:

> Unrecorded deposits were of two different natures: the so-called gray deposits, for which adequate documentation existed but had been recorded off–balance sheet, and the so-called black deposits, based on inadequate documentation, such as promissory notes and the like. Unrecorded deposits (gray and black) were a widespread practice in Paraguay before the crisis started, not only at the intervened banks, but at most Paraguayan banks and some foreign banks as well. (Garcia-Herrero 1997: 41)

Off–balance sheet holdings meant that in practical terms most banks kept several ledgers simultaneously. Banks issued promissory notes (*paragrés*) on different slips of paper (or none at all) to different classes of savers and borrowers, which also led to widespread accusations that Paraguay was a hub of money laundering.[29] This was not merely a localized practice in Paraguay either. A special class of deposits, denominated CC-5 accounts, facilitated money transfers to and from Brazil, which meant that gray and black deposits were part of a transnational system of parallel bookkeeping and off–balance sheet transactions.

The nebulous realm between bank deposit, promissory note, and credit instrument was rendered even more nebulous by the widespread practice of repurposing seemingly straightforward banking instruments—like personal checks—for the informal extension of credit. The postdated check as collateral on informal borrowing was a widely utilized, as elsewhere in the world, in Paraguay's informal credit market.[30] Tellingly, until the banking reforms of 1996 Paraguayan law prosecuted individuals who wrote checks against accounts without sufficient funds. Under Paraguayan law they were held criminally liable for "swindling"[31] and could be prosecuted in Paraguayan courts. In a sense, the informal credit market was parasitic on the Paraguayan legal system.[32] Instead of relying on Mafia-style enforcement techniques, creditors could simply require borrowers to sign a postdated check as collateral for a loan and cash it if the loan came due and the borrower did not pay. If there were not sufficient funds to cover the loan amount, then the creditor could initiate criminal proceedings to demand full payment. The practice was so widespread that in the 1990s criminal prosecutions involving checks written against accounts without sufficient funds constituted 10 to 20 percent of all criminal proceedings.[33] Moreover, a rediscount market developed for postdated checks; informal creditors could trade the collateral on their loans among one another, usually at a fraction of the face value of the check, in order to ensure the liquidity of the informal credit market.[34]

Put another way, even seemingly white and gray deposits in registered Paraguayan banks were tethered to outstanding liabilities in the informal credit market, with its own set of books parallel to the white/gray/black account books of registered banks in Paraguay.[35] This is precisely the type of perspectival liability that makes parsing contractual obligations far from clear, and certainly not merely an index of the degree of informality of the transaction. Depending on one's position within the financial system, a personal check might look like a perfectly legal promise of payment but from another perspective might seem like the guarantee on a line of credit, and from yet another seem like an investment bought cheap and sold dear.

In the wake of the financial crisis, depositors were supposed to be compensated if they held assets in failed banks.[36] Importantly, the new law covered depositors whose assets were recorded off the balance sheet as gray or black deposits. The banking regulations were referred to in Paraguay's national newspaper as the Whitewashing Law, *Ley de blanqueo,* because they whitewashed the discrepancies between banks' multiple account books and rendered all deposits white. Paraguay's major daily, *ABC Color,* gave a graphic account of the new law, depicting

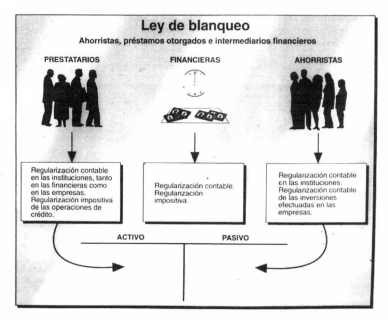

FIGURE 9. Paraguay's "whitewashing law," where borrowers and lenders face one another and neatly slot into assets and liabilities. *ABC Color,* June 27, 1995, 43.

borrowers (*prestatarios*), financial intermediaries (*financieras*), and depositors (*ahorristas*) (fig. 9).[37]

Borrowers (prestatarios) were represented as a group of people standing together, in contrast to the people who made that capital available through savings (ahorristas). Their assets neatly slotted into corresponding double-entry accounting columns labeled assets and liabilities (*pasivos* and *activos*). The stakeholders in the financial crisis were represented as distinct and contrastive, bunched as they were in separate groups. However, the neat division between borrowers, finance companies, and depositors depicted by *ABC Color*[38]—where all accounts can be "regularized" (*regularizado*) and tidily divided into assets and liabilities—did not follow seamlessly from the 1996 reforms, since borrowers in the formal sector were often creditors in the informal sector: indeed, creditors of the very people who are placed neatly across the column from them as depositors in the newspaper illustration. The lesson I hope to draw from this is *not* that the informal economy constantly interrupts the regulation and accountability of the formal banking system. Rather, given the copresence of multiple accounting practices and sites of liability, the nuts and bolts of Paraguayan banking means that the very concept of liability is seen by most people as a highly unstable category. Following important research in economic anthropology that cautions that the separation between formal and informal sectors should not be treated simply as an empirical problem (i.e., postdated checks are informal, deposits are formal),[39] I suggest that we must account for the repertoire of economic practices that render them separate.

This chronicle of Paraguay's informally formal financial system, and the formality of its informal credit market, is an effort to trace repayment in the broader financial system in Paraguay, including its important links to the wider world. As I argue, the conditions of being a creditor and a debtor in Paraguay are necessarily entailed one in the other, and the relation implicates intermediaries that do not fit easily into a single credit/debt twinship. This is not only a question of scale, as if microentrepreneurs have complicated and socially embedded financial strategies and large banks were rational and calculative businesses. Rather, the imbrications of savings and loans are a broader feature of credit/debt in Paraguay: namely, that the categories "lender" and "borrower" must be constantly separated, managed, and stabilized in social practice.

This is not a chronicle of the failings of Paraguay's financial sector to comply with best practices in banking. Paraguay's unusual banking system makes visible certain things about the economy that are present elsewhere, and thus indicative, I think, of financial processes more generally. For instance, it was precisely these sorts of overlapping liabilities that were the heart of the 2008 mortgage-backed securities crisis in the United States. In fact, Paraguay was actually a test case for banking regulation going back to the 1940s,[40] and it has been a laboratory for macroeconomic banking management and regulation ever since. If anything, Paraguayan financial sector is a paragon of liberal banking reform.[41] The lesson to draw from Paraguay's banking crisis and subsequent reforms is that pinning down and whitewashing—fully accounting for the debts owed in the banking system—hinged on deciding exactly what counted as assets and what counted as liabilities. I argue that this was by no means clear or obvious from the financial tools themselves, or apparent from the logics of the value sphere of finance.[42] Nor did those relationships necessarily preexist, or even extend past, the context of repayment. Rather, lending and borrowing are generally caught up in the *partiality* of economic perspectives: partial in the double sense that it was incomplete and also interested. Whitewashing was an act of persuasion. In other words, el doctor's effort to prioritize one perspective on liability over many others was not a symptom of micro-lending but rather continuous with broader debates about repayment.

MAKING THE RIGHT CONNECTIONS:
DEFAULT AND GROUP PAYMENT

In Paraguayan banking reform the clear separation of lenders and bor-rowers hinged on the regulatory purview of the Paraguayan state and its ability to formulate policy reordering formal and informal finance. In other words, the perspectival qualities of finance are not unique to the complex and socially dense micropolitics of development-oriented microfinance. Competing perspectives on repayment, though, certainly played an active role in the life cycle of microcredit loans. Continuing my study of crises of repayment, debt service was hotly debated in a case of group borrowing that threatened to destabilize the very idea of liability generated by social collateral. For this loan, the threat of defaulting on repayment was mobilized as a way to activate the obliga-tion of the Fundación as creditor. Borrowers sought to make visible the NGO's obligation to properly collect repayment from the appropriate debtors, which worked to redefine and reinvigorate the social unit of debt in the process.

The weather grew stormy as I arrived with a team of credit coun-selors at the periurban neighborhood of eighteen borrowers in a Com-mittee of Women Entrepreneurs. Although terminal default was very rare among committees, late payments were a constant problem. Coor-dinating and synchronizing the income streams and daily schedules of over a dozen women was a formidable challenge. What this really meant was that committees often missed payments. Credit counselors spent about half of their workdays traveling between Ciudad del Este's periur-ban barrios, making use of its baroque system of private bus lines to visit their borrowing groups and resolve payment issues. Often, so few buses connected these peripheral neighborhoods to the city center that a Fundación staff member was likely to encounter the president or treasurer of one of her committees on the bus ride itself, and most of the discussion about payments was conducted en route. Credit counselors were tasked with negotiating lateness and reactivating payments rather than serving collection notices like Doctor Gregorio.

By the time we arrived at the small grocery shop where the treasurer of the group—Doña Carmen—had convened the meeting, rain was

FIGURE 10. Despensas, or small neighborhood shops, were a common business activity for women who borrowed from microfinance companies.

pounding, and we could see sparks spraying from the transformer right above Carmen's home. Carmen's middle-aged mother, who lived with her in the single room behind the shop, dashed outside to flip the breaker, plunging the scene into murky gloom. We stumbled inside out of the rain as Carmen laid down cardboard on the floor in a futile effort to keep Ciudad del Este's ubiquitous red clay from soiling the clean cement in the shop. A handful of her fellow committee members had already arrived, and the rest of us stood uncertainly by the door, reluctant to get the floor dirty, as the rain blew in, soaking us from behind.

Doña Carmen's neighborhood grocery shop was nearly identical to the countless others that were the primary means of subsistence for most of Ciudad del Este's periurban residents (fig. 10). Managed almost exclusively by women, these small stores offered staple foods and goods for sale, as well as some fresh produce and dairy if the owner was prosperous enough to own a refrigerator and have an electrical connection. Importantly, their proprietors often had store credit at the central market with wholesalers and in turn would offer to sell their wares "a fiado"—on credit, a term derived from the word *fiar*, which means "to trust" or "to have confidence"—to their clients in the neighborhood. Since there were often half a dozen such stores on any given block, it was crucial to sell goods on credit to build long-term loyalty among its client base, an important function of credit itself. In many cases, the local grocer was given the responsibility of being the treasurer of the microcredit Committee of Women Entrepreneurs because she was thought to have accounting skills and the practical know-how to manage cross-cutting neighborhood debts.

As soon as Carmen noted the arrival of the Fundación Paraguaya staff, she turned the stream of loud complaints on Norma, the senior credit counselor who was there to mediate the dispute over lateness, although she was not in charge of this particular loan. Shouting, Carmen advanced, getting closer and closer until Norma was backed up against the doorframe. This was an impressive feat, since Norma is quite an imposing woman herself. With the pounding rain, the intensity of the debate and claustrophobia of the small shop made the encounter seem particularly combative, especially as group meetings were usually held on the more open and public patios in front of women's homes. In a single breath, Carmen recounted the numerous problems facing her committee while impressing the need to find an immediate solution. She began by acknowledging that the problems in the group had arisen because of her own difficulties with separating the tabs or bills from her grocery shop and the loan repayments to the Fundación. Some of her clients—she used the generic Guarani term *gentekuera* to avoid specifying whom—had running tabs at her grocery store that they had deferred paying for months, so her own debts were mounting. In the previous borrowing cycle she had solved her cash flow problem by deducting the outstanding bills owed by her neighbors from the loan disbursals to the women who owed her money and who were also in Fundación Paraguaya's borrowing group. In other words, participation in the microcredit program redrew the boundaries of local forms of credit by reorienting the economic interdependencies of the grocer and her neighbors. Women who might have successfully deferred paying their bills longer suddenly found that they had unexpectedly come due when the grocer had appropriated part of their microcredit loan. Carmen noted that, in retrospect, this had created a great deal of animosity within the group, especially since she had not consulted anybody in the committee before taking a unilateral decision about discounting the loans. However, she continued, this cycle seemed to be off to a better start as she had successfully separated her business from the accounts of the committee, and had begun to insist on more timely payments for the credit that she extended at her store.

Maria Elena had agreed to come along with Norma to help her resolve a difficult situation. She interjected a question, inquiring what the problem was now if Carmen seemed to have repaired relations with her committee and resolved the cash flow problems of her business. Carmen's voice began to rise again. As she told it, things had started off fine, but some people had started paying their weekly microloan quota late, so she had pulled money out of the cash register (*caja*) in order to make the payments for her group. In effect, she was offering credit to her neighbors so that they could pay off a different debt in the form of the weekly microcredit installment. She had begun doing it for some people because she knew them and knew that they would pay soon but understood that they did not have the cash on hand at that moment. Based on trust and without collateral, she gave them an advance from the money she had in her store. This seemed like an adequate stopgap until Carmen noticed that one woman was abusing her personal cash advances and now was three installments behind, which made Carmen wonder if she was going to (or was able to) pay either Carmen or the Fundación at all. From her perspective, Carmen had put in the money "from her own pocket" because the woman had complained, "Why won't you pay for me if you paid for all of my neighbors, all the other women from the committee?" Pointing an accusatory finger at both credit counselors, Carmen concluded that this was the reason she had called the Fundación with such urgency: "What was the Fundación going to do about it? Why didn't they solve this problem, since it was their own client who was owing [*debiendo*]?"

Norma's response was nearly identical to the answers she routinely gave to groups that were behind in their payments because one member of the group was in arrears.[43] Rehearsing a claim she often made while negotiating late payments, Norma countered that there was nothing the Fundación could do because it was the *committee's* problem—an internal problem—so as long as the group was meeting their group liability and making their payments on time, it was up to it to solve its own problems. This is why, Norma stated in a pedantic tone, the loan was called a "solidarity loan." Solidarity, in Norma's view, figured as an internal quality of the group and a feature of the committee as the social unit of debt. In other words, Norma deflected the accusation by pointing to the structural bonds of collective liability and refusing to mediate the actual relationships of interdependency—the animosities, betrayals, friendships, trusts, and shortcomings—that kept the group together.

Carmen nodded, impatient, and interrupted Norma's disquisition on solidarity. She declared that she had taken the promissory note (*pagaré*) for the group-based loan to the lawyer at her husband's work, and he had told her there was no way to mitigate the joint liability. The contractual obligation that bound the group together was legally unbreakable. However, Carmen turned the question from a contractual to an ethical issue that exceeded the social unit of debt defined in terms of membership. In Carmen's view, at the core this was an "injustice" (*injusticia*) and "it shouldn't be like this." In other words, if there was no legal remedy, she demanded to know how she could get the Fundación to intervene on her behalf and collect the unpaid debt from the group. Norma shook her head and responded with the same reasoning as before, observing that so long as the group was paying its collective installments, there was nothing they could do. Carmen crossed her arms and cocked her chin in anger. "Fine! That's all I need to know. We'll just stop paying you then! And then the Fundación will have to step in." The other women in her committee stood by quietly, observing the encounter unfolding between the credit counselors and Carmen. For her part, Norma responded firmly by reminding her that she was jeopardizing all of them if she made a rash decision and broke ties with the NGO. Maria Elena seemed content to observe. Carmen retorted that the decision was not rash: "Well, what else can we do?" From her final retort, the slippage was evident between her own financial perspective and the position of the group. By asking "what can *we* do," Carmen collapsed her own dilemmas about the cash shortfalls at her grocery store and the contractual liability of microcredit joint obligation.

Carmen used the threat of breaking social relations—the threat of default—in order to reactivate the obligation that she perceived the Fundación had to its clients. I suggest that it is precisely the instability of the personal bonds that anchor microcredit social collateral that challenges some readings of microcredit as structurally asymmetrical and exploitative.[44] The dramatic negotiations between Carmen and the credit counselors about what sorts of dependencies and interdependencies are internal to the group, or conversely also include the Fundación, are an effort to negotiate the nature and qualities of the multiple liabilities created by debt. Furthermore, based on the conflicting interpretations of debt debated by Carmen and Norma, I suggest that although debt does indeed restructure people's lives and choices, it is important not to take the common narrative of microcredit's economic progression—microcredit stepping in to remedy women's exclusion from credit systems—at face value. The critique of structural dependencies, though rightly pointing to the power effects of institutional authority, risks taking *microcredit* to be the only debt relations that restructures people's lives and choices. Carmen's efforts highlight the important ways borrowers are not a homogeneous group. Rather, I argue that social collateral often tracks social difference.

The shifting repayment relationships were dilemmas ardently contested by Carmen and her multiple creditors and debtors, not a single credit/debt twinship. Her threat of group default was not a protest against microcredit practices generally but rather an effort to connect, in her view, the correct creditors with the correct debtors. In other words, Carmen's project was to define and stabilize what she thought were the appropriate channels of repayment and link them to the social unit of debt defined in terms of group members. In practical terms, Carmen sought to connect the cash advances that she made to her neighbor to a group-based debt with Fundación Paraguaya rather than a running tab from her personal cash register. Default, which from one angle looks like an act of breaking social ties, was an effort to reactivate an entirely different lender/borrower relationship. It was an act of regeneration.

This dynamic became apparent when Carmen visited her credit counselor in the office the next day to request a copy of the asset contract (*garatía prendaria*) that each member signed to initiate the loan. This contract specified a household item that each would put up as a guarantee to the group in the event of default. Even though it was paperwork initiated, processed, and kept by Fundación Paraguaya, credit counselors emphasized that they themselves never collected the items: TV sets, refrigerators, washing machines, motorbikes. Instead, it was a guarantee for the group in the event of default, to cover the collective liability. The group was in charge of acting on seizing the collateral in the event of default. Carmen recounted that often her group members would voluntarily bring household items to her store to hold while they were still short on their payments, and she would keep them as collateral or pawn them while they put the cash together to make their debt payments. Again, debts proliferated other debts in wider financial interdependencies that resist categorization as straightforward exchange or repayment relationships. In fact, Carmen recalled that one woman even brought all of the blankets from her house to pawn, in the middle of winter during the harshest cold spell. "But still they brought their blankets to show that they were going to make good on their loan," Carmen said. This was how she had confidence that they were going to pay her back. It was a show of trust. Even when they were having a hard time, she reported, there were members who would bring cash in increments over the weekend, $2.50 at a time, a bit more when they could manage. Carmen reasoned that she needed the asset contract for the woman who was defaulting because she had never come by with anything as a show of confidence and had not demonstrated good intentions as her neighbors had done. Having a copy of the document was important to Carmen because it stood as a counterweight to the *other* important document: the contract of collective liability that her lawyer had evaluated and deemed unshakable. In her estimation, that asset contract would allow her to attach liability to the appropriate site and avoid the "injustice" of the Fundación's refusal to act on the late quotas.

PERPECTIVAL DEBT

Here I further theorize the social unit of debt by suggesting that the repayment mode of credit's lifecycle consists of constant work to define and stabilize the credit/debt twinship. The work of "gestionando"—of administering the loan as well as negotiating repayment—strove to twin credit and debt and fix both terms.[45] And importantly, while credit/debt does indeed bind ties over time, repayment spotlights the production and legibility of lender and borrower *priority*, as they are negotiated in the indeterminate middle period between credit access and the cancelation or renewal of a loan. In other words, when multiple overlapping credit/debt relationships coincide, the priority of one relationship in effect captures, reorients, and destabilizes other credit/debt twinships that might not even, on their face, appear to be connected in the same circuit of credit and repayment.

In Fundación Paraguaya's microfinance loans, gestionando highlights the risks and entanglements of liability that cross-cut differentiated social units. Part of the social drama at work in negotiating a loan settlement at the moment of collection hinged on the multiple and overlapping claims over the assets used to collateralize the loan. All of these were sites of competing valuations and claims to ownership, and only some could be put in service of repayment: land title, freezer, store tabs, and winter blankets. In the cases negotiated by Doctor Gregorio, the work of collection sought to disembed the asset from those other entanglements in order to repair *one* mutual entanglement. Gregorio prioritized the contractual interdependency of lender/borrower structuring the microloan between Fundación Paraguaya and its clients, which in turn refigured other forms of credit/debt defined by the Fundación as reciprocal kinship ties, or nepotism and theft.

As I argue, the obligation to repay was not merely located in the structural bonds joining borrowers in committees or simply in the contractual ties that bound together microcredit borrowers and the NGO that lends money and collects repayment. Instead, repayment—and the interdependencies attached to those relationships of liability—articulated across the whole regulatory field of microfinance. Liability, then, is both a subject position and a material relation. Put differently, persons and the debts they were answerable for are coemergent. This is especially clear from the position of Doctor Gregorio. Doctor Gregorio described himself as an astute interpreter of debt's many disguises and invisibilities. Indeed, of all the Fundación's staff members, he was one of the few who offered a metacommentary on the social meaning and relationality of credit. Given his expertise, Doctor Gregorio located himself as an observer and mediator of debt's multiple entanglements and layered interdependencies. As a consequence, of the many staff members at the Ciudad del Este branch of Fundación Paraguaya, he was uniquely self-possessed and independent. Why would that appear to be the case?

Doctor Gregorio was preternaturally attuned to the connections and differences enacted through credit relations, but for one end only. He was invested in prioritizing one debt over many others. On the one hand, he was immensely invested in cultivating personal relationships, which is why he spent a great deal of his professional life standing on the front porch of clients' houses discussing the messiness of their kinship and neighborly networks. In a way it seems counterintuitive that the debt collector was interested in forging social connections and repairing broken financial ties, while defaulting debtors were often keen to cancel their pending obligations and reach a zero balance owed so that they could disentangle themselves from their interdependencies with the Fundación and never hear from it again. However, it is crucial to note that Gregorio's self-identification as someone who knew "where and how to press" (*donde apretar*) positioned him *outside* the relationships that he manipulated like a puppeteer, pulling and tweaking debt's interdependencies to activate repayment but always unmoved by those relations. Doctor Gregorio was particularly adept at cloaking his own reliance on clients as contrastive subjects enmeshed in socially dense networks of obligations. By dint of drawing borrowers' relationships in relief as hypersocial, Gregorio's own outside interventions seemed straightforwardly technical and instrumental. In a sense, he made himself stand in for the Fundación's interests in collecting loans and thus came to embody the lender, even though his own finance capital was not at risk. Gregorio's professional *independence* relied on and reproduced the dense network of connections rendering the Fundación's borrowers *interdependent*. His success in stabilizing the terms of the lender /borrower relationship, and thereby defining liability, hinged on his unique professional role of pressing from the outside and convincingly articulating the perspective—and definition of debt—from the lender's point of view.

Part of the work of this chapter is to chronicle the daily triumphs and failures of credit counselors as they managed unwieldy microcredit loan portfolios. Their own professional fate was fundamentally tied to unruly, socially complex subjects: borrower's multiple credits and obligations, family connections, neighborhood ties, precarious income streams, chronic health and family problems, all of which intruded on the structured, contractual repayment of loans. In the repayment relations negotiated for the Committee of Women Entrepreneurs, Fundación Paraguaya's credit counselors were at a loss to parse the crosscutting debts that transected the committee and were adamant about their incapacity to intervene in the inner workings of the group. From Norma's repeated retreat to the idiom of solidary lending to the offloading of responsibility for managing repayment issues through the asset contract, credit counselors sought out ways to deploy social collateral to harden the boundaries around committees. The clear distinction that they made between internal matters and their own managerial identities at the Fundación marked a sharp contrast between the relationships that bound up the group and their own relationship to those dense sites of collective affiliation. Credit counselors, then, were only partially successful at asserting their independence from the social and economic entanglements of the Committees of Women Entrepreneurs.

The perspectival quality of financial instruments lead to a careful dance around repayment. This chapter has tracked the various instances when that careful dance around repayment stumbled: Not through terminal default, but rather through lateness. Social collateral drew together economic obligations that were very difficult to sever, even as the debate circled around who was included and left out of the social unit of debt. I suggest that social collateral is a good tool to think with, beyond the intimate debts of microfinance and their expression in Paraguayan development. In fact, from crises in the Eurozone to banking bailouts in the United States, something that looks a great deal like social collateral—including the delicate choreography of repayment—is becoming the basis for global finance capital.[46] Indeed, whitewashing in the financial sector dramatizes the way "too big to fail" notions of overly dense financial entanglements among the biggest banks in the global financial system now share remarkable similarities with "too small to fail" logics of microfinance and their intimate economic ties of joint liability. These massive socioeconomic shifts have made Paraguayans ever more dependent on financial products. The question of how these contingent and perspectival processes of financial capture and conversion take shape presses at this particular historical moment, when indebtedness is something contemporary capitalism both relies on and enables. In Ciudad del Este's smuggling economy—as in other financial contexts—regulating the line between finance, fraud, and family involves a great deal of financial labor from the Fundación and its clients. At the same time, acts of repayment make social collateral persuasive and possible in the Paraguayan banking system.[47] As I argue, loose-fitting perspectives on liability are generative forces in finance capitalism.

CHAPTER 5

Renewal

"We didn't know, they never told us that we had insurance in the case of a death," Lourdes said with apparent exasperation, relating the troubles her microcredit group had experienced recently in the course of their cycles of borrowing and repayment. It had been two years since I had last interviewed her microfinance group, and Lourdes had just been informed that her creditors now bundled a life insurance policy into their suite of finance services. Like many such groups throughout Paraguay—and part of a development model implemented in similar programs around the world—their microcredit loans brought small-scale credit to the periurban settlements of low-income families with few insurance options (*seguros*) in the Paraguayan financial system. Lourdes had been a long-standing client of Fundación Paraguaya. Like other Committees of Women Entrepreneurs, her group's loans were cross-guaranteed by the members who were collectively liable for their fellow borrowers. Lourdes's remark about the death of a group member underscored the hard realities of joint liability, where the loss of a member left the microcredit group to deal with the payment. The insurance policy was a relatively new addition to the financial services offered by Fundación Paraguaya starting in 2012, after I finished my long-term fieldwork. It came about because so many microcredit groups found it impossible to deal with the increased debt load that followed from the death of a borrower. I track some of those stories of loss and renewal in this chapter before returning to Lourdes's experience of the new policy.

Before life insurance was bundled in the suite of financial services offered by the Fundación, groups had to decide for themselves how to redistribute the debt. Like many social development programs—including *Ikatú* and its aim of entrepreneurialism—this was a case of evolving policies playing catchup with the everyday dilemmas generated by collective forms of debt.[1]

Lourdes's story of three borrowers who had died over the group's long credit history and her surprise at the Fundación's new insurance program "in the case of a death" are part of a larger story about value and its reproduction within families, neighborhoods, and financial organizations in Paraguay. Before the insurance policy came into effect, the committees had to figure out themselves how to cover the payments owed by a member who had died midcycle. The end of the three- or four-month microcredit cycle was not simply a matter of paying down and canceling a debt. Loan renewals offered an opportunity and a context to discuss how the relationships anchoring social collateral would be conserved or transformed for another cycle of borrowing. Conversion of debt—in an out of the financial obligations of microcredit—is also a transformation of value that in turn reformulates relations of dependency, obligation, and affiliation attached to and produced through those relations of exchange. It is precisely these conversions and materializations that so occupied Lourdes in her group-based microcredit payments.

This chapter traces the triangular relation between kinship, death, and formal financial indebtedness. This three-way relationship is especially important when all relationships were being knit and unknit through social collateral. What microcredit debates about the exploitative and coercive nature of extracting financial value from women's social ties often leave unremarked are the complicated and conditional ways in which the forms of interdependency at the heart of microcredit social collateral unfold as the loan itself moves through its life course.[2] Recent anthropological scholarship on new financial infrastructures has pointed to the tensions as well as the opportunities thrown up by innovations found at the bottom of the pyramid, especially as they are incorporated into the development world.[3] One site where financial practice and borrowers' relationships clearly come together is in the realm of kinship ties, many of which in Paraguay are reckoned in economic terms. I aim to track microcredit and mortuary practice to show how dense ties of obligation and financial accounting of debt service were not aligned in predictable ways, and offer some thoughts on the materiality of kinship relations reckoned in terms of financial debts. The importance of renewing social collateral while renewing loans from one cycle to the next was made obvious in crises of relatedness like the incorporation of the dead into collective loans. Building outward from the hard choices faced by women who borrowed through microfinance initiatives in Paraguay, I suggest that these collective debts generate a series of puzzles around relatedness. I document how the three-way link between kinship, death, and indebtedness goes beyond analogy; collective debt is not simply "like" a relationship of kinship. Instead, microcredit collective indebtedness offers a powerful context for people to grapple with the broader question of life span and the life-and-death human stakes of obligation.

In microcredit group-based loans, the limits of debts' life spans were put into focus most clearly when persons' lives ended abruptly and sometimes tragically. Although debts have structured biographies that are bound to the calendar,[4] microcredit offers an especially good vantage to think broadly about the (mis)aligned life course events of borrowers and their debts. For women who borrowed in microcredit-based Committees of Women Entrepreneurs from Fundación Paraguaya, the personal health crises of members constantly jeopardized the payments of the wider group. Importantly, microcredit social collateral made losing a member of the group especially complicated. In extreme cases, groups had to grapple with the death of one of their members and with what to do with their outstanding debts, a situation that highlighted the redistributive arrangements that helped the group remain solvent under normal circumstances. Death exposed the relationships that were attenuated, reinforced, or ruptured when the individual ceased to be but the group—and the debt—remained. Indeed, death, as Annette Weiner (1976: 85) reminds us, "finally makes apparent the reality that all social relationships are at best tenuous," and throws into relief the chains of mutual indebtedness that traverse the life span of valued objects and overcome individuals' life spans. Microcredit borrowers felt the hard edges of debt's life span most acutely when mortuary practices of commemoration and mourning were bound up with the practical task of shouldering the financial obligations of the dead. Here I work through the broader implications of debts' life cycles by looking at the credit histories compiled by Informconf. Then I turn to two instances where groups grappling with the death of a member and settlement of a loan before the insurance policy took effect. Their loan renewals united kinship and financial ties in unexpected ways.

"SOCIAL DEATH": READING FOR
BIOGRAPHY IN A CREDIT REPORT

I first began to contemplate the life spans of credit/debt twinships during my conversations with an executive at Informconf, Paraguay's private sector credit rating agency. The story of Informconf credit score reports is much more nuanced than it might appear at first from looking at the piles of paper printouts or the drab Web interface that the company packages and sells to Paraguayan businesses. Tracking how a credit score gets made, and the sophisticated social theory that goes into its making, tells a story of economic personhood. The social unit of debt that is assembled through a credit report intersects in complex ways with the narrative of living on credit told by the top managers at the company.

Gustavo, a vice president at the credit scoring company, routinely led a two-day seminar on managing credit risk. I attended one such seminar in Ciudad del Este in 2009. After discussing my research, he expressed interest in my work on social anthropology and invited me to attend a seminar on credit for microenterprises that he was leading in Asunción the following month. In between seminar sessions we sat down for an interview about his views on credit and debt. These topics were central to his career in the financial sector as well as to his deeper interest stemming from his Jesuit training in history and liberal arts. Informconf credit checks were usually used as technical tools by financial institutions, but Gustavo also suggested that at another level credit histories certainly invited more abstract reflections on the binding efficacy of debts. He was keenly interested in the social and ethical dilemmas that configured very concrete and material processes of credit and repayment. I discuss Gustavo's reflections on credit as, in his words, "a pathway to transcendence" with an eye to the ways his analysis of the durability and sensitivity of credit and debt resonated with and supported the corporate project of credit rating. Central to Gustavo's story is the question of what sort of obligations and responsibilities were made visible by Informconf and by his efforts to query the future-oriented character of loans. The temporal efforts and effects of debts illuminate the conditions and the consequences of repayment in Paraguay's most powerful credit institution.

Gustavo's primary role as senior vice president at Informconf was to supervise, market, and lead professionalization seminars that trained financial sector managers to understand and make use of credit assessment tools. He had been with the company for over fifteen years and had overseen the expansion of Informconf's credit training seminar series to become one of the largest certificate training programs in Paraguay. In a sense, it was ruthlessly self-serving for Paraguay's sole credit rating agency also to hold a monopoly on training and professionalization seminars for people employed in the banking and financial services sector. These seminars invariably touted the indispensability of credit scores—provided by Informconf—for loan officers making decisions about client creditworthiness. That said, Gustavo's informal poll at the beginning of each seminar revealed that most loan officers were already reliant on Informconf credit scores to make decisions about credit risk. The seminars familiarized financial managers with the accounting techniques made possible by the data provided by a credit history. In fact it was data they were already using in some capacity. Importantly, Gustavo's role at the company meant that his particular views on credit reached a broad audience of financial professionals. He personally led intensive training seminars several times a month, for audiences that often surpassed one hundred participants. Furthermore, Gustavo's views on Informconf's role in the credit market in Paraguay were particularly salient, since Informconf held a monopoly in credit services through their national financial database as well as business services including debt collection claims, telemarketing, audit and risk management, and professional training.[5]

When I met him in 2009, Gustavo was a slim, active man in his early forties. Although soft-spoken and mild-mannered, he was prone to decisive gestures and categorical statements, especially while lecturing groups of financial professionals. With perfectly cropped graying hair and a well-cut charcoal suit paired with a matching tie, he clearly was comfortable with the parlance of financial and professional authority, and he wielded impressive command of both the seminar room and the office workspace at Informconf headquarters. In my unstructured interview between seminar sessions and follow-up phone conversations and email exchanges, we discussed his professional responsibilities at Informconf at length and also his broader interest in the ethical contours of credit and responsibility. Gustavo began by noting that his intellectual formation had been indelibly marked by his Catholic upbringing and Jesuit schooling, which inspired him to continue his university studies in history and liberal arts. He came to work at Informconf after several years of teaching history at a Catholic school in Asunción. Like Doctor Gregorio, he had found greater success in the financial services industry than in the profession he had initially trained in. Given his background, however, Gustavo found resonance between my interests in society and culture and his own fascination with world history and civilization, positing that both intellectual projects were fundamentally concerned with the tension between cultural variation and human nature. His current position as an executive at Informconf was not as far from his core interests as one might suspect, he suggested, as credit is concerned with many of the same themes of futurity, responsibility, and subjectivity.

These themes appeared most prominently when I asked Gustavo why he thought people paid their debts, a question that at the onset I meant quite concretely. Given his role as executive at a credit rating agency, I had hoped for a tutorial in the regulatory force of Paraguayan civil law as well as the importance of credit history from the perspective of the credit rating agency that also managed debt collection services and several payment platforms. I was surprised, then, when Gustavo immediately steered the conversation toward broader reflections on credit and temporality.

C: It is impressive that people repay their credit even if their loan officer does a poor job [of managing the loan].

G: They pay in any case [*igual paga*].

C: And that leads me to think, why would it be that people pay back their credit? Because for a lot of people, there really are no bad consequences if they don't pay, if they enter into default . . .

G: Clearly, it does not matter if they default because they are the bottom [*está en el fondo*] [of the credit pool] and nobody gives them credit.

C: Yes, and their moneylender isn't going to cut them off if they enter into Informconf [as a defaulting debtor] . . .

G: And the usurer will not cut them off either.

C: Exactly, so why then would it be that people pay back their credits?

G: It's being human. All of human nature always leads you to think about the future [*Todo la naturaleza humana siempre te lleva a pensar en el futuro*] . . .

Gustavo turned the interview to what he saw as the essential qualities of debt relations as fundamental human characteristics and away from the economic motivations of moneylenders. In his estimation the impulse to repay one's debts emanated from anxieties and aspirations about the future: anxieties that he conceptualized as shared by all humans and an inescapable fact of the social writ large. Gustavo's answer to my question about why people pay back their loans moved seamlessly between rumination on the temporal orientation of credit and reflections on the material conditions of debt and repayment. In other words, his explanations of credit as a function of economic necessity segued into his explanations of credit as a natural human characteristic and worked to draw the two together. He continued by stating explicitly, "Credit is toward the future, right; it helps make human beings transcendent."

Perhaps sensing both my interest and my confusion, Gustavo quickly sketched a linear time line with a finger, leaving a smudge on the heavy wood seminar table in Informconf's glassed meeting room. In ghostly marks on the conference table he drew a time line beginning with the past, marking the present, and trailing off toward the future as he spoke. Explaining, he said, "This is today. This is the future. This is the past. The evolution of a basic [simple] man [*un hombre muy básico*] is up to the present, he looks at his present and does not think in the future, right? He looks at what he has lived, and at his present, the present." I surmised that his working sense of transcendence drew heavily on his Jesuit training, emanating from the reasoning mind's faculty of judgment, evidenced particularly in his clarification of transcendence as "something more than the material." His further observations about the properties of credit moved quickly, however, from its abstract principles to the material practices that stitch time together into the past, present, and future and into the smudged time line we were both peering at on the table. He concluded:

> Credit helps one *transcend* and go toward the future. Because a man is told, "Take this money, and you are going to pay me in a year." And he looks to the future and says, "Will it be that in ten months I'll still be working?" Or rather, that person who is fairly formed [*medianamente formado*], who is basically formed, that person evolves, credit invites him to evolve toward the future and say, "In a year, will I have—will I be able to sell my crops? For how much will I be able to sell my crops? Will the prices be the same?" So he thinks, to, well, to *progress*, right?

Thus in Gustavo's model of transcendence, it was precisely the practical concerns of crop prices and employment stability that invited his hypothetical "basically formed person" to evolve toward the future. His central example of credit's capacity to transcend the material hinged especially on credit as progress, which he located in the realm of the material. Transcendence appeared as an ethical imperative laminated onto the material conditions of progress, as they moved in tandem toward a future. His sense of personal evolution was, in other words, grounded in a person's personal economic project that sustained and built a livelihood from year to year. These concerns motivated Gustavo's sense of evolution and progress, too, which he further attributed to a need for "belonging" (*pertenencia*). These modes of attachment were something that Gustavo also posited as future-oriented and, again, were tied to the relationship between personal aspirations to go beyond and expand one's horizons and brought together with questions of access to material resources. Credit offered the promise of mobility in both an economic and a social sense, with the specter of paralysis and immobility for someone with no debts. This time his sketch took the form of a pyramid, drawing on the table as he spoke.

> G: People have a sense of belonging—what does that mean? I'm [down] here where usurers lend to me, and here [in the middle] they are where the finance companies are. And [up] here are where the banks are, and here they are where the credit cooperative are. So if he is [down] here, he wants to be [up] here, he wants to enter here [gesturing upward]. Once he entered here, he belongs to another group already. He is above his peers [*por encima de sus pares*] on top of this one [indicating the lowest level].
>
> C: And they always are trying to move up?
>
> G: And always, right . . . it's what they say here in Paraguay, who they call the "*rico pyahu*" [newly wealthy],[6] the person who has money—the man who was poor and starts to have money. . . . And so he scales up, natural in the human being, right. That same thing happens with credit, right.

At the heart of Gustavo's sense of credit's invitation to go beyond the present and open up the future is the implicit certainty that people's sense of belonging is always forward looking as well—that belonging is ultimately caught up in aspirations to go beyond the boundaries of one's current personal standing and context. However, Gustavo's sense of transcendence as synonymous with socioeconomic upward mobility invariably drew him back to a linear model of growth and improvement restricted to individual possibilities and limitations. He returned again and again to the idea of credit as profoundly enabling but always undertaken by and anchored in individuated people. This time unsatisfied with drawings smudged on the tabletop, he reached for my field notebook to mark out a time line: clear, decisive lines etched in blue ballpoint pen. His analysis of credit is worth spending time with because it resonates so powerfully with the story of social collateral.

> • I'm going to tell you something—credit is—this is your life [sketching the time line]. I always explain this to the financial analysts [loan officers he trained at seminars]. A person reaches twenty years here, and then he finds himself here at twenty-two years old, and they give you a credit [making

cross-hatches on the time line]. That credit invites you to think up to your death—your commercial death—that is to say, "I'm going to pay well now at twenty-two years old because when I turn thirty-seven, I *might* need credit. If I pay badly today, they won't give me that credit at thirty-seven years old. So I have to watch my name [cuidar mi nombre]." So he begins to watch his image, his "personal transcendent 'me'" [*su 'yo personal transcendente'*]. He begins to be a social being, he starts to belong to a social group that will observe him. And they will watch him. And they will evaluate him. If they see that he behaved in a way that is socially acceptable, they will lend to him again. If he did not, then they will exclude him. In other words, he enters into a new universe of relationships where he has laws that he was to obey. In other words, not only does he transcend, but also he relates to a group.

This is what you [loan officers] need to teach your clients. That he [the borrower] has to transcend, and not that, say, he has problems paying now, and there he goes and throws it all away [*ahí tirar por la borda todo*]. Because he'll have—he will be dead alive [*va a morir en vida*], this whole stage up until sixty-five years old [gesturing toward his time line, cross-hatched with commercial death at sixty-five], he won't *exist,* he will be dead, creditwise and socially. And that's a bit what I try to teach people, right?

In his sketch of the credit time line, the social (*social*) began with credit (*crédito*) at age twenty-two. Complicated looping lines and brackets link together, separate, and locate the different temporal positions, periods, and perspectives that emplace the borrower. He or she is represented in the scene as a little stick figure positioned over "today" (*hoy*) and contemplates the pasts and futures of borrowing. Through his diagram and explanation, then, Gustavo offered a way of narrating personal biography through the lens of credit. And further, in the decision-making calculus that Gustavo outlined, personal relationships flow from individual choices, with credit doing important work to socialize individuals into the norms of the group. Not unlike Adam Smith's classic liberal enlightenment treatise on stranger sociality in his *Treaty on Moral Sentiments* (2000), the sympathy felt for and garnered from others forms the basis for ethical action. These norms, incidentally, were codified and enforced by Informconf credit scores, public approbation that Smith described as "love of system" and, more famously, leading people "as if by an invisible hand."[7] For Gustavo, those social relations were of paramount importance precisely because they could help him make sense of and clarify his life as a time line of personal decisions up until "social death" (*muerte social*) at retirement age.

One could imagine many situations of multiple and overlapping debts where the "socially acceptable" orientation to payment or repayment,

FIGURE 11. Credit advertised with the slogan "We don't look at Informconf."

to borrow Gustavo's framing, is far from clear, and certainly not as decisive as his time line. Indeed the tangled repayment relationships described
in the previous chapter probably would not follow the neat logic of
credit, repayment, and reputation that Gustavo implicitly plays out in
his parable of the credit Everyman. And importantly, death here only
makes sense in terms of the singular relationship between the individual
borrower and the enigmatic "them" who evaluate their credit and repayment. Death, in Gustavo's formulation, is marked simply by, in his
words, the "absence of things to evaluate." In a sense, commercial death
at retirement and being "dead alive" as a defaulting debtor barred from
the credit market are equally about disentanglement from that singular
relationship with "a social group that will observe him." Both signal an
exit from debt—and its individuated social unit—but with different ori-
entations to the cross-hatched markers of a biographical life span.[8] In
the case of retirement, "social death"—marked at the far right of the
diagram—largely coincided with physical death, so the period of being
"dead alive" as a credit zombie was dramatically reduced. However,
defaulting earlier in the time line would mean years of "[being] dead,
creditwise and socially."

To conclude his tutorial on Informconf, Gustavo drew together the
threads of credit, biography, and sociability that he had been developing

in his discussion of the subject of credit and of social relationships. After I remarked that credit invites you to think in new ways, Gustavo said:

> And we, here at this company, it is an important component for us that this happen. Because we are like the judge that shows who behaved badly and who behaved well. Therefore it *creates* culture [*Entonces* crea *cultura*]. Creates culture. Why? Because it is a, it's a determinant to say that I judge—or that I am the path through which other people will get to know you. A path through which they will get to know you, and they will evaluate you, so it would be good for you to be alright with them. Because that path works [laughs]. That is life.

Perhaps unsurprisingly, the biography that Gustavo describes—the person who gets his first line of credit and imagines the pros and cons of repaying that debt—closely corresponds to the biography that can be read from an Informconf credit report. And it is in that sense that Informconf is "the path through which other people will get to know you." Individual credit histories are accessible to any company that subscribes to Informconf's national database. The standard printout begins with a brief summary of the personal data for the individual. The database is searchable by name, which can lead to ambiguity since there are several very common family names in Paraguay. It can also be accessed more precisely by personal national ID number (*numero de cédula*, CIN), which is a personal identification code that functions similarly to a social security number in the United States.[9] Credit scores are reported as a letter between A and Z. Directly below a listing of basic personal information, including gender, date and place of birth, marital status, is a listing of employment history. This only shows up if a person is lucky enough to find formal sector employment that is registered in the Informconf system. Following that, there is often quite a long list of all credit both applied for and contracted. Finally, at the bottom of the page, there is a list of information that is absent or does not register in the database. These can cover many facets of a person's livelihood, including informal employment, property, licenses, and permits, as well as unpaid debts. The collection notices that might be registered with Informconf can range widely from the types of credit listed in the section above but also late payments for monthly plans like utilities or payments to a property developer for a land title, late payments on installment plans, and so on.

What is remarkable about the human life course that can be read from an Informconf credit report is that it corresponds so felicitously with the type of person—and their dilemmas about futurity and belonging—sketched by Gustavo in his reflections on credit's place in forging social relations. This person enters into a series of consecutive individual contractual liabilities and arrangements with other parties, and those transactions can be neatly recorded on descending lines of a credit report. Even for jointly held liabilities like guarantor relationships, each party is listed on his or her own credit report. The obligation is not partible or attenuated even if it is distributed across multiple persons.[10] The crosshatches on a personal financial time line can be read directly from the line items on a credit report, as though each line were a snapshot of an event in a time line. Gustavo's observations about the possibility of "credit death" would be concretely enacted if Informconf recorded default, nonpayment, or disqualification. In such cases, no more lines appear on the credit report. The person ceased to exist, which rendered him or her unable to borrow from formal financial institutions in the future.

In eighteen months of daily observation of Fundación Paraguaya staff requesting, printing, and evaluating credit reports, I was confronted with many cases of people who hoped to rise from the dead, as it were, by submitting applications for group-based loans. Committees of Women Entrepreneurs provided special exemptions for women with blemished credit histories, so long as their fellow borrowers accepted them. Like bankruptcy proceedings, for these women part of the ritual of collective credit involved making public the financial biography that emanated from the Informconf system.[11] The gaps in the economic time line registered by their Informconf reports were particularly striking for me. In many cases, the binders of loan documents that were the basis for credit to Committees of Women Entrepreneurs included credit reports whose last line was recorded three or five years ago because the credit history barred women from borrowing at a bank or finance company. In other words, in institutional practice this type of biography— this means of capturing, accounting for, and describing a life span— stood out in relief as an important way of describing people and debts.

Gustavo's model of credit offers a provocative way of thinking about the covariance between death, debt, and entrance into or exit from financial relationships that he described as "the social."[12] His take on credit highlights the hard work of maintaining a line of sight on credit as it unfolds over time, changing as it goes and changing debtors along with it. It is useful to consider the subjective experience of credit and life span described by Gustavo as a way to further unpack the stakes of the periodization of credit for imagining the social unit of debt over differentiated time scales. These life spans are especially important because of the close resemblance between his credit time line and the biographical narrative of an Informconf credit report. In both cases, the gaps and caesuras in credit offer the unsettling prospect of dead-alive debtors. More broadly, the social, epistemological, temporal, moral, and political stakes of pledges and promises, of course, are classic themes in anthropological theories of value. Whether Adam Smith's reflections on the stranger relations that regulate judgment through shared moral sentiment or Georg Simmel's enthusiasm about money's abstraction from social ties as a universal solvent that corrodes those binding pledges and promises, the philosophical underpinnings of binding promises—as well as their monetization—have been amply explored in social theory. Gustavo's emphasis on individual credit histories is perhaps unsurprising since he is coming at it from a bird's-eye view of the Informconf *system*, which is an aggregate database of debtors in Paraguay. Microcredit loan renewals help us see how his important intuition that credit creates culture—especially a culture of self-responsibility—might ultimately have consequences for the social unit at stake in credit's binding pledges. It also helps us see the boundaries of inclusion and exclusion in practice, *given* the social field that Gustavo traced out. In other words, this way of describing a biography was important for generating and regenerating finance capitalism.

DEATH, DEBT, AND "BUYING THE FUNERAL" IN CIUDAD DEL ESTE

Ethnographically, I found that the culture creation effects of credit, to borrow Gustavo's turn of phrase, were not only mediated by Informconf and its capacity to inspire a particular orientation to an ethics of debtor responsibility. The theory of credit elaborated by Informconf rippled outward to other financial institutions in Paraguay. Tellingly, Fundación Paraguaya was also deeply invested in the futurity of credit liability as an important regulatory form. Here I turn to the life span of credit not in the abstract terms of credit scoring and its particular rubrics of personal responsibility but rather as dilemmas and choices faced by borrowing groups in the working out of credit repayment and renewal. Indeed, many residents of Ciudad del Este characterized their relationship to debt as bicycling (*bicicleteando*), where their livelihood was propelled by endless cycles of borrowing, often paying off one loan with another. Like Gustavo's credit time line, the ceaseless revolutions of pedaling credit can be thought of as extending a debt in spacetime.[13]

Instead of Informconf's story of personal progress over the years, the credit bicycle corresponds to a theory of movement and mobility that moves forward by coming around and around to the same place and the same process, again and again.

Importantly, in the world of microfinance borrowing, cycles of birth, death, and renewal were a constant point of discussion and not just for human actors. The cycles of borrowing and paying in women's microcredit loans—especially their "initiation" (iniciación), "cancellation" (cancelación), and "renewal" (renovación)—were a regular feature of economic life. In a striking parallel, Maurice Bloch and Jonathan Parry (1982a: 10) remark on the cyclicality of time as organized in mortuary practices in their classic work on death and the regeneration of life. There, they suggest that death holds together two different experiences of time: repetition and irreversible duration. Cycles of debt also hold together the regular repetition of payment with the irreversible duration of a credit history.

Returning to the scene of credit and mourning that led Lourdes to comment about the death of a borrower and repayment of a loan, the social personhood enacted through credit and recorded by Informconf took on new meaning amid many overlapping debts. In Lourdes's settlement of about eighty households located on the outskirts of the city, her neighbors were accustomed to dealing with death through relationships of lending and borrowing. These economic networks were rooted in daily practices of commercial exchange that stitched the settlement together. While not obviously connected to microcredit social collateral, other types of funerals in the neighborhood illustrate how kinship, economy, and value seep into one another. This is especially important as an alternative perspective on the economic time line sketched by Gustavo and made material in Informconf credit scores. For instance, neighbors often came together to "collaborate" (colaborar) though financial support and labor in support of a common funeral rite to mourn the death of a child, locally called a "fiesta de angelito" (little angel festival). The angelito, sometimes also called angeloro, was meant to be a celebratory occasion since an innocent child without sin was expected to pass immediately to become an angel in heaven.[14] Here, I show how the wider life cycle events of the neighborhood offer a window onto the ways kinship relationships shape broader economic practices. Among the predominantly Catholic residents of the neighborhood, these festivals participated in the borrowing and exchange networks that were so much a part of the commercial rhythm of Ciudad del Este.

On the few occasions when I was visiting the neighborhood during a fiesta de angelito, swarms of local children descended on the parents' home as word spread of the festival throughout the settlement. Munching enthusiastically on snack-sized packages of chips and sucking on sweets, the neighborhood kids seemed only vaguely aware of the unhappy circumstances that brought them together. The event was usually organized by the extended family of the dead child—especially grandmothers, ritual coparent godmothers (*comadres*), and older aunts—who often lived nearby and came to help with the festival.[15] A shared sense of matrilineal obligation animated the gathering, linking domestic groups to a wider web of relations in Ciudad del Este. In very practical terms, these female kin shouldered the expense and the labor of procuring the snacks and sweets for local children.

Folklore studies of Paraguayan popular religiosity have often focused on oral histories of mortuary rites, frequently citing the historical importance of both Catholic and Guarani religious practices. Some of these accounts shed light on the redistributive networks that sustain funerary practices like the angelito. Dionisio M. González Torres wrote in 1980 of his travels through Alto Paraná in eastern Paraguay, including the towns surrounding Ciudad del Este. In his ethnology of mortuary practice, he noted that "when a young 'innocent' child dies, the owner of a neighborhood store takes charge of the funeral and compensates the parents of the child with some sum of money. They often call this practice 'buying the funeral of the *angelito*.' The store owner's interests are served in that he or she can sell lots of stock during the funeral, especially food and beverages" (313). González Torres also cites an earlier newspaper account of the importance of neighbors and extended kin in "buying the funeral of the *angelito*." The article was published in *ABC Color*, Paraguay's leading daily newspaper, in a special report on the festival. The report noted, "Coins play an important role: it is a common ritual to place coins over the eyes of the little body, with the objective of keeping their eyelids closed. It is also common to place money on the chest, which will add up as more neighbors and family arrive. The money will be used to buy beverages and food for consumption during the wake, and it is a family member or neighbor who spontaneously takes charge of attending to visitors, serving [drinks], cigarettes, water, or sweets for the children."[16] The money piled on the child's body materialized the caring network and further was put to use to reproduce the next generation, especially through snacks and sweets. Unlike weddings, where the expense was usually expected to be borne by the immediate family, mortuary practices often incorporated a wide range of people in the work of "buying the funeral of the angelito," and to a lesser extent for funerals for adults, which are customarily spread across nine days (*novenarios*) of mourning. And as I talked with the women who busily handed out candy and plastic cups of soda during the neighborhood angelito funeral in Ciudad Jardín, the sense of "spontaneously taking charge" of the gathering was tangible. Each woman said that she did what she could to help out, often leveraging her business contacts with wholesalers downtown to supply food and toys for the gathering.

The financialization of these community events through programs like microinsurance and microcredit might seem at odds with the extemporaneous and dispersed set of neighborhood linkages that sustained mortuary practices in Ciudad del Este. However, recent anthropological scholarship on debt has underscored the importance of financial relationships in socially important life cycle rituals, including death and mourning. From Julie Chu's (2010) research on cosmologies of credit and the scales of value that prioritize U.S. dollars in Chinese spirit money gifts to ritualized gambling to pay off outstanding debts to the dead in Alan Klima's (2002) research on funeral casinos in Thailand, anthropologists have shown the numerous points of intersection between financial technologies and traditional mortuary practice.[17] Indeed, mortuary payment systems are a classic topic of anthropological inquiry (Bloch and Parry 1982b), especially in Pacific contexts. And just as the classic study of kinship has received renewed interest as the shared substances of kin have been denaturalized and defamiliarized by advanced reproductive technologies and global mobility, so too have classic anthropological notions of exchange received renewed interest in a moment of intensified global financial interconnection. The intersection of kinship and material relations with the dead in the credit worlds of microfinance, then, invites fresh analysis of classic questions of kinship and exchange.

In Paraguay, credit and debt often serve as the idiom and the practical mechanism through which people negotiate and sustain a whole range of obligations, including family ties and socially important life cycle events. It is important to keep in view, though, the legacies of using kinship and exchange as building blocks for anthropological theory. As Susan McKinnon (2001: 278) has argued, turning a critical eye to classic treatments of kinship theory shows "just how central 'enterprise' has always been in anthropological conceptions of kinship." Whether Lewis Henry Morgan's model of patrilineal kinship as the accumulation of

capital or Lévi-Strauss's logics of risk and return through market speculation, McKinnon suggests that "the analogy that focuses on the power
of paternity (and fraternity) to mobilize more 'natural' female resources
through the enterprising spirit of the market is not 'just' a metaphor but
an analogy central to the anthropological understanding of what kinship and the creation of culture are all about" (297). I understand
McKinnon's analysis of origin stories in anthropology as a further provocation to continue excavating the specific cultural-historical dynamics
that give these kinship narratives and frameworks such powerful appeal.
Indeed, microcredit debt illustrates the ways development NGOs conceptualize kinship relatedness *also* in terms of the power of others to
mobilize "natural" female resources through the enterprising spirit of
the market. Tellingly, social collateral is crafted around the assumption
that networks of women will mobilize themselves and one another in
order to make claims on financial resources. The "symbolic density of
the substances and codes that come to signify kinship," in the words of
Franklin and McKinnon (2001: 10) are reconceptualized by both lenders and borrowers as a resource in the repayment of financial debts in
microcredit programs and a key aspect of their durability.

THE INS AND OUTS OF "SOLIDARIDAD"

Microcredit social collateral worked as a powerful allegory of a broader
thematic of obligation and its limits—including mortality—that is at the
heart of women's understanding of kinship.[18] I couldn't help but think
that this was why the microcredit problems, especially regarding renewing loans, so excited issues of relation-affirming and relation-bounding
in the death context. The resources mobilized by Committees of Women
Entrepreneurs to pay their group loan installments were especially visible in the unusual contexts of late payments (morosidad) or difficult
loan renewals (*renovación*). Both situations were especially high stakes
when the borrowing group lost a member—through death but also
migration or illness—and had to go on making collective payments.

   In addition to my discussions with Lourdes early on in my fieldwork
and before institutionalized insurance was put in place, I encountered
several such groups that were paying off the debts of a dead borrower. In
one instance, I accompanied a team of credit counselors from Fundación
Paraguaya to a meeting with a borrowing group that was in trouble
because their president had died suddenly of a heart attack. Silvenia,
the credit counselor in charge of their loan portfolio, observed that the

problem would not be so difficult to overcome if the group's collective savings account were not unfortunately also registered in the name of the woman who had died.[19] Beyond the temporary caesura in the rhythm of repayment, the broader worry for both lender and borrower was the social reproduction of the group and its renewal for another cycle of borrowing. The group's future borrowing prospects were in jeopardy if they could not restart payment of their current loan as well as resolve the claims over the savings account. Group savings were among the institutional requirements for participating in the microcredit program and served as a sort of ad hoc collateral for the loan. In brute financial and administrative terms, the death of the member threatened the continuing *life* of the borrowing group and its potential renewal. Meanwhile, Fundación Paraguaya's insistence that the group continue paying the loan was not a general feature of small-scale banking in Paraguay. When I later asked a friend who was an informal moneylender what would happen if any of her clients were to die and leave behind unpaid bills, she laughed and said that she would not be able to pursue it any further unless she wanted to "hunt in the tomb itself," since extended family networks were not considered liable for outstanding debts. By contrast, Fundación Paraguaya's model of joint liability incorporated even the dead.

Silvenia and I pulled up at a lovely brick home surrounded by a carefully manicured lawn. Despite being quite a distance from the city center, the neighborhood had experienced a bit of a boom as real estate development companies sold off the lots and financed land purchases.[20] There were more than enough patio chairs to accommodate the whole gathering—a sign that the house was a central and prosperous node in neighborhood gatherings—and we sat shaded by a large willow tree that had been landscaped with a border of bright flowers. This was a thriving family, and the cornerstone of neighborhood life. The grim irony of the situation was that the substantial savings for the group corresponded to a long institutional history of borrowing from Fundación Paraguaya. The most advanced members of the group were authorized for a line of credit of about $300 for every four-month lending cycle.[21] Since the president was one of the most senior members of the group, her death had also left behind large weekly loan installment payments to the Fundación. Her very success in the microcredit program became a source of danger when her income streams and reliable payments were, on her death, no longer collateralizing her portion of the group loan.

As we sat on the shaded patio and discussed the situation with group members, Silvenia calculated that if each member paid about $4 per week—not an inconsequential addition to the amount that they already owed for their own loans—then they could pay at least the first few installments of the president's remaining debt and thus reactivate the group's collective payments. Fundación Paraguaya's credit counselor emphasized that the group itself had to decide right away, because they were falling further and further behind in their payments. Importantly, since the savings account was still unresolved they could not fall back on those funds to get back on schedule while they found a way to pay the dead president's debt. The group members seemed resigned to the fact that part of the outstanding installments would have to be added to their own weekly payments. The cyclicality of lending also meant that the group prioritized repaying the loan, since their approval for another cycle of credit in three to four weeks hinged on successfully completing the repayment of their current loan. The stakes were high for Silvenia as well, for her salary and commission bonuses were tied to the performance of her portfolio of clients, including successful loan payment and renewal.

The generally somber mood lifted briefly when the treasurer of the group announced that a woman who lived in the neighborhood had donated a thick winter blanket to the group to express condolences for their loss. In the deepening winter months, the blanket would be a valuable household item that the committee could use to generate income. Incidentally, the fleece blankets were an iconic feature of the transborder trade of Ciudad del Este. Smugglers hoping to cross the border without paying the Brazilian customs fees often slipped electronics like cell phones or even netbooks and computer games between the folds of the blankets, and that way hoped to avoid detection. In this case, the blanket was diverted from that transnational pathway and repurposed for its actual intended use as bedding. Surprised and delighted, the group hoped to raffle off the blanket and use the money to pay for their deceased group member's outstanding loan payments. This was a common fund-raising strategy among microcredit borrowing groups. Groups often invested in prizes—items ranging from a cell phone to an insulated cooler—and then sold raffle tickets in the neighborhood. A member of the group commented that raffling off the blanket would be a great help since they would get all of the proceeds from the raffle without worrying about covering their expenses for the prize. The generosity of a neighbor, then, would ameliorate some of the burden of the debt left behind by the group's president. In the broader logic of microcredit social collateral, committees relied on their neighbors but in a way that did not require regimented repayment schemes and strict loan install-ments. This case was particularly arresting because it was the spontane-ous mortuary gift for the group that was incorporated into the micro-credit payment scheme. Just as neighbors and kin would lend a hand in organizing an angeloro in the neighborhood, so too, apparently, might they lend a hand to the stricken microcredit group. The wider sense of matrilineal obligation and shared attachment to place that suffused mortuary rituals extended to the Committee of Women Entrepreneurs.

To wrap up the meeting, Silvenia addressed the group about their joint liability. She told them, "It is time to have solidarity with your deceased member but also to have solidarity among yourselves." In other words, the group members needed to have solidarity in order to pay their loan at the Fundación. Coming on the heels of the gifted blan-ket—a poignant recognition of the microcredit group as integral to the ties between extended female kin that are usually the site of mortuary rituals—the credit counselor's argument about solidarity was especially charged. What is more, solidarity implicitly extended to Silvenia herself, since her own livelihood and professional advancement were caught up in the group's loan payments to the Fundación.

Despite the fact that the Fundación presumed that "having solidarity among yourselves" meant structural bonds of joint liability among members—that is, the solidarity of collective indebtedness and repay-ment that would add $4 to each woman's weekly installment—the model of social collateral also included the latent possibility of interde-pendency that could not be neatly aligned along individual lines of responsibility. Indeed, the group started to look much more like family once it undertook the task of commemoration and mourning by having solidarity with their deceased president. The neighbor's donation worked concretely as a material support for the borrowing group. The committee mobilized its friends and neighbors to ensure its solvency and its continued line of credit. In effect, the blanket was a financial transfer that could be raffled off to pay a loan installment but also an expression of solidarity with both the deceased member and the micro-finance group that she left behind. In a sense, the mortuary gift recog-nized the deceased president's economic project—the committee, and her line of credit with the Fundación—as important not just for reasons of joint credit liability but also as an important site for collective eco-nomic and belonging anchored in their neighborhood.

The propensity of symbolic tokens, including money, to move between different regimes of value[22] can highlight tensions among varied exchange practices, from funerary rites to debt amortization. Importantly, particular moments in debt relations were reciprocally materialized through certain things: an envelope of cash thickened by an extra $4 from each member, a circle of chairs pulled onto a patio for a group meeting, a packet of raffle tickets, a warm winter blanket. More than a structuring relation, an object, or a calculative agency, credit and debt traversed people's lives as mobile contexts. Further, these valuation practices[23] were knit together by different formations and iterations of indebtedness. These overlaps as well as the loosely fitting perspectives on debt made some things—like the donated blanket—particularly amenable to slipping between different types of obligation, from a mortuary rite to a loan installment. One aspect of the multiple materializations at work in paying financial debts is, surprisingly, the materiality of an abstract concept like solidarity, which here came to be embodied and enlivened by a particular group of neighbors in Ciudad del Este.

FORGIVING BUT NOT FORGETTING

Studies of the possibilities and perils of solidarity in debt relations have deep roots. As Gustav Peebles (2010: 226) has traced in his review of the anthropology of credit and debt, much of this scholarship rests on the foundational Maussian insight that "credit and debt greatly contribute to the building of hierarchy and dominance, but are also the keys to building group solidarity." Further, Mauss's writing on group solidarity itself usefully points us back to certain ambiguities in the mutual obligations of credit and debt. As Jane Guyer (2012: 500) argues, it is precisely the life course, "in all its puzzling and uncontainable and indeterminate time horizons," that makes solidarity so thick with possibility and so prone to exceeding the structured terms of transactional reciprocity or arithmetic repayment. The materiality of loan installments and group membership was not always a solidarity based on amity. Even the extended kinship networks that were commonly the focus of debt relations in Ciudad del Este were often a site of tension and acrimony as much as spontaneous collaboration and mutual support. Returning to Lourdes's group, which had grappled with the deaths of several borrowers over the course of its credit history, heated debates over who was responsible for the debt exposed important asymmetries. Before Fundación Paraguaya began coupling credit with life insurance, Lourdes had managed tense relationships within the group as members disagreed about how to redistribute the dead woman's debts and who should shoulder those financial burdens. The crux of one such quarrel was how and to what extent kinship should be incorporated into micro-credit social collateral.

In this case a new borrower had died suddenly in childbirth after having paid just one loan installment. Her unexpected death left the group to deal with months of unpaid installments. As Fundación Paraguaya's credit counselor met with the treasurer of Lourdes's group, the treasurer made a strong case for asking for support from the brother of the deceased woman or from Lourdes herself, even though—or perhaps because—she was the president of the group. The dead woman's sister-in-law and brother lived nearby in the same neighborhood and thus were part of the diffuse reciprocal ties that formed the basis for many redistributive arrangements across kin and neighborly lines. Lourdes herself had also apparently been the woman's neighbor and business partner. They had managed an Avon cosmetics sales program together and lived on the same street. According to the group's treasurer, Lourdes had been an advocate on the woman's behalf when the group was making decisions about its membership and had even gone so far as to push through the membership paperwork at the last minute, just before the loan was processed.

The NGO's staff member was there on the scene to talk the situation over with the treasurer and strategize which relationships could be most easily activated to repay the outstanding debt. The case was especially tragic, both the treasurer and credit counselor agreed during their discussion, because the deceased member had left behind three small children. Her closest family, then, could not be expected to shoulder their mother's outstanding debts. In fact, mortuary practices usually tended toward the opposite: money, food, and labor were all marshaled to help the family of the bereaved. However, the treasurer was insistent that responsibility for the outstanding loan payments should be shared by the woman's kith and kin and not the remaining members of the group.

Lourdes had moved to Ciudad del Este as a teenager. Her mother passed away when she was very young, and she was raised by her father and his sister. When her aunt moved from their native town in southeastern Paraguay to Ciudad del Este in search of work in the mid-1990s, Lourdes followed. Her father and four siblings sold the family properties in the countryside and moved to Ciudad del Este shortly thereafter. After working as a cook and then later opening her own cantina where she prepared and sold pizzas, she met her husband, who was a regular client at the cantina and worked as a police officer. Soon the family decided that renting a room was too expensive, so they started looking for a plot of land in one of Ciudad del Este's outlying settlements. Lourdes ended up deciding to move to the neighborhood because a close friend had called to let her know that the settlement had just been opened up, so her friend would "move earth and sea if [Lourdes] would come, she would find a spot close to her." Lourdes noted that she had not yet arrived when the Ministry of Housing took a census of the neighborhood in order to deliver building material to build permanent structures.

> L: No, the only one that it [the subsidized building materials] reached was that one there [gesturing to a house at the end of the street]. They were in the census, they were counted when there was the census and we were not here. Up to there, that's why it didn't reach us. Surely we are going to come out *without* housing. But I prefer that it goes to those who need it more. Some people don't even have floors [gesturing to show the unevenness].
>
> C: But when it rains?
>
> L: And right, I prefer that [help] comes through for them first, I'm very satisfied [*yo estoy muy conforme*]. I thank God for what he has given me. But most people, the more they have, the more they want. The people who are doing well economically want *more*. And me, I prefer that my neighbors are doing well too. Those ones over there, for example, they do a lot, they were the first ones to arrive here. And that lady, who is my friend too. They lived underneath a tarp when they first got here, they say when this settlement started. Without anything. So I prefer that they give to them rather than to me. They are the ones who suffer most.

In her self-presentation, Lourdes's sense of prosperity was inextricably tied to a particular model of neighborliness and community. Partly this had to do with the fact that the neighborhood was full of her family and friends, who were surely part of her economic network of obligation and redistribution. In fact, her father lived in a small house behind hers until he built a larger structure down the block, her cousin lives across the street, and her comadres[24] and friends lived in the housing settlement. Being surrounded by friends and family was intimately linked to her sense of self-satisfaction that she did not want more because she was already "doing well." Undoubtedly, she was in a position to launch criticisms at the avarice of others precisely because she had an extensive network of support that served as her basis for being "very satisfied." Broadly speaking, Lourdes seemed quite invested in building a certain sort of community, which was tied to her sense of the proper durability of relationships. Indeed, she criticized people who took the opportunity to move into the settlement in order to take advantage of the land grant from the Paraguayan state, reasoning that even if that made good individual economic sense it came at the expense of people who really needed the houses and, by extension, might come into her permanent orbit within the neighborhood.

> L: You see, when the majority of people came here they already had a house somewhere else. And so that they pretend to be really poor, they come here and make a really precarious house. So when a lot of them realized they were going to take the lot away again, well then they had to sell the property to somebody else. That woman who sold me this property, she already had a beautiful house there on the other side of the highway. And so that is why she sold it to me, because she knew they were going to take this property away. And that's why the majority of these lots were for sale, because people had another house.
>
> C: A shame, because settlements seem really important for people without possibilities to . . .
>
> L: That's it, exactly it, so for me, for example, if I had a house in my own place, I would never take away the opportunity from somebody who doesn't have a place. Nothing will come of that [Así no da]. But people, like I told you, when they have, they want more. They don't think of others, they think of themselves.

Lourdes's use of the Spanish phrase "así no da" offers an important insight into her general orientation to the proper way to relate to her neighborhood, and especially her certainty that she was in a position to judge the appropriate ethical orientation to those forms of collective affiliation. The phrase can be approximately translated as "that's no way to do things," but it also connotes a common project, "nothing will come of that," with the implication that even if taking the opportunity to get a land title would benefit one person, nothing would come of it for the neighborhood. This same sense of common cause and group prosperity underpinned Lourdes's account of how she came to form a borrowing group with Fundación Paraguaya. She noted that the group began with just three women she knew, but then, like the neighborhood, she filled it with more and more of her friends and family: "After [those first ones] then I came in with my friend, and then we put in more people and more people." When I asked how many people were in the group now, she told me about the member who had recently died in childbirth. Lourdes noted that the group would respond to the tragedy by redistributing the remainder for her loan among the group in a similar sense of common cause that inspired her sense of neighborliness.

C: And what did you do, for your group?

L: And we had to—so we were then a group of thirteen and we had to, no, we were a group of twelve, and her [biweekly] loan installment was exactly $12 so we put in an extra dollar for each installment. To just exactly cover it. And to pay off all of her loan installments. And her daughter is just sixteen years old, the oldest. And the other is eleven, and the other is ten, and one is six or seven.

C: She wasn't with anyone?

L: No no no no no.

C: And what happened with her children?

L: And she is the mom now [the eldest daughter]. She works in Foz [across the border in Brazil], she—she's a minor, her daughter—works in Foz and supports her little brothers and sisters.

C: What a tragedy.

L: Very sad, but . . . That guy with the woman who runs the corner shop is her brother. Surely he will help them, and I didn't want to really ask—because he was so torn up about it himself—and ask him on top of that for her installment, well that's no way to do things [pues no daba]. And that's why, because I talked with the ladies, with the group, and they said that yes they would contribute for the woman. She had paid one single installment, and then she died.

C: And so she ended up owing almost the whole thing, and the kids would not be able to pay . . .

L: No, impossible. When that happened, the [eldest] girl wasn't even working.

C: And they didn't inherit anything?

L: No, no. I think they had very limited resources.

C: And so you were in a group of only twelve.

L: Right, twelve of us, and then one more came in [in the next cycle], and now there are thirteen of us again.

In this instance, it seems as if forgiving the loan meant *not* forgetting about the deceased borrower. The group had the choice to approach the woman's brother but decided instead to "contribute for the woman." In other words, part of the mutual obligations that bound the group together involved caring for the children of their deceased member by redistributing their mother's debts among themselves rather than expanding the bounds of joint liability to include her family. While the treasurer of the committee, Doña Cristina, had observed that the woman probably had kin who would recognize the member's obligations and pay her installments, in Lourdes's view forgiving the debt was an important way of remembering and honoring the importance of those kinship ties and expressing the grief of losing a family member. Remembering the obligation and choosing to collectivize it was an important part of "doing things correctly." Indeed, Lourdes used the same phrase—"Así no da, pues no daba"—she had used to describe the proper way to distribute resources in the settlement.

When I later spoke with Lourdes to inquire how the debt had been resolved, it turned out that in the end the group had covered the remaining payments. She emphasized that this was a way of showing solidarity with the family of their deceased member. In a telling reversal, Lourdes claimed that the group had solidarity with the deceased member by *not* claiming any community or family resources that had been directed to mortuary rites for the deceased. She argued that it would be inappropriate to insist on payments by the woman's sister-in law and brother, who were now caring for the children and grief-stricken by the loss of their close family. Thus Lourdes concluded that the family was so devastated by the death that she couldn't possibly ask them for money, even though that was precisely the logic and nature of microcredit social collateral. By calling this decision "solidarity with the family," Lourdes drew on traditions of mourning that channeled community moneys to mortuary rites, but she redirected those resources to the collective pot of money for debt repayment. In a sense, this recognized the financial reality that microcredit loans incorporated even the dead. In effect, Lourdes's framing of solidarity with the family actually emphasized solidarity with the member, since the dead woman remained present among the group through the duration of installment payments.

In this instance, emphasizing the bonds of joint liability became a way for Lourdes to articulate broader interdependencies and recognize the forms of kinship that traversed the boundaries of the microcredit group and its loan. She reworked the social unit of debt through her judgments about the correct way to arbitrate relation-affirming and relation-bounding decisions. It is important to note, however, that it was the president of the group who imposed her vision of kinship, mourning, and neighborliness that ultimately resulted in this particular form of redistributing the debt: forgiving the loan by not forgetting their group member. The treasurer of the group was keen to recognize family, too, but particularly the responsibilities of the family *to the group* rather than the other way around. For Lourdes, the collective repayment was a way of mourning the woman's death and aligning with her family. However, this claim of solidarity was a counterpoint to the treasurer's initial strategy of pinning the debt on Lourdes, since she was considered to be responsible for the dead woman as part of a broader matrilineal kinship network. Widening the circle of family and neighbors bound by the ties of the microcredit group—all the way out to the mourning family of the deceased group member—had the consequence of muting the claims of individual responsibility that were the focus of the treasurer's discussions with the Fundación. The outcome of the renewed social unit of debt meant that each member of the group found her debt burden increased over the amortization cycle of the loan.

From Lourdes's perspective, Fundación Paraguaya provided the financial instrument—the microcredit group-based loan—around which she built her sense of interdependency. These expressions of solidarity extended far beyond the instrumental ties of mutual surveillance, peer pressure, and joint responsibility that figure prominently in public and academic discourses surrounding microcredit. I want to underscore the fact that it was precisely the terms of the *microcredit* that became a mode or instrument for expressing caring and supportive relationships to other people within the community—the children of the dead woman, her brother who was mourning her death, the grief felt by her neighbors who were also her friends and comadres—and an important way of ritually commemorating rupture in the group and its subsequent renewal. The microcredit instrument, of course, had complex effects, since the social collateral of the group-based loan was harnessed by one member of the group to crystallize her vision of kinship and obligation, which she did over and against the opposition of other, competing visions, including that of the treasurer.

Microcredit was one of many different credit relationships that shot through and bound up obligations in the neighborhood. What is most surprising, perhaps, is Lourdes's turn to the highly regimented and institutionalized credit relationships of microfinance to enact the most intimate obligations of mourning and grief in the wake of a tragic loss. With a whole range of credit relationships that expressed and sustained mutual obligation, the group-based borrowing at Fundación Paraguaya was uniquely available to convey support and help for the deceased borrower and her surviving children because the social collateral model could enlist group members—sometimes coercively—in a social unit of debt that was not strictly circumscribed by the boundaries of the group.

The often acrimonious discussion in borrowing groups put into focus the stakes of social collateral for realigning and cementing the authority in the borrowing group and also across the neighborhood.

Those shared burdens might perhaps be a central reason why, three years after my long-term fieldwork when I met again with Lourdes in 2013 and asked how her microcredit group was faring, she immediately remarked on Fundación Paraguaya's institutionalized life insurance program. Not only did this new program cancel the debt of a borrower who had died, but it also included financial compensation to the immediate family. In some ways, this policy broadened the horizons of solidarity yet further, to include Fundación Paraguaya in the circuit of redistribution that was materialized when a borrower died. Credit counselors already shared complex financial interconnections with their clients. Now the institution was thickening its ties with borrowers as well. However, the life insurance policy simultaneously redefined kinship quite narrowly—as a nuclear heteronormative family whose members can claim benefits—which figured as a policy that was in many ways at odds with important neighborhood-based mortuary rituals, of which microcredit sometimes, surprisingly, played a central part. Now that she was aware of the policy, Lourdes surmised that in the future it would be a simple matter of recalculating the group's weekly payments. The group would not miss a beat in the rhythm of credit access, repayment, and renewal. In a sense, the insurance program materialized financial debt, most tangibly in the diminished group installment and the cash for the life insurance payment. In doing so, the program also *dematerialized* kinship as the appropriate site of and context for working out shared obligations, financial and otherwise.[25] Indeed, financial debt was no longer a socially important condition that was debated, disputed, and borne by a wide network of neighbors and extended family in the wake of death and mourning. Solidarity was only equated with economic joint liability.

RENEWING CREDIT

The disjunctive life spans of overlapping debts in microcredit practice offer a framework for understanding different formations of social interdependency. By way of conclusion, the life cycles of people and credits presents an opportune occasion to revisit Weiner's classic essay, "Reproduction: A Replacement for Reciprocity" (1980). She focuses on reproduction to understand a community's processes of creating and *life insurance is taking away the chance for social solidarity*

sustaining value that are not automatic or habitual: they must be carefully cultivated. In the case of microcredit social collateral, reproduction and renewal worked across multiple scales: individual life cycles, the life cycles of microcredit committees, the cycles of loans and repayment. Of course, the futurity of exchange relationships is a sustained interest in economic anthropology, particularly drawing inspiration from Melanesian ethnographies of gift exchange[26] and the cosmological time imagined and materialized through long-term relationships of reciprocity.[27] Weiner's contribution to feminist theories of exchange is particularly invested in exploring the central role of reproduction and women's role in sustaining community value over cosmological rather than generational time.

For Weiner, *reproduction* refers to the cultural work invested in creating something new; and *regeneration* refers to the "renewal, revival, rebirth, or re-creation" of things previously created through processes of reproduction (Weiner 1980: 71). Exchange is important because it both reflects and is constitutive of these reproductive and regenerative processes. Weiner uses a curious metaphor of feeding the system through exchange, a process that she catalogs through highly localized and culturally specific ethnographic examples from Melanesia. As an invitation to understand these processes more generally, Weiner notes schematically that "the flow must be 'fed' or the system (or part of it) begins to collapse. The modus operandi of this 'feeding' is exchange" (72). Could credit—especially the moving connections of the credit bicycle—feed systems of reproduction and regeneration in an analogous way? Further, if credit is one way to feed systems of interdependency, then the different life cycles of credit and debt are especially important as they often chafed against one another. As I have shown throughout this book, the microcredit proffered by Fundación Paraguaya was but one of many credits in the commercial economy of Ciudad del Este. Indeed, for Weiner, the system must be fed because all material resources have their own life cycles, and regeneration reflects a social effort to offset loss and decay because "each element [material and immaterial resources] moves through it's life cycle or trajectory organized around the cultural meaning of loss" (72). She makes the crucial point that the complexity of exchange relationships is oversimplified if it is simply labeled generosity or balanced reciprocity, since these do not attend to long-term cycles,[28] and miss how value is built up and accreted in others over many iterative transactions. Indeed, these exchange relationships may constitute a long-range set of obligations particularly because those material and immaterial resources may be reclaimed, even after both parties have died. In the case of microcredit social collateral, there were different ways to reclaim the material and immaterial resources of the dead, and indeed, different sorts of death to reckon with: dead-alive debtors, lively committees, and ghostly members.

In these several cases, the groups' mortuary practices—the donated blanket, and the fraught solidarity of the treasurer and president with their neighbor—upended the conventional logic of social collateral that animated the Fundación's debt and repayment. According to the model of social collateral put forward by the Fundación, these other interdependencies should become features of the group and not the other way around. It was thought of as perfectly reasonable for borrowing groups to rely on family members for support in their loan payments, but programs like life insurance needed to protect groups from becoming too entangled with wider kinship affiliations. For the purposes of Fundación Paraguaya's bottom line, the group was imagined to encompass these other relations, affiliations, commitments, and rituals of mourning and to domesticate them in service of debt repayment. The ambivalent position of kinship ties in microcredit groups hints at the ways social collateral might be inverted: the social unit of debt becomes a feature of kinship obligations rather than the other way round. Tellingly, Fundación Paraguaya was also captured by that wider network of relations, from credit counselors like Silvenia to the insurance program.

One consequence for anthropology of studying kinship work-in-progress[29] in the realm of debts is that it exposes other criteria for social difference beyond the putative difference of naturalized biologizing assumptions about sexual reproduction. Indeed, the "mutuality of being" that Marshal Sahlins (2011) has famously claimed as the basis for kinship actually takes different forms in different contexts, which calls into question any hard and fast distinctions between kinship and other modes of relating.[30] The stitching together of credit and kinship in Paraguayan microfinance highlights other forms of durable asymmetry at the heart of social solidarities, kin-based, debt-based, and otherwise. Namely, we can see the politics of interdependency in neighborhoods, between credit counselors and clients, leadership within microcredit commissions, business partners in Avon sales schemes. The contingent and provisional insertion of microcredit into the range of economic practices that sustain mortuary rituals exemplifies the fact that the processes of accounting for debt within the relational space of the borrowing group also is a process of materializing kinship that cross-cuts and exceeds the boundaries of mutual indebtedness. The differences at the heart of relational belonging expose the asymmetries in kinship *and* credit systems. In other words, the interdependencies of families and borrowing groups highlight both the possibility and the peril that relationships of credit and debt might terminate, attenuate, or crystallized into new terms, with deepening inequalities. Both the encumbering and enabling qualities of interdependency become visible through the vexed solidarities of kinship and credit.

The renewal of loans, which kept the pedals of the credit bicycle spinning, offered an opportunity for all involved to debate the triangular relationship between kinship ties, death, and formal financial indebtedness. The precise contours of that three-way relationship went to the heart of creating and maintaining social collateral. Three ostensibly disparate things—relatedness, death, and debt repayment—were all made mutually interpretive of one another. Debt was a kind of death, as Gustavo's story of Informconf credit scores and "credit death" showed. Relatedness was also a kind of death, as the cyclical effort of renewing committees constantly dramatized. And death was also a kind of relatedness, as the poignant inclusion of ghostly members in borrowing groups attested. This was so for the women doing the work of maintaining kinship ties and financial repayments in practice. Social collateral set up these difficult analogies and mediations, and they were puzzled out in the dilemmas women faced in seemingly mundane and quotidian practices. For all of the financial dilemmas thrown up by microfinance—including the potential for exploitation—I suggest that social collateral also works powerfully as a context for considering and contesting a broader thematic of obligation and its limits. Although microcredit programs are eminently worthy of critique, they also offer a provocation to rethink the life spans of relatedness, and by extension the social writ large.

Conclusion

In the past two decades, microcredit—and the broader suite of pro-poor financial services that coalesced under the moniker "microfinance"—has emerged as a cornerstone of global development. Taken together these financial products reach millions of borrowers annually and coordinate the support, research, and investment of institutions internationally. Microfinance has increasingly shed the mantle of specialized aid as "bottom of the pyramid" lending has proliferated in the commercial credit market.[1] In this book I have built outward from ethnographic research in Paraguay on the centrality of credit and debt in microcredit borrowers' and lenders' daily efforts to build and sustain economic livelihoods. Their everyday dilemmas bring into focus the tensions within microcredit in its relationship to social life and broader development policy, particularly in Latin America.

What I hope to show by chronicling the successes and travails of living on credit both in and out of institutionalized microfinance are the complex and indeterminate factors that position microcredit vis-à-vis other sources of formal and informal credit in Paraguay. This is especially important because it allows us to begin disassembling the taken-for-granted understanding both in development policy and broader academic debates that there is a natural fit between women and microcredit. In both types of accounts—policy and scholarly critiques—women in microcredit are figured as always already hypersocial and encumbered by obligations. Therefore, it may come as no surprise to (1) find that women participate in these programs in astonishing numbers and (2) find interdependency at the core of this financial technology. However, taking social collateral for granted comes at an important cost. My effort to denaturalize the interdependencies at the heart of microcredit social collateral calls both of these features of microcredit—its feminization and its hypersociality—into question and launches crucial new lines of inquiry. That is not to say that we should ignore the seemingly unproblematic fit between women and microcredit. To the contrary, it is especially important to look at interdependency not just in places where we presume autonomy: finance capitalism, the entrepreneurial neoliberal risk-bearing subject, *homo economicus,* and so on. Indeed, this has been the dominant anthropological move as scholars working on and in financial contexts have contributed research that broadens our understanding of the dense social networks that undergird and sustain contemporary global finance.[2] In that sense, I advance a research agenda that is already well under way.

Microcredit, by contrast, challenges us to ask why we presume interdependency where it seems most natural. By pointing to the ways in which social collateral tracks social difference (i.e., who is included and excluded from the interdependencies of microcredit and under what conditions), interdependency emerges as an analytic framework that cuts across and exposes other dimensions of social life, especially normatively disciplined expectations regarding gender, labor, value, and development. Since groups of women borrowers are often presumed to be homogeneous, how financialization creates figurations of difference, contrastive categories, and strained aspirations are questions too rarely posed in debates about microcredit. For example, in the assessment of creditworthiness, feminized labor and forms of mutual support were captured, converted, and transformed into a financial relationship through various administrative techniques, including the loan documents assembled to manage loan disbursal and repayment, the punitive arithmetic of credit scores, and the dramatization of group unity in recurring bureaucratic rituals. In contrast, the management of creditworthiness for both unmarked individual micro-borrowers and the short-lived and disastrous "men's committees" worked to define interdependency as an individual quality of borrowers rather than distributed across a collectivity, as with women's microcredit committees. Moreover, the interdependencies of microcredit repayment brought into focus not only the complex economic lives of the treasurers and presidents of committees that borrowed from Fundación Paraguaya but also the NGO staff such as credit counselors who worked in pink-collar financial services, Doctor Gregorio who displaced his own interdependencies onto the social collateral of his clients, and Martín's independent entrepreneurialism that served as an elusive model for the organization. Given the contingent link between Paraguayan women and Fundación Paraguaya's lending program that I have emphasized here, we miss the politics of interdependency by focusing only on the end users of financial tools and on the individual choices or preferences of women who borrow.

THE REGULATORY WORK OF INTERDEPENDENCY

One of the central claims of this book is that microcredit is not positioned in predictable ways vis-à-vis the formations of collectivity and cohesion that organize and sustain daily economic life in Ciudad del Este. The constitutive tension between joint liability and individual entrepreneurialism regulated many such processes of financialization. These were performative cultural productions that generated profit margins, portfolio metrics, and routine accounting practices in the back offices of banks and development organizations. Simultaneously, they were subtle, everyday material practices that created collective account books and shared bills that stretched across the city from downtown to the contraband economy to Ciudad Jardín (fig. 12). Women used relationships of debt to buoy their businesses along with the rising commercial prosperity of the frontier economy. Meanwhile, many of those relationships were strained and broken by investments that did not pan out and opportunities that fell short of expectations. Collective indebtedness constantly pressed for further precision in specifying how these debts were assembled using particular social units. The point is not just an analytic one for anthropology of finance and development. Joint liability set up these difficult mediations for actors in the Paraguayan financial system. And importantly, there was nothing "natural" about the social unit of debt or its particular figurations of gender. Specific financial interventions—creditworthiness, repayment, and renewal—made collective debt persuasive and possible in contemporary commercial capitalism and microfinance economies.

But what of social collateral? Even if social collateral appears to be everywhere once we know to look for it, microcredit seems uniquely able to capture and deploy the language of joint obligation to anchor its claims about credit and debt. In the final analysis, social collateral

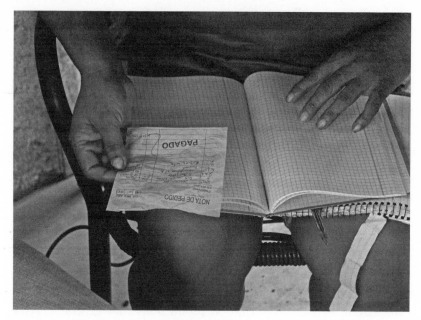

FIGURE 12. A receipt marked "Paid" being filed in the collective account books of a Committee of Women Entrepreneurs.

names a set of arguments about the appropriate forms of social and economic obligation that people harness in everyday economic practice. Challenges to joint liability emerge from within the financial practices themselves. Worries about strangers (persona ajena), discussions of eating collective moneys (comiendo la plata), and negotiations over late payments (morosidad) are everyday mechanisms though which the social units of social collateral are produced. The gendered and gendering work of knitting and unraveling interdependencies is a crucial means through which debt and "the social" mutually constitute one another. Meanwhile, by reifying microcredit and its peculiar financial forms, we miss the fact that those financial forms—joint indebtedness, group-based borrowing, social intimacy through economic ties—can be found across multiple sites and scales in the contemporary commercial and financial economy, from cross-border trade to Ponzi schemes to U.S. treasury bills to bank bailouts.[3] By granting microcredit a conceptual and practical monopoly on social collateral, we miss how contingent and unstable the financial form is in practice.

Microcredit seems uniquely able to spark these concerted debates about joint indebtedness and social justice because the financial tool is still emergent in both the financial and development arenas. Financial tools, of course, are moving targets, as recent work in the anthropology of finance has illustrated. However, the outsized place microcredit occupies in development policy and practice—that is, in programs focused explicitly on social justice and economic inequality—can obscure the broader processes of valuation that go beyond microcredit and its particular place in both global finance and global development. By highlighting the prominence of interdependency in the hyperliberalized Ciudad del Este special customs zone, the specific context of the Paraguayan frontier allows us to see the debates over value worked through everyday dilemmas of credit and debt not as they pertain only to specialized development programing but rather as a feature of commercial credit more generally. The distinctiveness of the site provides a particularly useful vantage from which to address the larger implications of these arguments over the politics of interdependency vis-à-vis changing regimes of finance in the contemporary global economy.

As David Graeber (2011) has pointedly argued, the asymmetries of credit relations have sparked outrage around the world and fueled much of the anger that drove the Occupy protests and the Strike Debt movement. Indeed, Graeber posits that wealth and poverty maps onto struggles around credit and debt: "For thousands of years, the struggle between rich and poor has largely taken the form of conflicts between creditors and debtors—of arguments about the rights and wrongs of interest payments, debt peonage, amnesty, repossession, restitution, the sequestering of sheep, the seizing of vineyards, and the selling of debtors' children into slavery" (8). For Graeber, what he calls "human economies"—"ones in which what is considered really important about human beings is the fact that they are a unique nexus of relations with others"—begin to break down when humans are abstracted from their web of relations and rendered equivalent and tradable: a process that he considers necessarily violent (208). Credit and debt in Ciudad del Este, as I show, is certainly inflected by violence and by intractable economic inequality. That social collateral so often tracks social difference highlights the figurations of gender, class, kinship, and nation that place difference at the heart of relational belonging.[4] It is for that very reason that I am wary of drawing a sharp divide between webs of human relations, on the one hand, and financial relationships, on the other. Social collateral illustrates precisely how those economic interdependencies can be profoundly enabling and debilitating. Further, this contractual and quantified view focuses on debt as a singular relationship between a creditor and a debtor connected by mutual arrangement. Instead, I document debts that do not inhere in one single relationship but rather cut across and join together broader interdependencies, as well as creating contexts of economic independence. As I argue, it is precisely the constant management of people's unique nexus of relations with others that gives social collateral its particular density. This book, then, builds on current research on human economies[5] by examining the broader stakes of various interdependencies—an especially complex task since so many seemingly straightforward "human" relationships are co-constituted with financial relationships.

In Ciudad del Este, the agonistic debates among borrowers and their creditors about the role of microcredit social collateral within Paraguay's commercial economy help us think how (1) the form of microfinance is produced both as a global asset class and an object of development discourse and, more broadly (2) when we talk about "financial instruments," we are naming a set of arguments about the value(s), terms, and life course of the shared economic substances we call debt. Rather than try to parse underlying or preexisting models, logics, or interests that drive capitalism I suggest that a better approach is to interpret the many ways gender, kinship, personhood, and social reproduction help constitute, and are themselves shaped by systemic economic processes. This is not just (or primarily) about broadening the scope of anthropology of finance or anthropology of development. Instead, I suggest that it is a project of reembedding commercial capitalism—and all of its vexed interdependencies—in its social context but with an eye to how the embeddedness of economic subjects is also differentially experienced and deployed throughout the financial system. Ciudad del Este provides an exemplary case of the pervasiveness of credit politics in contemporary capitalism because these forms of social interdependencies are a constitutive part of financial relations at the heart of liberalized laissez-faire commercial markets.

Might it be possible to redraw the boundaries of social collateral in order to remake development aims and finance capitalism? This question bears heavily at a moment when mounting debt—from student loans to mortgages to sovereign borrowing—simultaneously emerges out of and also challenges wider processes of financialization. In Paraguay these mounting debts go to the heart of life on the credit bicycle. And as economic inequality has become a flashpoint in discussions about the distributional politics of contemporary capitalism, the act of breaking ties through default (whether via a debt collective or a national referendum) has also become a powerful mechanism for comparing, interpreting, and disrupting the massive disparities in accumulation and wealth that debt-based financial products enable. Other avenues are available. The story of social collateral points to an alternative and complementary way forward. Social collateral offers an invitation and a provocation to do more than consider how to free debtors from their creditors. Instead, by specifying how interdependency is generated and regulated, we gain a critical vocabulary to discuss the productive powers that re-create and renew jointly liable collectivities by offering recourse to the repertoire of obligations that are internal to financial products themselves.

Both scholars and practitioners of community development projects have frequently taken the regulatory work of development interventions as a sign of program failure. That is, they see constraints on women's lives due to microcredit as a sign of coercion and, therefore, the failure of development programing. Success, for development practitioners, hinges on more choices and freedoms for program participants. These two types of critiques—of microcredit failing to empower people to individual gain and of microcredit ensnaring people in extractive relationships—are, in fact, the same critique but for very different analytic purposes, and as such they make very strange bedfellows. My research shows that the simple version of this interpretation misses the ways the multiple claims that we hold over one another are an important feature of economic sociality. More useful than the task of assessing whether microcredit binds women too tightly to one another and/or to a predatory market is to ask how, and under what conditions, do we wish to be bound by others or by a community, through collective liability. Social collateral provided an explicit framework for women in Ciudad del Este to take up and contest the terms of credit. And as I show here, joint obligation was structured around important moments in the life course of loans where the terms of debt were unstable and up for grabs. The moving connections of credit congealed around social collateral, which also became a framework for disputing the conditions of collectivity and cohesion bound up in shared debt. Can we say the same for the rest of our (conventional) debts? I suggest that anthropology has an important role to play in taking seriously interdependency as a crucial but indeterminate factor in arguments about credit politics and inequality today.

Notes

INTRODUCTION

1. All names are pseudonyms unless otherwise noted. The leadership of Fundación Paraguaya, the NGO where I conducted long-term fieldwork, explicitly asked me to use the name of their organization and the biographical information of Martín Burt, founder and director of the NGO; my usage of the identifying information about Fundación Paraguaya throughout this book reflects Martín's request and our ongoing discussions and collaboration since 2006.

2. Unless otherwise noted, all currency is converted from Paraguayan guaranis to U.S. dollars at an exchange rate of Gs. 4,700 equals US$1 (the average exchange rate during my fieldwork from February 2009 to September 2010).

3. There has been extensive scholarship on Paraguay's unequal land distribution and the struggle to formalize land titles for many rural and periurban residents. *Asentamiento,* or housing settlement, describes the informal land tenure as communities move through state bureaucracies to title their properties. For an in-depth ethnographic study of these campesino practices at the interface with state agencies and technologies of information, see especially Hetherington 2009, 2011, 2012a, 2012b.

4. This is a classic insight from the anthropology of kinship, perhaps best exemplified in David Schneider's *American Kinship* (1980) and as his critical retheorization of kinship studies (1984).

5. I draw on Megan Moodie's (2008) research on microfinance and gender in India, which makes a related claim about the insertion of women's "empowerment" loans into a wider field of social and economic practices. She writes, "I have had to see microcredit not just as an 'economic' arrangement but also, and maybe primarily, as a social project. This social project introduces new ideas and languages that interact with many others in the cultural terrain of rural Rajasthan. . . . This cobbling together of frameworks provides women in Debaliya

with platforms for critiquing these very same exchanges and transactions; such a critique is one of the main activities within loan groups" (455). My research advances this conversation by specifying how social collateral in Paraguayan lending becomes key to this process of cobbling together some frameworks and excluding others.

6. Zelizer 2010: 303.

7. In Spanish, these trajectories were talked about as *avanzando* or *progresando,* advancing or progressing.

8. Indeed, Marx hinted obliquely at the importance of timing in these equivocal financial arrangements in his writings on credit and banking in his third volume of *Capital.* There, he famously referred to the dense and drawn-out relations between merchants and bankers in the East India Company commercial trade as "a method of creating fictitious capital" (Marx 1993: 537), particularly as a "fraudulent procedure" where both sides exploited ambiguities regarding when the debt would fall due. The relationships that for Marx—writing primarily on commercial and bank arrangements—appeared to be the purview of "mutual advances by producers and merchants [that] form the real basis of credit" (525) now appear in all sorts of places throughout the financial system. And importantly, since arguments about what is and is not social collateral play out on a power-laden social field, there is also power that can be harnessed analytically in distinguishing between its different—and competing—formations. Movement, especially across the life cycles of loans, is a crucial dimension.

9. In the wake of the 2008 financial crisis, the concept of financial collateral has been one of the few aspects of global finance that has not been subjected to intensified scrutiny (Riles 2011). In her anthropological study of law and finance in Japan, Annelise Riles (2011: 1) suggests that physical collateral has persisted, largely unquestioned, since it is seen by many as "a technical little sideline item" relegated to the byzantine world of property law. By contrast, development programs engaged in small-scale lending have long placed collateral front and center in their lending programs, though social collateral, too, is often treated as a "technical little sideline item" based on borrowers' presumed preexisting social networks. Julia Elyachar (2005) has documented the ways relational value was transformed into financial value, especially using the idiom of "values" itself, in early experiments in Egyptian microfinance programs.

10. Moodie 2008; Sanyal 2009; Rankin 2002.

11. See Harper 1998.

12. On the *Portfolios of the Poor* project, see Collins et al. 2009. Elsewhere I have written with Sohini Kar on the comparative methodology in microfinance research (Kar and Schuster n.d.). This approach is the centerpiece of important research collaborations housed at MIT's Abdul Latif Jameel Poverty Action Lab and led by Esther Duflo. The Yale Innovations for Poverty Action collaboration and the IMTFI at the University of California, Irvine, are projects also undertaking this sort of comparative study.

13. See Ardener 1964; Wu 1974.

14. Roy 2010.

15. Cooper 2008. C.A. Gregory (1997) calls this the era of post–gold standard global financing based on trust and obligation "savage money."

16. This has been a widely debated point in anthropological discussions of microfinance. A.R. Rahman's (1999) early ethnography of the Grameen Bank challenged the widespread presumption that microfinance was empowering. From there, numerous scholars have turned a critical eye to the gendered assumptions (Keating, Rasmussen, and Rishi 2010; Moodie 2013; Karim 2011), NGO politics (Elyachar 2005; Karim 2001; Rankin 2001), and staggering commercial profits (Appadurai 2011; Kar 2013) made possible by microfinance.

17. Peebles 2010: 234.

18. Scholars working on emerging biotechnologies and their commodification within capitalist markets have put this concept to generative use. *Lively Capital* summarizes much of this conversation (Rajan 2012), including the important intersections with theories of governmentality and knowledge production. A related debate focuses on the commodification of lively processes, including artisanal cheese (Paxson 2012), algae (Helmreich 2007), and mushrooms (Tsing 2009). My focus on the life course of loans is not meant to unpack and theorize the agency of financial objects as if they were biotechnologies or bioorganisms. Rather, I suggest that the unfolding of loans offers a window on economic practices as they are patterned around particular regular (and regulated) conditions, or "terms" in the world of lending and borrowing. I draw inspiration from the important intervention made by Sunder Rajan and others, however, in that they focus our attention on objects, processes, and sites that escape and exceed the purely transactional logics of capitalist exchange.

19. Maurer 2006. His review article—in concert with his broader research on money and finance—is a masterful contribution to rethinking and challenging precisely that presumption about the abstracting and homogeneizing logics of the money form.

20. To borrow the anthropologist Anna Tsing's (2009: 351) term for the coproduction of capitalist standardization along with value produced though diversity and niche.

21. I draw particular inspiration from the collective of feminist scholars in economic anthropology, organized by Sylvia Yanagisako, Karen Ho, and Laura Bear. The "generating capitalism" manifesto first presented at the 2014 American Anthropological Association annual meeting in Washington, DC, builds out of feminist and substantivist traditions in studies of capitalism; I draw upon and ally with that collaborative project in my research of microfinance. See Bear et al. 2015.

22. For a discussion of anthropology's role in reiterating the common notion that money is a universal solvent that corrodes traditional social bonds and moral reasoning in service of instrumental logics of transactional exchange, see especially Bill Maurer's (2006) review of "The Anthropology of Money." Ethnographic work on economic practices in service of projects that go beyond capitalist logics (Cattelino 2008; Chu 2010; Muehlebach 2011; Stout 2014) has been an especially fruitful avenue for research on money and markets. Feminist anthropologists have systematically theorized the "grip and slip" (Tsing 2009, 2015) of capitalist markets that coproduce universal principles like accumulation, standardization, and production with deeply social relations like sentiments, intimacy, and diversity (Tsing 2005; Yanagisako 2002).

23. Appadurai 1986; Kopytoff 1986. See also Appadurai 2011.

24. Scholarship in economic anthropology has made important steps forward in analyzing exchange practices as fundamentally *political* (i.e., an expression of authority) rather than dictated by a static and normative cultural order. In these studies, regimes of value are located, analytically at least, at a high level of generality. For instance, Jane Guyer's (2004: 21) contribution to theories of value centers on the "logical and socio-logical consequences of multiple emergent valuation scales," where each scale of value is organized around its own cultural logic. Indeed, it could be argued that in this vein of analysis, regimes of value are only perceptible systemically from the top down, as it were, at the level of cultural principles, even if, following Ferguson's (1992) research on the politics of wealth, we know that those cultural principles originate from and operate on a power-laden field.

25. In other words, I suggest that power and inequality are not only discernible at the level of socially acceptable "regimes of value" as "paths [that] are made and maintained by those with the power to do so" (Ferguson 1992: 59). Within the regular and regulated pathways loans take, asymmetries track alongside the terms of credit and debt, especially social collateral.

26. My immense thanks to Alex Blanchette, fellow traveler in studies of social relations and political imaginaries under capitalism, for helping me to see these connections.

27. Munn 1992.

28. Chu 2010.

29. On the one hand, economists have focused on gender as an explanatory variable for microcredit success and have long found a strong correlation between women borrowers and various metrics for human development, including improved outcome for children, improvements in medical access, and household income (Faraizi 2011; Lemire, Pearson, and Campbell 2002; Khandker et al. 1998). There is considerable nuance in many of these studies, including surprising conclusions about the durability of Indian men's misogyny in their perceptions of their wives, even after women became successful borrowers in Grameen Bank programs (Pitt, Khandker, and Cartwright 2006). On the other hand, anthropologists and feminist scholars have pointed to the way microcredit programs assume and capitalize on the gendered positionality of their borrowers. Studies show how women's caring and reproductive labor is enlisted in microcredit schemes, often in ways that can be violent and coercive (Rankin 2001; Keating, Rasmussen, and Rishi 2010; Moodie 2013; Karim 2011; Roy 2010, 2012). Microcredit, in this formulation, has been created to be especially effective at capturing and appropriating the (hitherto nonfinancialized) value of women's social networks and affective labor. I build on both of these approaches to show how the two explanatory models—it's something about women; it's something about microcredit—are two sides of the same coin. By building outward from the hard work of producing social collateral, I focus on how the social unit of debt emerges in microfinance, *including* its gendered sociality.

30. Pitt, Khandker, and Cartwright 2006; Collins et al. 2009. For further discussions and criticisms of the commercialization and financialization of

microcredit, see Bastiaensen et al. 2013; Wagner 2012; Wagner and Winkler 2013.

31. This is the dominant move in anthropology of microfinance. A substantial body of scholarship explores the processes that extract value from the social relationships of poor people and derive financial value from them, giving special attention to the way women's caring relationships are especially vulnerable to exploitation by these loans (Karim 2011; Keating, Rasmussen, and Rishi 2010; Moodie 2013; Roy 2012; Weber 2002; Rankin 2001). My research builds outward from this intervention, especially on scholarship that focuses on the particular effects of microfinance within the social worlds of borrowers in Latin America (Bedford 2005; Lazar 2004; Brett 2006; Barber Kuri 2010; Han 2012; Stoll 2012; Villarreal 2014). There is also a parallel set of debates about the broader discursive frames that justify women's enrollment in microfinance, including the tropes of vulnerability and economic marginalization that focus the work of financial inclusion on women (Moodie 2008; Black 2009; Roy 2012), which intersect with broader discussions of the banking technologies that make global microfinance possible (Schwittay 2014; Roy 2010). Julia Elyachar's (2002, 2003, 2005, 2006) research on the insertion of World Bank logics of enterprise and markets into local workshop culture in Cairo pioneered ethnographic analysis that combines with wider theorization of microfinance within international development and Egyptian national economic policy.

32. I owe thanks to Kregg Hetherington for his generous suggestions for clarifying this aspect of the argument.

33. Here I follow the pathbreaking work of Leslie Salzinger, *Genders in Production* (2003), identifying the processes through which productive labor within capitalist systems also produces gendered sociality (see also Salzinger 2004a, 2004b). Important feminist and queer theory scholarship has further critiqued the deeply gendered and gendering modalities of capitalism, including J.K. Gibson-Graham's critical studies of globalization (Gibson-Graham 2006, 2014; Cameron and Gibson-Graham 2003) and Carla Freeman's (2001) analysis of the consequences of these gendered assumptions for anthropological theory.

34. One way to rephrase this story about the life course of loans might be to borrow a Deleuzian framing, where "the unity-in-movement produced by a context, may be captured and induced into a network of repetition (variation) called 'power'"(Massumi 1992: 31). The terms of credit are precisely this network of repetition and variation that help us understand the power effects of a credit context.

35. Social studies of finance have breathed fresh life into economic anthropology by bracketing the question of social embeddedness versus determining logics of economic structure (in classic formalist/substantivist debates), and engaging instead with the sociality of markets. Many of these works focus on the political and social boundaries erected through the institutionalization of markets in financial firms (Cetina and Preda 2004; Zaloom 2006; Ho 2009; Riles 2011; Miyazaki 2012). Others draw inspiration from Actor Network Theory and renewed interest in the networked objects and forms of reasoning animating finance (Callon 1998; LiPuma 2004; Lépinay 2011). Finally, the epistemological principles of financial knowledge and expertise have been

studied by anthropologists engaged with the logics of money and markets (Maurer 2005; Elyachar 2010).

36. The long-standing debates in economic anthropology that cleaved along formalist and substantivist lines are far too large to discuss in depth here. I follow the rich scholarship in practice theory that draws inspiration from Pierre Bourdieu (1977), which focuses on cultural production rather than the determining logics of economic or social structures. More broadly, I am interested in what Sylvia Yanagisako (2002: 7) has described as "[leaving] open the possibility of the coexistence in any geo-political space—whether local or translocal, national or global—or heterogenous capitalist practices, all of which are culturally mediated."

37. Interdependency in debt relations of course has a storied history in anthropology, from the foundational work of Marcel Mauss to the masterly analysis of David Graeber. If interdependency is a feature of credit/debt relations (and the obligation to return more broadly), then it is instructive to track its conditions of possibility and consequences of those interdependencies. I use interdependency in Jessica Cattelino's (2008) sense, building out of Iris Marion Young's feminist political theory that criticizes the individual rational actor at the root of sovereign theories of self-determination.

38. I draw inspiration from feminist economics (Barker and Kuiper 2003; Barker 2005; Bedford 2005, 2007) as well as the crucially important—though often overlooked—theorization of gender, labor, and exchange in feminist anthropology (Rosaldo, Lamphere, and Bamberger 1974a; MacCormack and Strathern 1980; Strathern 1990; Yanagisako and Collier 1987) and queer theory (Cameron and Gibson-Graham 2003).

39. Rubin is concerned with unpacking the way compulsory heterosexuality tracks alongside women's subordination within kinship as a productive and reproductive system. Sex in microfinance also hinges on women's position in heteronormative reproduction; counterintuitively, this is especially the case for *individual* loans that stand in for the unmarked heterosexual family household. As I describe in chapter 2, the particular way that women become responsible for large pots of collective money means that they are enlisted in broader reproductive systems based on family affiliation. Microfinance thus regulates sexual subjects (see Bedford 2005) and is gendered not just in the sense that loans primarily target women.

40. Salzinger 2003; Yanagisako 2002.

41. Thayer 2010.

42. For a breakdown of Fundación Paraguaya's credit program from 2005 to 2009, see their publicly available audit submitted to a global microcredit ratings clearinghouse (MixMarket 2009).

43. The group-based lending format also meant that the Foundation undertook a fivefold increase in borrowers in as many years (from 6,281 in 2004 to 36,651 in 2009). Further, these group-based loans for committees were handled by a special category of bank functionary—*asesor(a) de créditos,* or credit counselors—rather than the loan officers, or *oficiales de créditos,* who had previously handled all of FUPAs lending operation. This signaled a massive institutional expansion, with more expensive personnel costs and administrative overhead, as well as a growing loan portfolio.

44. Roitman 2005.

45. Peebles 2010: 228.

46. Schuster 2010.

47. Cattelino 2010.

48. Anthropologists and political scientists have underscored the difficulty of diagnosing these arrangements as fraudulent, especially in the context of emerging financial technologies and new profit-making opportunities. Both Smoki Musaraj's (2011) research on Albanian pyramid schemes and Kellee Tsai's (2004) research on curb markets in China point to the slippages between—and coproduction of—putatively fraudulent schemes and emergent forms of institutional finance and juridico-political regulation. In the world of development, see especially Cox 2011, 2013 on fast money schemes in Papua New Guinea.

49. For a wider discussion of the ways microcredit captured, disciplined, and in many cases destroyed these local lending practices, see, e.g., Rahman 1999; Roy 2010; Karim 2011.

50. According to Mariela, the founder of Elite Activity had learned about the process from Paraguay's Mennonites—a community widely regarded as both hyperinsular and very successful in their business ventures. Their commitment to community and to helping one another was cited as the source of their fantastic wealth, real or imagined. The details, however, seemed far less direct and neighborly than the inspirational rhetoric she used to sell the new cooperative. It was all managed online—all you need is an email address to sign up—through direct bank transfers using a credit card.

51. This was true beyond the microfinance world as well, as several acquaintances discussed the Elite Activity scheme with me, though the buzz just as quickly died away. Elite Activity's blog included posts advertising the scheme:

> Ahora en Paraguay! Te gustaría recibir ingresos extras sin tener que dejar ni descuidar tu trabajo actual y duplicar o triplicar tus ingresos?? No Es Negocio, No Es Multinivel, No Es Venta. Somos una organización con tiene 10 años de antigüedad, en sus comienzos nos manejabamos en forma manual y por medio de fax, hasta que en el 2001 se informatizaron haciendo presencia en Internet. Contamos con un programa de rastreo y seguimiento que brinda soporte, ayudando a prosperar de forma equitativa a todos, mientras sigamos participando. Esta constituida legalmente en USA, bajo el apartado de donaciones y la enmienda constitucional: "Const. Amendment XIV states." Somos una de las pocas oportunidades que fácilmente puedes estar recibiendo regalos de 100, 250, 500,1000, 2000, 4000, 6000 dólares directamente en tus manos y de forma ilimitada (si ya sos miembro deja tu testimonio para que otras personas en asunción crean, confien y se sumen a Elite Activity Paraguay). (http://paraguayactivity .blogspot.com/, accessed October 20, 2013)

The scheme apparently was briefly popular in the capital city of Asunción as well, as evinced by advertisements for an informational meeting about the program (http://asuncionciudad.olx.com.py/reunion-informativa-de-elite-activity-iid-37033388, accessed October 20, 2013).

52. Clara Han's beautifully detailed ethnography of the conjuncture of family life, mental health, and consumer credit in a marginalized neighborhood describes the pervasiveness of debt in Santiago, which feels very familiar in Ciudad del Este. See also Han 2004, 2011. In South Africa Deborah James

(2014) has similarly described consumer credit as the key to middle-class aspirations and identity formation.

53. I draw inspiration from Viviana Zelizer's (2010: 307) practice theory account of economic life. She states that these highly regulated financial practices participate in "circuits within commerce," which "involve multiple actors creating and maintaining distinctive form of economic activity."

54. Miranda Silva 2007.

55. Abente, pers. comm., 2013; Hetherington 2011, 2013.

56. What is more, nearly all of the statistics generated on the economic conditions of the tri-border area are caught in a circular citational loop around reporting of organized crime and terrorism in the region (Goldberg 2002; Hudson 2003; Lewis 2006; Abbott 2004; Sverdlick 2005). A series of articles cite one another with regard to the estimate of 60 percent, and it is unclear where the original statistic derived from. All of this is to say that basic sociological information about Ciudad del Este's economy is itself an open question and constantly debated and contested both in Paraguay and abroad.

57. Rabossi 2003, 2010, 2012. I use "duty-free" to describe the tax framework that organizes commercial trade in Ciudad del Este's downtown. Brazil and Argentina both specify limits on the value of goods that can be imported duty-free by shoppers traveling back across the border.

58. For a sustained discussion of the Régimen Tarífa Únificada (RTU), see, e.g., Rabossi 2010; Aguiar 2012.

59. Alexander Dent's (2012) research on piracy in Brazil highlights the close connections between the "counterfeiters" in Paraguay and the informal street markets in Brazil where consumers ultimately purchase those commodities. He writes, "Any pejorative sense of piracy seems to reach its epistemological limit at the Popular Shopping Center. . . . As Marcos of box 384 tells me, as he stamps my DVD purchases with the name and number of his stall, shop owners take pride in their "guarantees"; if something doesn't work, he'll replace it. Similarly, the owner of a nearby electronics kiosk informs me that he can now even take things all the way to the original stores where he bought them in Paraguay. These guarantees are often confirmed by those who purchase goods. Shoppers inform me that if, for example, they had to deal with Sony's customer service representatives when their digital camera broke, they'd be waiting for weeks. And they would be disappointed at the end of the process. Here, however, they simply return to the booth where they bought the offending product and exchange it for a new one" (40–41). In addition, Fernando Rabossi's finely textured ethnography of street vendors (*mesiteros*) in Ciudad del Este in the early 2000s underscores the long-term relationships between sacoleiros and their Paraguayan vendors (Rabossi 2003, 2010, 2012).

60. The discursive link between empowerment and microfinance has been brilliantly analyzed by Elyachar (2002). In Brazil, the purchase that empowerment has in stitching together the broad organizational goals of feminist NGOs, local offices, and program participants has been well explored by Millie Thayer in her book, *Making Transnational Feminism* (2010).

61. Discourse analysis of microfinance aims and goals, especially articulated in self-consciously translocal forums like big development conferences or

reports or statements that aspire to global circulation, often note the felicitous fit between microenterprise and neoliberal governmentality (Roy 2010; Schwittay 2011). While not denying the rise of microfinance as a popular development tool in the context of neoliberal economic restructuring, I follow Elyachar and Freeman in questioning the specific deregulatory policies and macroeconomic theories used to justify particular configurations of national and local development. As with Freeman's (2007, 2014) discussion of the contingent alignments between Caribbean notions of reputation and neoliberal entrepreneurial self-making in Barbados, entrepreneurship in Ciudad del Este was not a straightforward outgrowth of a global development assemblage.

62. On the tightening control of Paraguay's border with Brazil, see Rabossi 2012; Aguiar 2012.

63. See, e.g., Aguiar 2010, 2012; Ferradas 1998, 2004, 2013. Ieva Jusionyte (2013) offers a detailed analysis of those engaged in cross border smuggling from the Argentine side of the triple frontier, especially the media representations produced by those involved.

64. I have benefited from conversations with many people in this group, especially Christine Folch, whose fieldwork coincided with my long-term research in Ciudad del Este, and with Kregg Hetherington and John Tofik Karam, both of whom generously shared their ideas and research with me when I was just starting this project. While Paraguay has long been understudied, partly because of its marginality in Latin America (and Latin American studies), the conversation among area specialists doing ethnography in Paraguay is especially vibrant at present. See especially Bessire 2011; Folch 2012, 2013; Hetherington 2011; Jusionyte 2013; Karam 2004.

65. Sahlins 1972.

66. Feminist scholars have in fact reexamined some of the classic anthropological theories of exchange in order to understand the gender dimensions of value production, especially in Melanesian contexts, from which much of the ethnographic record in economic anthropology has historically been drawn (Weiner 1976; Munn 1992; Strathern 1990). Similarly, feminist retheorization of classic debates such as spheres of exchange (Ferguson 1985; Hutchinson 1992) has challenged assumptions about gender and prestige economies.

67. Louise Lamphere's (1985) pathbreaking studies of workplace culture and social reproduction retheorized the public/private distinction, a long-standing focus of feminist research in economic anthropology (Rosaldo, Lamphere, and Bamberger 1974b). I also draw inspiration from Susan Gal's (2002) linguistic anthropology of social reproduction and the politics of the public/private distinction.

68. Hetherington 2011, 2012a, 2012b.

69. Within the division of labor at the Ciudad del Este office, three credit counselors oversaw microcredit group-based loans and three more loan officers managed individual small-business clients. Credit counselors had far lower professional credentialing requirements than did more senior loan officers. These young women—and they were all women during my fieldwork, though other offices had some male credit counselors—were unmarried and had recently graduated from either high school or a bachelor's degree program. Loan officers

were required to have some background in financial management, such as a professional degree in accounting, management science, or business. Instead of business training, the post of credit counselor prioritized "people skills" and personality, and credit counselors were hired on that basis. This was the first long-term, steady employment for all of the credit counselors. By contrast, loan officers moved laterally to other financial institutions with apparent ease. During my research at the office, one loan officer left for Visión Banco Microfinanzas and was replaced by another financial professional coming from Visión, and some were transferred between regional offices of the Fundación. A secretary and a teller, both young women, staffed the office. Don Edgar managed the Ciudad del Este branch; he had worked his way up through the ranks of the organization, beginning as a loan officer and now supervising a regional office. In the nationwide network of microcredit offices, senior male staff managed all of the regional branch offices.

70. Schwittay 2014; Roy 2010.

71. See Collins et al. 2009.

CHAPTER 1. ENTREPRENEURSHIP

1. At Fundación Paraguaya this was talked about as *emprendedurismo*, which was used to gloss entrepreneurialism as well as general business savvy. In advertising material, the Fundación also referred to *el espíritu emprendedor*.

2. Carla Freeman holds together feminized labor with global processes of production and consumption in her research on "pink collar": "The concept of 'pink collar' is central to my insistence that the dialectics of globalization/localization, production/consumption, and gender/class be analyzed in a way that keeps them linked. 'Pink collar' denotes two major processes within informatics and its workers. The first is the feminization of work such that informatics is itself gendered, not only because it recruits women workers almost exclusively, but also because the work itself is imbued with notions of appropriate femininity, which includes a quiet, responsible demeanor along with meticulous attention to detail and quick and accurate keyboard technique. The second process is the linking of work and clothing—production and consumption" (Freeman 2000: 3–4). My aim here is to show how the gendered administrative space of encounter (or pink-collar work) between credit counselors and Committees of Women Entrepreneurs exposed tensions between an unmarked subject position of financial professional and multiple feminized entrepreneurships.

3. I draw especially on Jessica Cattelino's usage of valuation practices—as distinct from ideology or form of calculative reason—developed in *High Stakes* (Cattelino 2008). Cattelino's analysis of political interdependency through Seminole claims to sovereignty is the conceptual basis for my analysis of economic interdependence and independence.

4. Schumpeter [1942] 1975: 82–85. For a discussion of popular media treatments of Schumpeter and the concept of entrepreneurial innovation as it has been taken up in both economic and lay treatments of the recent financial crisis, see especially Gudeman 2010.

5. See Sheryl Sandberg's assessment of Silicon Valley culture in the age of Facebook, "Sheryl Sandberg: By the Book," *New York Times Magazine*, online, www.nytimes.com/2013/03/17/books/review/sheryl-sandberg-by-the-book .html?pagewanted= ll&_r=0; accessed March 27, 2013.

6. The fault line that separates these two models of microcredit is nicely glossed by Ananya Roy in her book *Poverty Capital* (2010). Roy differentiates between what she calls the CGAP (Consultative Group to Assist the Poor) model of microcredit, which is particularly concerned with financial benchmarks of portfolio sustainability as the fundamental criteria for evaluating microcredit's success, and what she calls the Bangladesh consensus, which broadens the scope of microfinance initiatives to include social initiatives, advocacy, and aid. CGAP is a microcredit best practices watchdog and research clearinghouse headquartered in Washington, DC, and loosely affiliated with the United Nations Development Program (UNDP). The central criteria for CGAP auditing and evaluation protocols are financial benchmarks: returns on investment (ROI), measures of portfolio risk, and market coverage. The Bangladesh consensus spearheaded by the venerable microcredit Grameen initiative and BRAC in Bangladesh, according to Roy's reading, calls into question the ascendency of financial measures for microcredit success and seeks to innovate new modes of assistance that build on but are not limited to the provision of credit services. The at times vitriolic debate between these two positions on microfinance distills to a basic disagreement over the power of credit *on its own* to serve as a poverty alleviation tool.

7. For an analysis of the centrality of training seminars in Brazilian development programming and the NGO sector, see Millie Thayer's *Making Transnational Feminism: Rural Women, NGO Activists, and Northern Donors* (2010).

8. Thayer 2010; Alvarez 2009.

9. In practice, a variety of other projects were attached to this three-pronged organizational structure. The microcredit program was especially amenable to serving as the institutional framework for other development initiatives that were passed from the Fundación's head office in Asunción to the eighteen branch offices of varying sizes, which oversaw microloans to clients throughout Paraguay. Credit served as the core program to which other initiatives could be tethered. However, these social projects constantly fluctuated as they were subject to the whims and vagaries of international donors and trendy development initiatives. In other words, microcredit was the Fundación's workhorse program, with a dedicated staff of credit counselors, loan officers, branch managers, administrative support, and permanent offices throughout the country. That permanent administrative infrastructure had been financially self-sustaining since the organization received generous financing from the Inter-American Development Bank in the early 2000s, which allowed the microlending business to achieve sufficient scale to cover the program's overhead costs.

10. Anthropology's concern with entrepreneurship and multiplying forms of risk harkens to Foucault's genealogy of neoliberalism; his work on governmentality charts the emergence of the entrepreneur as a politico-economic subject within the discursive field of Western—and particularly Anglo-American—

political economy. In his account of "the enterprise form of society," Foucault (2008: 219) found that the American focus on human capital implies two processes: "one that we could call the extension of economic analysis into a previously unexplored domain, and second, on the basis of this, the possibility of giving a strictly economic interpretation of a whole domain previously thought to be non-economic." *Homo economicus,* in this framing, serves as the grid of intelligibility for emergent forms of governance and social regulation. For a fine-grained assessment of anthropology's intersection with rational choice theory and the discipline of economics in the United States, see especially Chibnik 2005, 2011.

11. Ong 2006; Comaroff and Comaroff 2001. In Latin America, see Paley 2001; Goldstein 2004; Han 2011. Specifically within the anthropology of development and microfinance, see Stoll 2012; Kar 2013. Scholars have highlighted the way people and communities caught up in development interventions are called on to shoulder the risks of the free market as clients, stakeholders, and microentrepreneurs.

12. For example, Monica DeHart's (2010) study of ethnic entrepreneurs in Latin America traces the reimagining of local indigenous communities under the rubric of entrepreneurship, transforming them into valuable development subjects. In her account, development policy under neoliberal logics was remodeled to incorporate—and appropriate—the value produced by communities previously excluded from national projects of modernization. Similarly, scholars focusing on the feminized forms of access and inclusion brought about by women's incorporation into financial markets highlight the ways risk is read through the lens of gender.

13. See Lazar 2004; DeHart 2010; Paley 2001; Han 2011; Postero 2007; Goldstein 2004.

14. Here, I follow DeHart (2010) in focusing on the specific dynamics through which entrepreneurship comes organize development interventions. In her study of "ethnic entrepreneurship," DeHart argues that the pairing of development with ethnicized models of entrepreneurship "questions the multiple, contradictory ways that class and gender are invoked to explain and incite different understandings of community and who holds agency within it" (7). The tensions within microcredit, too, illuminate the ways gender and class were invoked to regulate social solidarity within an overarching imperative of entrepreneurialism.

15. Nussbaum 2002, 2011; Evans 2002; Sen 1999.

16. Young 2001.

17. As minister of the interior, Ynsfrán was granted executive power to oversee efforts to secure Paraguay's eastern border. In tandem with the police chief Col. Ramón Duarte Vera, Edgar Ynsfrán worked to ensure that political opposition to the regime was effectively silenced, often violently, and cemented Stroessner's complete political control throughout the country. Ynsfrán's central role in planning and developing Paraguay's "march to the east" was intertwined with his role in state surveillance and control through the powerful Interior Ministry.

18. This passage is often cited, including in Gilberto Ruiz Carvallo's *The Portentous Alto Paraná* (2010). As Ynsfrán wrote:

I remember the profound impression that I had on that first encounter with the immensity of the forest, that we got not long after we passed [the town of] Coronel Oviedo and that did not stop until that irregular line, much later, of the river that separated us from Brazil. We made a pass over the Yguazú waterfalls and later we flew south-southwest, bordering, at a relatively low altitude, the banks of the Paraná. . . . That flight influenced me in a singular manner. It was a live lesson in geography and geopolitics, which also evoked in my mind that old chimera of our whole generation, and of generations before: find another outlet to the sea for [exports for] our country, in order to finally be able to count on an alternative to the one option we had [i.e., river transit through the port of Buenos Aires]. (1999: 91–92)

19. Gesturing back to the initial overflight in the old Catalina bomber, Ynsfrán later commented in an interview, "Without a doubt, the foundation of a city is a relatively simple task. Basically, it is a matter of fixing on a map of the country a point that you suppose has a geopolitical interest, and whose possible connections with other points confirms the reasonable prediction of its future importance, and later, go through the rituals and formalities in order to found the city. *But the city is not there. That city has to constitute itself* [Esa ciudad tiene que erigirse]" (108; my emphasis). Even though the city project would bear President Stroessner's name, and thus have the full weight of institutional authority behind it, planners faced the pragmatic challenge of constructing it. His diagnosis of the Alto Paraná frontier as a space amenable to prognostication actually became the model of development at the heart of Puerto Presidente Stroessner. Along similar lines, Anna Tsing (2005) has argued that the frontier defies a linear logic of intensification and logical development. She writes, "The frontier is not a philosophy but rather a series of historically nonlinear leaps and skirmishes that come together to create their own intensification and proliferation. As these kinds of moves are repeated, they gain a cultural productiveness even in their quirky unpredictability" (33). Those nonlinear leaps and skirmishes that come together to create their own intensification and proliferation became the development model that animated Ynsfrán's frontier as reflexive verb (*erigirse,* constitute itself). See also Ruiz Carvallo 2010: 136.

20. For a sustained analysis of the politics of development theory articulated by CEPAL and other hemispheric policy analysts, see, e.g., Sikkink 1997, 1988.

21. This section of his memoir was aptly titled, "Planning for Development," where he noted that large areas of newly cleared land "quickly transformed into a commercial barrio" (119). For an excellent urban planning analysis of the history of commercial development and contemporary governance strategies in Ciudad del Este, see Tucker n.d.

22. *ABC Color,* "Editorial: Zona franca comercial en Puerto Pte. Stroessner," Asunción, Friday, December 18, 1970, 8. When the bill's sponsor was questioned about the source of the $75,000 to be invested in the project, Senator Masulli, the bill's sponsor, noted that Bussines Company SRL was run by "three Brazilians, residing in São Paulo; two from Buenos Aires; and one from Singapore."

23. The editorial opinion page of Paraguay's leading newspaper expressed outrage at the private business interests that were put in charge of the Zona Franca's development. The editorial railed: "Our understanding is that all

Paraguayan law has the mission of contributing to making all capital invested in our country recognize an obligation [*sentirse comprometido*] to the destiny of the nation, an obligation to serve it, obligation to defend it, with everything in its reach. But if love and affection cannot be imposed by law—and they cannot—then at the very least our legislation should oblige capital—all capital—to maintain the maximum respect toward the Paraguayan nation." The editor suggested that it was especially problematic to establish a haven for "capital that has no nationality" on Paraguay's eastern frontier, since, "Puerto Presidente Stroessner is in and of itself a result of an ideal vision of the nation, created as an example of directed [national] willpower." The second part of the opinion piece, published the following day, further explained the concerns about the special customs zone, especially the propensity for illegality and smuggling in similar reexport zones established throughout Latin America. Put another way, what the editors seemed to be worried about was the fact that the regulatory regime (minimal as it was) on the border would automatically generate illegal trade and smuggling; capital, in this view, was always unfettered and beyond the regulatory ken of the state. What went unspoken in the opinion article was the state's power to control—violently, through the supreme political authority of the "Stronato"—both "the ideal vision of the nation" that inspired the urban project on the border and the project of national development undertaken through international commerce.

24. The concept "commercial society" has deep roots in liberal political thought. Julia Elyachar (2012), building on the work of J. G. A. Pocock (1975) and Albert O. Hirschman (1977), has described the centrality of credit relationships in producing political individuality, suggesting that "That notion of political individuality arose in a context where anonymous mechanisms of credit and new forms of "imaginary property" were giving birth to "commercial society," before the "triumph of capitalism" (Hirschman 1977). These new forms of interaction via credit and debt, in turn, helped develop "economic and intersubjective man" (Pocock 1975, 466)." Elyachar concludes that eighteenth century debates about debt were related to the rise of the modern state and commercial society. I suggest that the nexus of debt, commerce, and state power in Paraguay highlights a similar debate about transformations in contemporary market society.

25. Strathern 1990.

26. See Wilber 2001; Hochachka 2007.

27. In the hour-long speech he summarized the project's intellectual commitments to integral theory, calling it the *marco teórico* (theoretical framework) for the project. He noted that "poverty is com-pli-cated . . . and has objective elements and subjective elements," which made integral theory and psychological approaches particularly apt. All translations from Spanish are mine unless otherwise noted.

28. Martín borrowed much of that language from the management theory book on positive deviance, which seeks to "leverage positive deviants—the few individuals in a group who find unique ways to look at, and overcome, seemingly insoluble difficulties. By seeing solutions where others don't, positive deviants spread and sustain needed change" Pascale, Sternin, and Sternin 2010.

29. For further ethnographic study of these approaches to development, see especially Mosse 2005, 2013; Mosse and Lewis 2005. In contrast, see APEX 2012 for a summary of Fundación Paraguaya's method and its insertion in national development policy.

30. Moodie 2013; Keating, Rasmussen, and Rishi 2010; Black 2009.

31. Elyachar (2010) discusses this infrastructure of sociability as "phatic labor," which then becomes the basis for various projects, from development programming to new payment technologies. I share her concern for the hard social work of building and maintaining these pathways of social connectivity, especially appreciate her insight that gendered sociality is the basis for this social infrastructure (which then can be harnessed to pursue unmarked or masculinized economic projects). However, I focus on the people who undertake this labor—and particularly the way institutionalized forms of social collateral render women individually liable for maintaining those connections while also assuming that they are inextricably enmeshed in them—rather than the infrastructure of connection itself, and thus depart slightly in my analytic focus.

32. The name of the neighborhood has been changed in order to protect the confidentiality of residents.

33. "*Compañera*" in Spanish. Claudelina would often talk about her microcredit borrowing groups as her *socias* too.

34. This is 2.9 million Guaranis. In mid-October 2009, the default rate was 8.54 percent, though the office manager noted that it had risen slightly since the close of last month, to 7.22 percent.

35. For a wider discussion of the cultural politics and history of terer é in Paraguay, see Folch 2010.

36. I follow Cattelino's (2010: 236) usage of "double bind," defined as "competing possible paths to overcoming the dilemma negate one another, posing a contradiction and leading to no possible resolution," drawn from her analysis of the double bind of need-based sovereignty for indigenous polities in settler states.

37. Cisco Entrepreneurship Institute online, http://ciscoinstitute.net/index .php?page=96810, accessed March 8, 2012.

CHAPTER 2. LIABILITY

1. The *Oxford English Dictionary* defines liability as, "**a.** Bound or obliged by law or equity, or in accordance with a rule or convention; answerable (*for,* also const. †*to* with the same sense); legally subject or amenable *to.*" In Paraguay the common term for liability, *compromiso,* captures both the binding spirit of obligation implied by the English-language legal term and the broader sense of "equity," *responsable,* in a jurisprudence sense, referring to "recourse to general principles of justice."

2. Munn (1992: 9) discusses value in the following terms: "differential levels of *spatiotemporal transformation*—more specifically, in terms of an act's relative capacity to expand what I call *intersubjective spacetime*—a spacetime of self-other relationships formed in and through acts and practices. The general value of an act or practice is specified in terms of its *level* of potency, that is,

what I sum up here as the relative expansive capacities of the spacetime formed." I follow Munn in suggesting that the spacetimes of entrepreneurship and liability are produced through action—or economic agency—though not strictly through exchange relationships.

3. A vernacular mixture of Spanish and Guarani commonly spoken by most Paraguayans, and especially widely used in cities, whereas "pure Guarani," as it was often explained to me, was thought of as dominating the rural countryside.

4. For a thorough ethnographic account of the way debt enabled aspirations to a middle-class identity while also further entangling South Africa's poor in exploitative financial arrangements, see Deborah James's *Money from Nothing* (2014)

5. See also Weiner 1992.

6. Which I translate from *comprometer* in Spanish, which can also mean wider obligations.

7. See Chu 2010: 169.

8. Indeed, anthropologists have suggested that a renewed discussion of "modern time" can be a fruitful site for theory building and might reveal new aspects of our own conceptual frameworks (Bear 2014).

9. It was followed by several accounts by Paraguayan historians elaborating on the basic argument (Laíno 1976; Galeano Perrone 1986).

10. The history of the war has been the primary focus of scholarship on Paraguay, and narrative tropes of the war continue to figure prominently in Paraguayan popular media, including advertisements aired during Paraguay's successful 2010 World Cup campaign (Lambert and Nickson 2013). For excellent resources on the military history and political economy of the war, see especially Lambert and Nickson 2013; Kraay and Whigham 2004. For a discussion of historical demography and what it reveals about the catastrophic consequences of the conflict and its aftermath, see Whigham and Potthast 1999, 2002.

11. The story of the archival research that revealed the full extent of Paraguay's devastation in the war is itself remarkable. After years of lively debate among military historians and historical demographers, Thomas Whigham and Barbara Potthast became aware of a complete census in the newly opened archive of the Ministry of Defense, available to the public for the first time with the political reforms that followed the fall of the Stroessner dictatorship (see Folch 2013). As they note, the circumstances for conducting a census were desperate but were a top priority of the Provisional Government as it took stock of Paraguay's circumstances: "The implications of the [census figures] are striking. First of all, between 72 and 74 percent of the prewar Paraguayan population was gone, a figure far higher than historians had hitherto imagined. Several thousand of the missing individuals might have been alive in 1870 as prisoners in far-off Brazil or Uruguay. A few Paraguayans might even have been hiding in the hills or swamps of their own country. But the great majority almost certainly had met their death on the battlefield or fallen victim to the epidemic diseases and malnutrition that accompanied the war. Proof of the overall demographic catastrophe can be seen in the numerical breakdown by gender, with women in the *joven* [young] category regularly outnumbering men of military age by four or five to one" (1999: 181).

12. As Michael Tomz's (2007) thorough account of sovereign borrowing and the consequences of reputation illustrates, first-time borrowers had much higher borrowing costs since investors were uncertain about how governments would approach repayment. With no credit history, Paraguay, like other new borrowers, "faced higher yields *because* they had not yet demonstrated, through years of [debt] service, their willingness to honor debt contracts" (227; original emphasis).

13. *Financier,* May 19, 1874; collected in CFB scrapbook, microfilm reel 138, p. 32.

14. This was familiar rhetoric from the British financial community at the time. Tomz's (2007) account of the importance of reputation in expert opinion emphasizes that it was precisely bondholder organizations like the Corporation of Foreign Bondholders (CFB) that sought to contextualize the financial decisions of borrowing nations by excavating the reasons behind any particular default. The CFB offered a corrective to these ethicizing discourses by focusing attention on external shocks that would explain interruptions in payment.

15. *Financier,* December 4, 1874; collected in CFB scrapbook, microfilm reel 138, p. 86.

16. *Daily Recorder,* November 25, 1874; collected in CFB scrapbook, microfilm reel 138, p. 80.

17. To recall Galeano's (1973: 188) framing.

18. Prospectus, "The River Plate Land & Trading Company, Limited with applications available the 1st of May, 1875"; collected in CFB scrapbook, microfilm reel 138, p. 137.

19. Ibid.

20. The prospectus notes under Terms of Purchase: "A favourable contract has been made with the Vendors for the purchase of these extensive and valuable Possessions, with all Concessions, Rights, Privileges and Franchises connected therewith, for £150,000, to be paid as follows viz.:—£100,000 thereof in fully paid up shares which the Vendors agree to retain for twelve months after allotment: and £50,000 in money" (ibid).

21. A report on the proposed River Plate Land and Trading Company that accompanied the prospectus in the scrapbook also insisted on a full account of the economic history of Paraguay but did not provide a similarly robust account of the political history in that country. For example, the report acknowledges, "It is impossible to refer to Paraguay without recalling the prejudices created by the position of the loans so recently brought out. But so far as the project now before us is concerned, it must be noted that a legitimate private enterprise in what is now acknowledged as one of the River Plate Republics, under the protection of Brazil, has nothing in common with past State intrigues, and Paraguayan bondholders have a direct interest in furthering the legitimate development of the country's wealth." According to the report, the recent history of Paraguay hinges on the scandal of default and the subsequent reclamations of British bondholders. The status of the "prejudices," however, emerges from the chronicle of debt service as evinced by the cessation of coupon payments, rather than the myriad other prejudices recently experienced by Paraguay. The form the scrapbook takes, however, makes visible the suspension of debt service—the serial list of bonds drawn up for payment notably does *not* appear after 1874—but does not chronicle other

suspensions (say, of political self-determination). If Paraguay was recently utterly devastated "fighting for a shadow," then only a shadow of that trauma appears in the CFB archive. The events worthy of chronicling are those related to the credit history of that nation and its ramifications for future investments.

22. *Financier,* April 24, 1875, collected in CFB scrapbook, microfilm reel 138, pp. 178–79.

23. The situation was particularly dire because Paraguay had been saddled with massive war debts imposed as a condition of the armistice. Presumably, a portion of the Public Works loan had been set aside to pay these war debts to members of the Triple Alliance. However, for a decade the bonds languished in default, and Paraguay could not borrow any further capital on European bond markets.

24. This sort of conditional lending, though closely associated with structural adjustment policies undertaken by the International Monetary Fund (IMF) in the 1970s was already widely used by private bondholder associations in Europe to renegotiate the terms of lending with states that had defaulted on their debts. The major difference was that usually bondholders and sovereign states were both asked to make compromises in these deals since there were various Exchanges that nations could look to for borrowing; the IMF by contrast had nearly total domination of international lending.

25. Warren 1965, 1989; Lambert and Nickson 2013.

26. Prospectus for the Paraguay Land Company, Limited, issued January 1, 1889; collected in the CFB scrapbook, microfilm reel 139, p. 399.

27. The settlement in 1885 publicized the concession of lands: "The holders of such Warrants shall be entitled forthwith, or at any time within six years from the present date, to explore any or all of the fiscal or public lands of the State referred to in the preceding Article, and to select therefrom the lands to be conceded as aforesaid, in exchange for the Warrants." Issued in 1885, collected in the CFB scrapbook, microfilm reel 139, p 125.

28. *South American Journal,* April 20, 1889.

29. "A Golden Notice," *Buenos Ayres Standard,* February 13, 1887, CFB archive microfilm reel 139, 149r.

30. See Rist 2002: 109–22; Sikkink 1997.

31. Thus, latifundios—large estates—came to be the dominant form of land tenure in eastern Paraguay (see Hetherington 2009, 2011) dating to the economically convulsive postwar period. Diego Abente (1989, 1993) one of the few historians of Paraguayan political economy researching this period, situates the dominance of foreign capital within a broader framework of liberal politics in Paraguay between the War of the Triple Alliance (1870) and the Chaco War (1932). He finds that, "during this period capital accumulation developed exclusively in the private domain, economic policies were informed by laissez-faire doctrines, and the political arena embodied, if mostly theoretically, the liberal principles of public contestation and elite competition" (Abente 1989: 61). Abente's central claim is that Paraguay faced structural dependencies based on its geographic, economic, and geopolitical positioning vis-à-vis Argentina and Brazil; the liberal republic pursued "a thorough process of denationalization" (63) in the economic sector that intensified these forms of dependence by opening up Paraguay to foreign capital accumulation.

32. "Esto demuestra que el Paraguay es serio": "Franco anuncia histórica colocación de bonos," *ABC Color,* January 17, 2013, www.abc.com.py/nacionales /historica-colocacion-de-bonos-528900.html; accessed July 1, 2015.

33. "Este año se pagarán US\$ 313 millones por deudas," *ABC Color,* January 25, 2013, www.abc.com.py/edicion-impresa/economia/este-ano-se-pagaran-us-313-millones-por-deudas-531658.html; accessed June 18, 2015.

34. Riles 2010.

35. See Howell 2003.

36. See Elyachar 2010. This is an important argument within feminist theories of exchange, including Gayle Rubin's (1975) important intervention in her essay on the traffic in women. The way that women are mobilized within a broader reproductive system is key to understanding the political economy of sexual systems. On this line of analysis, see also Gibson-Graham 2006.

37. Cattelino 2009.

38. Nor should we be surprised by the specificity this performance takes in Fundación Paraguaya's lending programs. It is not merely because microfinance is an idiosyncratic "small-time" set of banking practices. But rather, as Tsing (2000: 119) suggests, "conjuring is always culturally specific, creating a magic show of peculiar meanings, symbols, and practices. The conjuring aspect of finance interrupts our expectations that finance can and has spread everywhere, for it can only spread as far as its own magic. In its dramatic performances, circulating finance reveals itself as both empowered and limited by its cultural specificity.".

39. In Guaranies: "3 million, one million, 600,000, another million."

40. For similar discussions of indebtedness, nervousness, and "a time of waiting" in Chile, see Han 2011.

41. Ross 2014.

42. Here I join a conversation in social anthropology that seeks to specify, analyze, and ultimately enable "human economies" as the basis for collective sociality (Hart, Laville, and Cattani 2010; Hann and Hart 2009). By offering an analytic vocabulary to talk about interdependency, I add to their discussion of the commodification of social life and the deepening inequalities that brings to many communities. However, I fear that a facile reading of the project opposes "good" sociality and interdependency to "bad" individual and transactional exchange. My study of the social density of liability—especially how it incites fraud and theft—challenges some of the more bucolic sketches of interdependent social worlds. I draw inspiration from Hart et al. in finding interdependency immensely fruitful to think with but further ask how and when those mutual obligations take hold and with what effect. Moreover, the hyperfeminization of social collateral calls for a better understanding of the gender dimensions of human economies as an analytical and political project.

CHAPTER 3. CREDITWORTHINESS

1. On Kiva.org's publicity campaigns, web presence, and social media outreach, see Anke Schwittay's (2014) ethnography of microfinance and new information technologies emerging from California's Silicon Valley tech culture.

2. I develop a condensed version of this argument in "The Social Unit of Debt: Gender and Creditworthiness in Paraguayan Microfinance" (Schuster 2014).

3. For a detailed ethnographic account of the temporalities of commerce in Ciudad del Este, see especially Rabossi 2003, 2010, 2012; Tucker n.d.

4. MixMarket 2009.

5. Elsewhere (Schuster 2015) I have written on the complex relationship of social collateral to a sense of home and place.

6. Khandker 1998; Pitt, Khandker, and Cartwright 2006. I build on Megan Moodie's (2008: 455) research on microfinance in Rajasthan, which questions the international development framing focused on women's empowerment to "better understand not why microcredit projects fail but why they seem to be so successful—not only on a global scale but on the ground as well."

7. Or what Margaret Atwood has evocatively termed the credit/debt "twin-ship" in her wide-ranging work *Payback* (2008).

8. See Gregory 2012.

9. There is a long tradition in economic anthropology that paves the way for this type of analysis. I follow Annette Weiner (1976) and Nancy Munn (1986) in documenting how value, and its reproduction, is inextricably linked to for-mations of gender, especially the invisibility of women's labor and wealth in generating value through exchange networks.

10. For an analysis of gender and labor in the context of neoliberal develop-ment interventions aimed at crafting the entrepreneurial self, see DeHart 2010; Bedford 2007.

11. Thayer 2010.

12. See Grandin 2009.

13. Rabossi 2003.

14. Masi 2000.

15. In the informal sector, income generated from small businesses and microenterprises tends to be very low: 16.4 percent of workers in small busi-nesses and 41.3 percent of microenterprises earn income that puts them below the national poverty line (Geoghegan 2008: 79).

16. On gender ideology and labor discipline—especially the assumption of women as "nimble" and "docile," which also structured labor practice in maq-uiladoras—see Salzinger 2003; Wright 2006.

17. Geoghegan 2008: 80.

18. Barker and Kuiper 2003; Barker 2005.

19. Ferradas 1998.

20. Cited in Freeman 2014: 19.

21. Gregory 2012: 381.

22. MixMarket 2009.

23. For an excellent discussion of the day-to-day bank labor involved in making commercial microfinance work in India, see Sohini Kar's (2013) ethno-graphic research on Kolkata. I owe a great deal to our conversation about the similarities and differences between these two microfinance models. For an account of the development discourses animating both the Bangladeshi model of social development and the move to commercial microfinance, see Roy 2010a, 2012.

24. *Grupos,* sometimes simply referred to as committees (*comités*).

25. Individual loans were made for a period of twelve months with an interest rate of 33 percent. Group loans were repaid on twelve- to fourteen-week week cycles and carried an interest rate of 10 percent per cycle. In effect, this was an APR of about 34 percent, since the loan was amortized quarterly. Although the rates might seem quite high compared to consumer credit in the United States, this was standard for finance companies in Paraguay. In a comparatively small credit market still recovering from a banking crisis in 1994, the interest rates for microfinance were not unusual.

26. For more information about the Kiva International program, which pairs individual investors with partner organizations around the world, see their website, www.kiva.org, as well as recent scholarly material discussing Kiva lending: Black 2009; Moodie 2013; Roy 2012.

27. Black 2009; Moodie 2013.

28. See Gregory 2012; Han 2012.

29. During my long-term fieldwork in Ciudad del Este I experimented with an "economic diaries" project (see Collins et al. 2009) with some of my closest research contacts in women's borrowing groups. After a long series of frustrations on both sides, we realized that it was most common to account for daily economic life in terms of payments (Maurer 2012) rather than exchanges. Women measured what they owed in a week or a month for a variety of bills and debts rather than account for daily expenditures.

30. Han 2011, 2012.

31. Poon 2009.

32. For a comparison to morosidad in Chilean credit scores and their link to social and economic inequality, see Han 2011.

33. The ability of microcredit groups to solve "information problems" in banking services has long been a central tenet of microfinance. The alienation of banking surveillance and risk downward to the clients had been conceptualized by Yunnus and the Grameen Bank group as a way of resolving an issue that had long prevented conventional banks from lending to the poor: namely, conventional banks were not equipped to measure the fitness of poor people as borrowers, which justified exclusionary lending practices. Microcredit members were reconceptualized as a resource, since their local knowledge of prospective borrowers was put in service of determining creditworthiness and bearing the risk of making poor decisions (they would be responsible for the loans of unreliable payers).

34. Indeed, there is a robust literature in feminist political economy that tracks how women's caring relationships are recruited into microfinance. See Keating, Rasmussen, and Rishi 2010; Karim 2011; Roy 2010b.

CHAPTER 4. REPAYMENT

1. For an anthropological treatment of this theme, see, e.g., Gustav Peebles's (2010) review of the anthropology of credit and debt and Chris Gregory's (2012) response.

2. Gregory 2012; Graeber 2009. Here Gregory is discussing Peebles's (2010) review of the anthropological conversation on gift, debt, and exchange in an

effort to theorize the moral valences that Peebles's notes are often attached to credit (positive) and debt (negative).

3. The repayment aspect of credit/debt, and the ensuing exchange relationships, has been especially emphasized by David Graeber (2009, 2011, 2012). The violence of equivalence is caught up in the commensuration processes that reconcile monetary debts and their payments.

4. Thanks to Kregg Hetherington for helping me clarify this aspect of the argument.

5. I have a slightly different focus from the conversation in economic anthropology around debt as a product of quantification and calculation, as Graeber (2011) has persuasively argued. Instead, I argue that focusing on the life course of loans helps us track obligations in process and repayment as far from automatic.

6. Rudnyckyj 2014.

7. Indeed, Alexander Dent (2012a) has argued that the effort to make and maintain boundaries is a central feature of discourses on piracy. As he writes, "one of the primary reasons that piracy is simultaneously *au courant* and *passé* is that it seems to have arisen at moments when boundaries have not been quite clear, and those moments abound. Today the term *pirate* is levied at (or awarded to, depending on your perspective) those operating on the Internet but also in the context of newly 'discovered' properties of rainforests, the human body, and even outer space" (660). The ambiguous boundaries around commerce in Ciudad del Este are precisely what provoke the term *pirate* or *contrabandista*. This is especially the case in boundary zones like Remansito, given its geographic location on the triple frontier, as Carmen Ferradás (2013) argues. See also Dawdy and Boni 2012; Gaynor 2012.

8. Janet Roitman (2005: 3) has convincingly argued that economic instruments are themselves regulatory forms: "economic concepts, such as tax and price, are political technologies that serve to constitute 'that which is to be governed' or, in [the Chad basin], a field of regulatory intervention based on a set of presuppositions about the nature of economic life and economic objects."

9. Kar 2013; Ho 2009, 2014; Orta 2013.

10. Critiques of microcredit-based development initiatives, and development interventions generally, often make the general argument that the powerful financial interests behind debt-based programs articulate their mission in the name of poverty alleviation but in the end benefit the banks and development agencies running these programs, which undoubtedly they do in many instances (Roy 2010, 2012; Goldman 2005; Elyachar 2002). For this line of analysis, the rendering technical (Mosse 2005, 2013; Mosse and Lewis 2005) of development expertise—particularly in the financial idiom of portfolio at risk and returns on investment—is a key aspect of masking the interested nature of these programs. The importance of the work of *gestionando* as a repertoire of relational practices complicates the critics' account of development expertise and its unmediated capacity to extract economic value from local people interpellated into development programs, since the direct influence of technical financial tools on client payments was tenuous at best.

11. *Cierre mora,* or percent of the portfolio in arrears at the end of the last month's closing.

12. Peebles 2010.

13. This has been the dominant move in anthropology of finance and an important and necessary corrective to orthodox economic studies that presume self-regulating markets. By populating the offices and trading room floors of major financial institutions, we gain new insights into how the existing forms of hierarchy and exclusion are written into financial markets (see Ho 2009; Zaloom 2006; Fisher and Downey 2006; Miyazaki 2003). I add to this body of literature by showing how finance is embodied and enacted in the margins as well as the centers of global finance. That is not to say that Paraguay is a less financialized site than Wall Street. Rather, we can see how those financial technologies increasingly are absorbing and reconfiguring financial practices in regional economic centers such as Ciudad del Este.

14. "Apreciado cliente: El Pago al día des sus cuotas le permitirá recibir su próximo crédito el mismo día en el que cancela el actual, y recuerde que con su pago puntual USTED MISMO APRUEBA SU PRÓXIMO CRÉDITO."

15. For an analysis of similar logics of scaling and encompassment at a macroeconomic level, see, e.g., Guyer 2004, 2014.

16. On the moral judgments around debt as negative and credit as positive, see Peebles 2010; Gregory 2012.

17. This is not at all unusual in the microfinance world (see Karim 2008, 2011) or in the wider world of debt collection generally (Porter 2012; Rivlin 2010).

18. Elyachar 2012.

19. Other salient connections might include wage labor work; commercial arrangements with merchandise wholesalers in the central market (*mercado abasto*); family ties to other neighborhoods; and occasional cross-border arbitrage exchanges. However, this most often took the form of locals leaving the barrio to pursue commercial ventures and then returning with the proceeds. Politicians and legal or health authorities were generally the "official" personnel who had reason to enter a barrio and for a discrete project. However, local forms of credit relied on an extended network of *cobradores,* or bill collectors, to lubricate the gears of credit and repayment. Since there was not a standardized financial tool for making payments, companies hired contractors to visit clients in their homes to pay for purchases on installment plans, monthly phone and utility plans, etc. Thus the presence of a person seeking payment did not automatically signal lateness; it was often part of a recognized "circuit within commerce" (Zelizer 1997).

20. I note that this is in marked contrast to many critiques of microcredit (see chapter 3 above) that criticize these loans for commodifying the social connections of local neighborhoods and extracting economic value from those social relations (Elyachar 2002; Roy 2010; Keating, Rasmussen, and Rishi 2010; Karim 2011). While this is certainly an important critique, I add to this set of debates by outlining the ways in which microcredit staff members are also implicated in the regulatory work of interdependency.

21. One explanation for the differences between formal and informal finance follows logics developed in Paul Bohannan's (1955) foundational work on

spheres of exchange, and especially the near-impossibility of converting value across separate spheres. Stephen Gudeman's (2008, 2010) research on forms of economic reasoning and value spheres centers on the cultural matrix that organizes multiple "overlapping and conflicting spheres of value and practices that include markets" (2010: 4). He argues that these value spheres are dialectically related: "The domains are separate but mingle; their relative prominence changes over time; and they represent competing interests and perspectives" (4). I depart from this line of inquiry. In Paraguayan microcredit I find it helpful to highlight the unexpected continuities across different economic practices rather than, as Gudeman does, focusing on their difference and contextual convertibility.

22. Peebles (2012) tracks the "national whitewashing rituals" encoded in bankruptcy law in the nineteenth century in order to ritually cleanse deviant debtors and return them to the social. He underscores the spatial dimensions of these rituals: "Should it refuse to offer legal techniques that can cleanse its citizens or subjects of their debts, these same citizens or subjects, when faced with insurmountable debts, will often opt to decamp for a new life abroad, or even, as we shall see, for an oddly debtless life inside the debtors' prison. In other words, debt-forgiveness rituals are designed not only to cope with misfortune or malfeasance, but also to cope with the threat of escape into asociality by the otherwise hopeless debtor" (430). I suggest that Paraguay's whitewashing law allows us to see the process of becoming liable as it is negotiated in and through whitewashing rather than necessarily preceding those modes of accounting. Rather than spatial idioms of escaping and absconding, banking collapses spotlight the difficult negotiations undertaken when flight is impossible, mostly because creditor and debtor are one and the same.

23. See Insfrán Pelozo 2000: 11. Mercosur was also ratified in 1991, leading to greater regional integration. Insfrán Pelozo and other economists at the BCP explain the explosion of financial institutions as a necessary corrective to Stroessner's macroeconomic policies of supporting and stabilizing private sector investment in agroexports, with few financial instruments aimed at public savings or consumer credit.

24. Insfrán Pelozo 2000: 8.

25. See Elyachar 2003.

26. Franks et al. 2005.

27. Nickson and Lambert 2002; Lambert and Nickson 1997.

28. Garcia-Herrero's (2004: 34) IMF working paper on the Latin American financial crises of the 1990s notes that these reforms include "the unification of the exchange rate and floating of the guaraní, the liberalization of interest rates during 1990–91, the introduction of market-based monetary instruments, and the elimination, at least partially, of selective credit controls." Another important reform was the decision in 1993 to transfer deposits from public sector pension plans and social security programs from the Banco Central de Paraguay and instead invest them in the private sector banks. The IMF lamented the unintended outcome of this orthodox macrofiscal restructuring—namely, that these substantial increases in deposits in the private sector "continued to operate in large part through the informal financial sector, a major channel of financial

intermediation in Paraguay" (34)—even as the IMF oversaw the liberalization of Paraguay's financial environment.

29. This aspect of Paraguay's smuggling economy has been analyzed with zeal by a subset of security studies specialists in the United States. Many express anxiety about Paraguay as a "terrorist black spot" (Abbott 2004; Hudson 2003; Lewis 2006; Sverdlick 2005). What these reports leave out is the way international banking policy, including IMF economic policy making, was a central part of the story.

30. For comparative cases in the United States, see Drysdale and Keest 1999; Austin 2003.

31. Straub and Sosa 2001.

32. See especially Bazán 1986, 1991; Giménez Cabral 1986.

33. Straub and Sosa 2001: 297.

34. The failure in 1995 of several banks that dealt heavily in postdated checks led to a crisis in the informal credit market as well. The market for post-dated checks never fully recovered due to changes in banking regulations that required minimum balances for many checking accounts as well as new laws that relaxed the penalties for issuing checks without sufficient funds. This has led to a greater formalization of the credit market and might partly account for the sharp increase in loans issued by finance companies and credit cooperatives since 1995. However, two important links remain between the formal and informal credit markets: (1) informal lenders acting as intermediaries between formal lending institutions and their clients who lack collateral to secure bank loans and (2) the continuing (though reduced) use of postdated checks to guar-antee loans in the informal credit market.

35. Following Kellee Tsai's (2004) research on financial instruments for entrepreneurs in China, I find that formal and informal economies are mutually constitutive rather than mutually exclusive. Tsai argues that China's "curb mar-ket" cannot be fully explained by microeconomic theories of formal sector credit supply failing to meet demand because of political, regional, and gen-dered constraints on financing that result in a variety of financing choices between entrepreneurs facing the same market conditions. I build on Tsai's insight and consider how banking in Paraguay relies on financial instruments that cannot easily be schematized as formal and informal; treating the two as empirically separate misses the opportunity to track how and under what con-ditions some financial instruments are anchored in the "formal economy" while others resist the auditing, management and visibility of formal banking.

36. I describe the diversion of these funds, made available through the "Chi-nese Bonds," in chapter 2.

37. *ABC Color,* June 27, 1995, 43.

38. Ibid.

39. My research on the informal economy suggests that it is much more interesting to track the accounting practices that come to be characterized as more or less formal. Further, the IMF's outrage at the informality at the heart of Paraguay's formal banking sector is itself instructive. Elyachar gives a fine-grained account of the World Bank's hand in redefining Egypt's informal sector, which historically has included everything from unlicensed housing to migrant

remittances to Islamic finance to petty craftsmen. She concludes that "the state cannot always be so neatly located outside informality" (Elyachar 2003: 576); instead, she uses informality as a diagnostic to better understand the power relations between local NGOs, international organizations like the World Bank and the Egyptian Social Fund, and the Egyptian state. She notes that the analytic tool kit of World Bank staff was heavily skewed toward orthodox economics, which meant that it was unsurprising that their measure of informality—which they found correlated with small business ownership—ultimately defined the informal as an economic phenomenon. Similarly, since the IMF has long overseen Paraguay's financial sector liberalization, it is unsurprising that analysts at the Fund would be troubled by the immanence of their object of intervention and its ersatz informal other. Just as the Egyptian state and informality cannot be so easily separated, so too are the formal banking sector and informal credit market in Paraguay difficult to distinguish.

40. Triffin 1946.

41. The ultimate outcome of the financial crisis was a contraction in the financial industry. Paraguay had just over one-third of the number of financial institutions in 2005 that it had at the onset of the crisis a decade earlier. Paraguay's banking reforms of the 1990s led to new legal regulations of the banking industry but perhaps more important generated the sense that more stringent accounting practices, management techniques, and risk assessment were necessary both to deal with the aftereffects of the crisis and to prevent acute liquidity problems in the future. There seemed to be a general consensus that a new management culture in the banking industry was in order. The IMF lauded the transformed financial landscape after the crisis as a "flight to quality" (Garcia-Herrero 1997), where clients of the most troubled financial institutions sought out stabler banks. Thus policy makers concluded that the shock of the crisis ultimately rewarded sound financial management. Of course, "quality" was itself perspectival, since bank bailouts that generated those financial qualities and stability were negotiated through the whitewashing law. The broad trend (whether flight was to "quality" or not) was overwhelmingly of consolidation and merger. The resultant "low level of bank density in the economy" has led to a small amount and high cost of credit from banks (308). The new management culture, which prioritizes risk assessment in lending, has led overall to a contraction in the availability of credit, particularly for small and medium-sized businesses (PYMEs, *pequeñas y medianas empresas*), which dominate the Paraguayan economy.

42. Gudeman 2010.

43. The same logic of "internal problems" was rehearsed in credit counselors' regulation of borrowing committees' mandatory joint savings account, which I detail in chapter 2. Committees were required to maintain an external fund equal to 10 percent of the total amount borrowed. This served as a cushion against late payments and as a de facto guarantee of the loan collateralized (at least in part) by physical assets. When groups ran afoul of the 10 percent savings requirement, credit counselors routinely noted that it was an internal affair that should be resolved by the committee.

44. For example, based on fieldwork with a microcredit NGO in Bangladesh, the anthropologist Lamia Karim (2001: 93) has argued, "Credit . . . is a

most powerful dynamic in the relationship between the NGO and its poor beneficiaries, for it represents the ability to restructure people's lives and choices
through debt relations, and, as is well known, debt relations are relations of
dependence."

45. Munn 1986; Weiner 1985; Parry and Bloch 1989; Graeber 2001, 2009;
Hann and Hart 2009; Hart 2000a; Guyer 2004; Riles 2010.

46. For an analysis of "generating capitalism" within financial systems, I am
especially indebted to the Gens Collective and the ongoing work of Bear et al.
(2015) to articulate, in their framing, a "feminist manifesto in the study of
capitalism." As they argue, "While our generating capitalism approach tackles
head-on the massive socio-economic shifts that have made institutions, natural
resources, governmental entities, education, retirements, etc., increasingly
dependent on financial products, measurements, and values, we also insist that
the processes of finanicalization are uneven, specific, and contingent." I document and interpret exactly this double move in microfinance. Social collateral
involves a massive socioeconomic shift that has made individual women, families, communities, organizations, and governments increasingly dependent on
financial products. At the same time, I emphasize how processes of financial
capture and conversion—and especially repayment—rely on contingent and
uneven repertoires of economic practices to generate liability.

47. I owe a great to the conceptual framing of Cattelino's (2015) research on
valuing nature, which advances critical theorizations of value under systems of
political and economic liberalism. See also Appel 2015; Bear et al. 2015; Stout
2015; Rofel 2015; Tsing 2015; Zhan 2015.

CHAPTER 5. RENEWAL

1. Portions of the argument developed in this chapter appear in Schuster
2016.

2. For an account of family strategies in loan repayment, see Brett 2006.

3. Elyachar 2012: 109.

4. Guyer 2012: 491; see also Graeber 2011, 2012.

5. For a similar discussion of credit scoring and the way certain companies
dominate the content services aspects of financial infrastructures, see especially
Martha Poon's (2009) work on FICO scores in the U.S. credit market and Nigel
Thrift's anthropological analysis on electronic reporting systems within credit
markets (Leyshon and Thrift 1999).

6. *Pyahu* is the Guarani word for "new" or "emergent"; *rico* means
"wealthy" in Spanish.

7. Smith develops this analysis in Part IV, "Of the Effect of Utility upon the
Sentiment of Approbation." *The Theory of Moral Sentiments* is available online
at http://econlib.org/library/Smith/smMS4.html (accessed July 1, 2015).

8. A related dynamic might be the sort of exit from indebtedness analyzed by
Gustav Peebles (2013) in his work on nineteenth-century bankruptcy law. In his
archival research on debtor's prisons, the phenomenon was discussed by oppo-
nents as a sort of internal barbarism: "This Other was marked by his failure to
responsibly grasp the meaning of his financial obligations, whether as creditor

(by cruelly seizing bodies) or as debtor (by disdaining debts in various nefarious ways)" (703). The ritual cleansing of bankruptcy was thought of as rehabilitation into the social, while the "social death" of the debtor's prison precluded that sort of rehabilitation.

9. But interestingly, credit reports are not accessible to individuals; that is, people only become aware of their credit history as chronicled by Informconf after they apply for a loan. This seems important to note as a part of the relationship of "I" to "them" as it points to yet another "them"—the formal lender. Since Informconf is a private company rather than a public service, the data they collect and disseminate, though highly personalized, are vexed as to their public/private nature. You have to subscribe to the database service in order to have access.

10. See Strathern 2004.

11. See Peebles 2012, 2013.

12. As famously observed by Bourdieu in his essay on the biographical illusion, "Trying to understand a life as a unique and self-sufficient series of successive events (sufficient into itself), and without ties other than the association to a 'subject' whose constancy is probably just that of a proper name, is nearly as absurd as trying to make sense of a subway route without taking into account the network's structure, that is the network of objective relations between different stations" (Bourdieu, in Du Gay, Evans, and Redman 2000: 304). One might be tempted to stop there and dismiss Gustavo's account as too invested in producing a biographical illusion (and extracting profits from it) and condemn the credit-scoring agency as inspiring a certain ethic of social responsibility through the "cultural effects" of credit. However, I also think Gustavo has an interesting take on the perspectival nature of liabilities, especially as these liabilities unfold over personal and financial life spans. In other words, biography was itself implicated in the processes of financial capture and conversion described by Bear et al. (2015) as generative forces in capitalism or by Tsing (2015) as "salvage accumulation" that folds nonmarket value into processes of capitalist accumulation.

13. Here I am drawing on semiotic approaches to space and time that build out of Mikhail Bakhtin's literary theory (Bakhtin and Holquist 1981) and are elaborated in linguistic anthropology (Silverstein 2005). Nancy Munn's masterly analysis of value and social reproduction in *The Fame of Gawa* (1992) brought that analytic vocabulary and interpretive framework to economic anthropology.

14. Bondar 2012; Pedrozo 2003; González Torres 1980.

15. While census data in Paraguay suggest that 54.2 percent of families are nuclear, with another 32.4 percent living in extended families, the statistics only tell part of the story. In everyday life, while urban and semiurban families might generally share a household with their children, concentric rings of kin often live nearby, in the same neighborhood or even on the same plot of land (Céspedes 2004, 2006).

16. Mauricio Cardozo Ocampo, "El angelito y el angeloro," *ABC Color,* March 16, 1975.

17. There is a much wider debate about death, regeneration, and exchange that is too broad to fully capture here. Maurice Bloch and Jonathan Parry

survey major themes in their volume, *Death and the Regeneration of Life* (1982), and link those questions of short- and long-term cycles of regeneration to money and exchange practices in their later volume, *Money and the Morality of Exchange* (1989).

18. I would like to thank an anonymous reviewer from the journal *Social Analysis* for clarifying this point for me and provoking further consideration of the three-way connection between kinship relations, death, and financial indebtedness.

19. Paraguayan banking law prohibits nonprofit organizations from holding the savings of clients at the institution. In order to manage client savings in-house, Fundación Paraguaya would have to relinquish its nonprofit status and reregister as a finance company, or financiera. As a consequence, Committees of Women Entrepreneurs were required to open a savings account with a financiera—usually registered in the name of a single member of the group who handled the collective payments and savings—and present an account statement to their credit counselor during important institutional moments like loan disbursal (*desembolso*) and renewal (*renovación*).

20. These land developers are called *imobiliaria*. They broker real estate purchases and often finance land purchases as well. For a comparison with real estate purchases in Argentina (also undertaken with development companies), see especially Nicholas D'Avella's (2014) research on Buenos Aires after the crash.

21. As discussed earlier, Fundación Paraguaya's loans started at about $60 per borrower and increased incrementally from one cycle to the next. The five-fold increase in the president's line of credit reflected a very long credit history with the Committee of Women Entrepreneurs.

22. Keane 2001: 69.

23. See Cattelino 2008.

24. Her children's coparent godmothers, common in Catholic kinship practice.

25. See Goldfarb and Schuster 2016. In the introduction to a special section of the journal *Social Analysis* we develop the concept of materializing and dematerializing kinship using anthropological theories of value and semiotic analysis. The special section emerges from an American Anthropological Association panel in 2012 coorganized with Kathryn Goldfarb on the theme "(De)materializing Kinship."

26. Malinowski 1984; Mauss 1990; Munn 1986; Weiner 1976, 1980.

27. Parry and Bloch 1989; Akin and Robbins 1999; Hart 2000; Chu 2010.

28. See Parry and Bloch 1989.

29. Franklin and McKinnon 2001: 9.

30. I would like to thank a second anonymous reviewer at the journal *Social Analysis* for making this point especially clear.

CONCLUSION

1. For further discussions of the important intersections between microfinance and commercial banking, see Bastiaensen et al. 2013; Wagner 2012; Wagner and Winkler 2013.

2. See Ho 2009; Knorr-Cetina and Preda 2005; Zaloom 2006; Riles 2010.

3. See Cooper 2008, 2010.

4. I develop this argument with Kathryn Goldfarb (2016) in the introduction to our special section of the journal *Social Analysis* titled "(De)materializing Kinship: Holding Together Mutuality and Difference."

5. See also Hart, Laville, and Cattani 2010.

Works Cited

Abbott, Philip K. 2004. "Terrorist Threat in the Tri-Border Area: Myth or Reality?" *Military Review* 84(5): 51.

Abente Brun, Diego. 1989. "Foreign Capital, Economic Elites and the State in Paraguay during the Liberal Republic (1870–1936)." *Journal of Latin American Studies* 21(1): 61–88.

———. 1993. *Paraguay en transición.* Caracas: Editorial Nuevo Sociedad.

Aguiar, José Carlos G. 2010. *Stretching the Border: Smuggling Practices and the Control of Illegality in South America.* New Voices 6. Global Consortium on Security Transformation (GCST). www.securitytransformation.org/gc_publications.php (accessed July 1, 2005).

———. 2012. "Cities on Edge: Smuggling and Neoliberal Policies at the Iguazú Triangle." *Singapore Journal of Tropical Geography* 33(2): 171–83.

Alkire, Sabina. 2010. "Human Development: Definitions, Critiques, and Related Concepts." OPHI Working Papers (ophiwp036). Queen Elizabeth House, University of Oxford.

Alvarez, Sonia E. 2009. "Beyond NGO-ization? Reflections from Latin America." *Development* 52(2): 175–84.

Appadurai, Arjun. 1986. "Introduction: Commodities and the Politics of Value." In *The Social Life of Things: Commodities in Cultural Perspective,* ed. Arjun Appadurai, 3–63. Cambridge: Cambridge University Press.

———. 2011. "The Ghost in the Financial Machine." *Public Culture* 23(3): 1–24.

Ardener, Shirley. 1964. "The Comparative Study of Rotating Credit Associations." *Journal of the Royal Anthropological Institute of Great Britain and Ireland* 94(2): 201–29.

Atwood, Margaret Eleanor. 2008. *Payback: Debt and the Shadow Side of Wealth.* CBC Massey Lectures Series. Toronto: Anansi.

Austin, Regina. 2003. "Of Predatory Lending and the Democratization of Credit: Preserving the Social Safety Net of Informality in Small-Loan Transactions." *American University Law Review* 53: 1217.

Bakhtin, Mikhail M. 1981. *The Dialogic Imagination: Four Essays*. Trans. Caryl Emerson. Austin: University of Texas Press.

Barber Kuri, Carlos Miguel, ed. 2010. *Microfinanzas en América Latina*. Mexico City: LID.

Barker, Drucilla. 2005. "Beyond Women and Economics: 'Rereading' Women's Work." *Signs: Journal of Women in Culture and Society* 30(4): 2189.

Barker, Drucilla, and Edith Kuiper. 2003. *Toward a Feminist Philosophy of Economics*. New York: Routledge.

Bastiaensen, Johan, Peter Marchetti, René Mendoza, and Francisco Pérez. 2013. "After the Nicaraguan Non-Payment Crisis: Alternatives to Microfinance Narcissism." *Development and Change* 44(4): 861–85.

Bazán, Francisco. 1986. *Régimen jurídico del cheque: De acuerdo al Código Civil*. Asunción, Paraguay: Revista de Derecho y Jurisprudencia.

———. 1991. *El cheque: Su régimen penal*. Asunción, Paraguay: Revista de Derecho y Jurisprudencia.

Bear, Laura. 2014. "Doubt, Conflict, Mediation: The Anthropology of Modern Time." *Journal of the Royal Anthropological Institute* 20: 3–30.

Bear, Laura, Karen Ho, Anna Tsing, and Sylvia Yanagisako. 2015. "Gens: A Feminist Manifesto for the Study of Capitalism." *Fieldsights—Theorizing the Contemporary, Cultural Anthropology Online*, March 30. www.culanth .org/fieldsights/652-gens-a-feminist-manifesto-for-the-study-of-capitalism.

Bedford, Kate. 2005. "Loving to Straighten out Development: Sexuality and Ethnodevelopment in the World Bank's Ecuadorian Lending." *Feminist Legal Studies* 13(3): 295–322.

———. 2007. "The Imperative of Male Inclusion: How Institutional Context Influences World Bank Gender Policy." *International Feminist Journal of Politics* 9(3): 289–311.

Bessire, Lucas. 2011. "Apocalyptic Futures: The Violent Transformation of Moral Human Life among Ayoreo-Speaking People of the Paraguayan Gran Chaco." *American Ethnologist* 38(4): 743–57.

Black, Shameem. 2009. "Microloans and Micronarratives: Sentiment for a Small World." *Public Culture* 21(2): 269.

Bloch, Maurice, and Jonathan P. Parry, eds. 1982. *Death and the Regeneration of Life*. Cambridge: Cambridge University Press.

Bohannan, Paul. 1955. "Some Principles of Exchange and Investment among the Tiv." *American Anthropologist* 57(1): 60–70.

Bourdieu, Pierre. 1977. *Outline of a Theory of Practice*. Trans. Richard Nice. Cambridge: Cambridge University Press.

———. 2000. "The Biographical Illusion." In *Identity: A Reader,* ed. Paul Du Gay, Jessica Evans, and Peter Redman, 299–305. London: Sage.

Brett, John A. 2006. "'We Sacrifice and Eat Less': The Structural Complexities of Microfinance Participation." *Human Organization* 65(1): 8–19.

Callon, Michel, ed. 1998. *The Laws of the Markets*. Sociological Review Monograph Series. Oxford: Blackwell/Sociological Review.

Cameron, Jenny, and J.K. Gibson-Graham. 2003. "Feminising the Economy: Metaphors, Strategies, Politics." *Gender, Place & Culture: A Journal of Feminist Geography* 10(2): 145.

Cattelino, Jessica. 2008. *High Stakes: Florida Seminole Gaming and Sovereignty.* Durham, NC: Duke University Press.

———. 2009. "Fungibility: Florida Seminole Casino Dividends and the Fiscal Politics of Indigeneity." *American Anthropologist* 111(2): 190–200.

———. 2010. "The Double Bind of American Indian Need-Based Sovereignty." *Cultural Anthropology* 25(2): 235–62.

———. 2015. "Valuing Nature." *Fieldsights— Theorizing the Contemporary, Cultural Anthropology Online*, March 30. www.culanth.org/fieldsights /654-valuing-nature.

Céspedes, Roberto L. 2004. "Familias en Paraguay: Análisis sociohistórico de estructuras familiares y pobreza." In *Familia y pobreza en el Paraguay: Resultado de investigaciones.* Serie Investigaciones-Población y Desarrollo, Fondo de Población de las Naciones Unidas (UNFPA)-ADEPO. Asunción, Paraguay: Serie Investigaciones—Población y Desarrollo.

———. 2006. "Estructura familiar en Paraguay (1982–2002)." *Revista Paraguaya de Sociología* 43(125–26): 51–66.

Cetina, Karin Knorr, and Alex Preda. 2004. *The Sociology of Financial Markets.* Oxford: Oxford University Press.

Chibnik, Michael. 2005. "Experimental Economics in Anthropology: A Critical Assessment." *American Ethnologist* 32(2): 198–209.

———. 2011. *Anthropology, Economics, and Choice.* Austin: University of Texas Press.

Chu, Julie Y. 2010. *Cosmologies of Credit: Transnational Mobility and the Politics of Destination in China.* Durham, NC: Duke University Press.

Collins, Daryl, Jonathan Murdoch, Stuart Rutherford, and Orlanda Ruthven. 2009. *Portfolios of the Poor: How the World's Poor Live on $2 a Day.* Princeton, NJ: Princeton University Press.

Comaroff, Jean, and John L. Comaroff. 1999. "Occult Economies and the Violence of Abstraction: Notes from the South African Postcolony." *American Ethnologist* 26(2): 279–303.

———. 2001. *Millennial Capitalism and the Culture of Neoliberalism.* Durham, NC: Duke University Press.

Cooper, Melinda. 2008. *Life as Surplus: Biotechnology and Capitalism in the Neoliberal Era.* Seattle: University of Washington Press.

———. 2010. "Turbulent Worlds Financial Markets and Environmental Crisis." *Theory, Culture & Society* 27(2–3): 167–90.

Cox, John. 2011. "Deception and Disillusionment: Fast Money Schemes in Papua New Guinea." PhD diss., University of Melbourne. http://minerva-access .unimelb.edu.au/handle/11343/37058. Accessed January 6, 2015.

———. 2013. "The Magic of Money and the Magic of the State: Fast Money Schemes in Papua New Guinea." *Oceania* 83(3): 175–91.

D'Avella, Nicholas. 2014. "Ecologies of Investment: Crisis Histories and Brick Futures in Argentina." *Cultural Anthropology* 29(1): 173–99.

Dawdy, Shannon Lee, and Joe Bonni. 2012. "Towards a general theory of piracy." *Anthropological Quarterly* 85(3): 673-99.

DeHart, Monica C. 2010. *Ethnic Entrepreneurs: Identity and Development Politics in Latin America.* Stanford, CA: Stanford University Press.

Dent, Alexander S. 2012a. "Introduction: Understanding the War on Piracy, or Why We Need More Anthropology of Pirates." *Anthropological Quarterly* 85(3): 659-72.

———. 2012b. "Piracy, Circulatory Legitimacy, and Neoliberal Subjectivity in Brazil." *Cultural Anthropology* 27(1): 28-49.

De Soto, Hernando. 2002. *The Other Path: The Economic Answer to Terrorism.* New York: Basic Books.

Drysdale, Lynn, and Kathleen E. Keest. 1999. "Two-Tiered Consumer Financial Services Marketplace: The Fringe Banking System and Its Challenge to Current Thinking about the Role of Usury Laws in Today's Society." *SCL Review* 51: 589-616.

Du Gay, Paul, Jessica Evans, and Peter Redman, eds. 2000. *Identity: A Reader.* London: Sage.

Elyachar, Julia. 2002. "Empowerment Money: The World Bank, Non-Governmental Organizations, and the Value of Culture in Egypt." *Public Culture* 14(3): 493-513.

———. 2003. "Mappings of Power: The State, NGOs, and International Organizations in the Informal Economy of Cairo." *Comparative Studies in Society and History* 45(3): 571-605.

———. 2005. *Markets of Dispossession: NGOs, Economic Development, and the State in Cairo.* Durham, NC: Duke University Press.

———. 2006. "Best Practices: Research, Finance, and NGOs in Cairo." *American Ethnologist* 33(3): 413-26.

———. 2010. "Phatic Labor, Infrastructure, and the Question of Empowerment in Cairo." *American Ethnologist* 37(3): 452-64.

———. 2012a. "Next Practices: Knowledge, Infrastructure, and Public Goods at the Bottom of the Pyramid." *Public Culture* 24(166): 109-29.

———. 2012b. "The Passions of Credit and the Dangers of Debt." *Fieldsights—Theorizing the Contemporary, Cultural Anthropology Online,* May 15. www.culanth.org/fieldsights/337-the-passions-of-credit-and-the-dangers-of-debt.

Evans, Peter. 2002. "Collective Capabilities, Culture, and Amartya Sen's Development as Freedom." *Studies in Comparative International Development* 37(2): 54-60.

Faraizi, Aminul Haque. 2011. *Microcredit and Women's Empowerment: A Case Study of Bangladesh.* Routledge Contemporary South Asia Series. Abingdon: Routledge.

Ferguson, James. 1985. "The Bovine Mystique: Power, Property and Livestock in Rural Lesotho." *Man* 20(4): 647-74.

Ferradás, Carmen. 1998. "How a Green Wilderness Became a Trade Wilderness: The Story of a Southern Cone Frontier." *PoLAR: Political and Legal Anthropology Review* 21(2): 11-25.

———. 2004. "Environment, Security, and Terrorism in the Trinational Frontier of the Southern Cone." *GIDE* 11(3): 417-42.

———. 2013. "The Nature of Illegality under Neoliberalism and Post-Neoliberalism." *PoLAR: Political and Legal Anthropology Review* 36(2): 266–73.

Fisher, Melissa, and Greg Downey, eds. 2006. *Frontiers of Capital: Ethnographic Reflections on the New Economy.* Durham, NC: Duke University Press.

Folch, Christine. 2010. "Stimulating Consumption: Yerba Mate Myths, Markets, and Meanings from Conquest to Present." *Comparative Studies in Society and History* 52(1): 6–36.

———. 2012. "The Flows of Sovereignty: Itaipu Hydroelectric Dam and the Ethnography of the Paraguayan Nation-State." PhD diss., City University of New York.

———. 2013. "Surveillance and State Violence in Stroessner's Paraguay: Itaipú Hydroelectric Dam, Archive of Terror." *American Anthropologist* 115(1): 44–57.

Foucault, Michel. 2008. *The Birth of Biopolitics: Lectures at the Collège de France, 1978–79.* Basingstoke: Palgrave Macmillan.

Franklin, Sarah, and Susan McKinnon, eds. 2001. *Relative Values: Reconfiguring Kinship Studies.* Durham, NC: Duke University Press.

Franks, Jeffrey, Valerie Mercer-Blackman, Randa Sab, and Roberto Benelli. 2005. *Paraguay: Corruption, Reform, and the Financial System.* Washington, DC: International Monetary Fund.

Fraser, Nancy. 2009. "Feminism, Capitalism, and the Cunning of History." *New Left Review* 56(7): 97–117.

Freeman, Carla. 2000. *High Tech and High Heels in the Global Economy: Women, Work, and Pink-Collar Identities in the Caribbean.* Durham, NC: Duke University Press.

———. 2001. "Is Local:Global as Feminine:Masculine? Rethinking the Gender of Globalization." *Signs: Journal of Women in Culture and Society* 26(4): 1007–37.

———. 2007. "The 'Reputation' of Neoliberalism." *American Ethnologist* 34(2): 252–67.

———. 2014. *Entrepreneurial Selves: Neoliberal Respectability and the Making of a Caribbean Middle Class.* Durham, NC: Duke University Press.

Galeano, Eduardo H. 1973. *Open Veins of Latin America: Five Centuries of the Pillage of a Continent.* New York: Monthly Review Press.

Galeano Perrone, Horacio. 1986. *Paraguay: Ideología de la dependencia.* Vol. 9. Asunción, Paraguay: Ediciones La República.

Gal, Susan. 2002. "A Semiotics of the Public/Private Distinction." *Differences: Journal of Feminist Cultural Studies* 13(1): 77–95.

García-Herrero, Alicia. 1997. "Banking Crisis in Latinamerica in the 90s: Lessons from Argentina, Paraguay, and Venezuela." IMF Working Paper 97/140. http://papers.ssrn.com/sol3/papers.cfm?abstract_id=882703. Accessed February 12, 2015.

Geertz, Clifford. 1962. "The Rotating Credit Association: A 'Middle Rung' in Development." *Economic Development and Cultural Change* 10(3): 241–63.

Geoghegan, Verónica Serafini. 2008. *La liberalización económica en Paraguay y su efecto sobre las mujeres.* Buenos Aires: CLACSO.

Gibson-Graham, J.K. 2006. *The End of Capitalism (as We Knew It): A Feminist Critique of Political Economy*. Minneapolis: University of Minnesota Press.

———. 2014. "Rethinking the Economy with Thick Description and Weak Theory." *Current Anthropology* 55(9): S147–S153.

Giménez Cabral, Arnaldo. 1986. *El cheque sin fondo*. Asunción, Paraguay: El Foro.

Goldbar, Kathryn, and Caroline Schuster. 2016. "(De)materializing Kinship: Holding Together Mutuality and Difference." *Social Analysis* 60(2).

Goldman, Michael. 2005. "Tracing the Roots/Routes of World Bank Power." *International Journal of Sociology and Social Policy* 25(1–2): 10–29.

Goldstein, Daniel M. 2004. *The Spectacular City: Violence and Performance in Urban Bolivia*. Durham, NC: Duke University Press Books.

González Torres, Dionisio M. 1980. *Folklore del Paraguay*. Asunción, Paraguay: Editorial Comuneros.

Graeber, David. 2001. *Toward an Anthropological Theory of Value: The False Coin of Our Own Dreams*. London: Palgrave Macmillan.

———. 2009. "Debt, Violence, and Impersonal Markets: Polanyian Meditations." In *Market and Society: The Great Transformation Today*, ed. Chris Hann and Keith Hart, 106–32. Cambridge: Cambridge University Press.

———. 2011. *Debt: The First 5,000 Years*. Brooklyn, NY: Melville House.

———. 2012. "On Social Currencies and Human Economies: Some Notes on the Violence of Equivalence." *Social Anthropology* 20(4): 411–28.

Grandin, Greg. 2009. *Fordlandia: The Rise and Fall of Henry Ford's Forgotten Jungle City*. New York: Metropolitan Books.

Gregory, Chris A. 1997. *Savage Money: The Anthropology and Politics of Commodity Exchange*. London: Taylor & Francis.

———. 2012. "On Money Debt and Morality: Some Reflections on the Contribution of Economic Anthropology." *Social Anthropology* 20(4): 380–96.

Gudeman, Stephen. 2008. *Economy's Tension: The Dialectics of Community and Market*. New York: Berghahn Books.

———. 2010. "Creative Destruction: Efficiency, Equity or Collapse?" *Anthropology Today* 26(1): 3–7.

Guyer, Jane I. 2004. *Marginal Gains: Monetary Transactions in Atlantic Africa*. Lewis Henry Morgan Lectures. Chicago: University of Chicago Press.

———. 2012. "Obligation, Binding, Debt, and Responsibility: Provocations about Temporality from Two New Sources." *Social Anthropology* 20(4): 491–501.

———. 2014. "The Gross Domestic Person?" *Anthropology Today* 30(2): 16–20.

Han, Clara. 2004. "The Work of Indebtedness: The Traumatic Present of Late Capitalist Chile." *Culture, Medicine and Psychiatry* 28(2): 169–87.

———. 2011. "Symptoms of Another Life: Time, Possibility, and Domestic Relations in Chile's Credit Economy." *Cultural Anthropology* 26(1): 7–32.

———. 2012. *Life in Debt: Times of Care and Violence in Neoliberal Chile*. Berkeley: University of California Press.

Hann, Chris, and Keith Hart, eds. 2009. *Market and Society: The Great Transformation Today*. Cambridge: Cambridge University Press.

Hart, Keith. 2000a. "Kinship, Contract, and Trust: The Economic Organization of Migrants in an African City Slum." In *Trust: Making and Breaking Cooperative Relations* (electronic ed.), ed. Diego Gambetta, 176–93. Oxford: University of Oxford Press.

———. 2000b. *The Memory Bank: Money in an Unequal World*. London: Profile Books.

Hart, Keith, Jean-Louis Laville, and Antonio David Cattani. 2010. *The Human Economy: A Citizen's Guide*. Cambridge: Polity.

Helmreich, Stefan. 2007. "Blue-Green Capital, Biotechnological Circulation and an Oceanic Imaginary: A Critique of Biopolitical Economy." *BioSocieties* 2(3): 287–302.

Hetherington, Kregg. 2009. "Privatizing the Private in Rural Paraguay: Precarious Lots and the Materiality of Rights." *American Ethnologist* 36(2): 224–41.

———. 2011. *Guerrilla Auditors: The Politics of Transparency in Neoliberal Paraguay*. Durham, NC: Duke University Press.

———. 2012a. "Agency, Scale, and the Ethnography of Transparency." *PoLAR: Political and Legal Anthropology Review* 35(2): 242–47.

———. 2012b. "Promising Information: Democracy, Development, and the Remapping of Latin America." *Economy and Society* 41(2): 127–50.

———. 2013. "Beans before the Law: Knowledge Practices, Responsibility, and the Paraguayan Soy Boom." *Cultural Anthropology* 28(1): 65–85.

Hirschman, Albert O. 1977. *The Passions and the Interests*. Princeton, NJ: Princeton University Press.

Hochachka, Gail. 2007. "An Introduction to Integral International Development." *AQAL Journal of Integral Theory and Practice*. https://foundation.metaintegral.org/products/introduction-integral-international-development. Accessed July 1, 2015.

Ho, Karen. 2009a. "Disciplining Investment Bankers, Disciplining the Economy: Wall Street's Institutional Culture of Crisis and the Downsizing of 'Corporate America.'" *American Anthropologist* 111(2): 177–89.

———. 2009b. *Liquidated: An Ethnography of Wall Street*. Durham, NC: Duke University Press.

———. 2014. "Commentary on Andrew Orta's 'Managing the Margins': The Anthropology of Transnational Capitalism, Neoliberalism, and Risk." *American Ethnologist* 41(1): 31–37.

Howell, Signe. 2003. "Kinning: The Creation of Life Trajectories in Transnational Adoptive Families." *Journal of the Royal Anthropological Institute* 9(3): 465–84.

Hudson, Rex A. 2003. *Terrorist and Organized Crime Groups in the Tri-Border Area (TBA) of South America: A Report*. Ed. Library of Congress. Washington, DC: Federal Research Division, Library of Congress.

Hutchinson, Sharon. 1992. "The Cattle of Money and the Cattle of Girls among the Nuer, 1930–83." *American Ethnologist* 19(2): 294–316.

Insfrán Pelozo, Jorge A. 2000. *El sector financiero paraguayo: Evaluando 10 años de transición*. Asunción: Banco Central de Paraguay.

Iris Marion Young. 2001. "Martha C. Nussbaum, Sex and Social Justice." *Ethics* 111(4): 819–23.

Iván Bondar, César. 2012. "Angelitos: Altares y entierros domésticos. Corrientes (Argentina) y sur de la región oriental de la república del Paraguay." *Revista Sans Soleil—Estudios de la Imagen* 4(1): 140–67.

James, Deborah. 2014. *Money from Nothing: Indebtedness and Aspiration in South Africa.* Stanford, CA: Stanford University Press.

Jusionyte, Ieva. 2013. "On and Off the Record: The Production of Legitimacy in an Argentine Border Town." *PoLAR: Political and Legal Anthropology Review* 36(2): 231–48.

Karam, John Tofik. 2004. "A Cultural Politics of Entrepreneurship in Nation-Making: Phoenicians, Turks, and the Arab Commercial Essence in Brazil." *Journal of Latin American Anthropology* 9(2): 319–51.

Karim, Lamia. 2001. "Politics of the Poor? NGOs and Grass-Roots Political Mobilization in Bangladesh." *PoLAR: Political and Legal Anthropology Review* 24(1): 92–107.

———. 2008. "Demystifying Micro-Credit." *Cultural Dynamics* 20(1): 5.

———. 2011. *Microfinance and Its Discontents: Women in Debt in Bangladesh.* Minneapolis: University of Minnesota Press.

Kar, Sohini. 2013. "Recovering Debts: Microfinance Loan Officers and the Work of 'Proxy-Creditors' in India." *American Ethnologist* 40(3): 480–93.

Kar, Sohini, and Caroline Schuster. n.d. "Comparative Projects: Ethnography and Microfinance in India and Paraguay." Unpublished manuscript.

Keane, Webb. 2001. "Money Is No Object: Materiality, Desire, and Modernity in an Indonesian Society." In *The Empire of Things: Regimes of Value and Material Culture,* ed. Fred R. Myers, 65–90. Santa Fe, NM: School of American Research Press.

Keating, Christine, Claire Rasmussen, and Pooja Rishi. 2010. "The Rationality of Empowerment: Microcredit, Accumulation by Dispossession, and the Gendered Economy." *Signs: Journal of Women in Culture and Society* 36(1): 153–76.

Khandker, Shahidur R. 1998. *Fighting Poverty with Microcredit: Experience in Bangladesh.* Oxford: Oxford University Press.

Klima, Alan. 2002. *The Funeral Casino: Meditation, Massacre, and Exchange with the Dead in Thailand.* Princeton, NJ: Princeton University Press.

Kopytoff, Igor. 1986. "The Cultural Biography of Things: Commoditization as Process." In *The Social Life of Things: Commodities in Cultural Perspective,* ed. Arjun Appadurai, 64–94. Cambridge: Cambridge University Press.

Kraay, Hendrik, and Thomas L. Whigham, eds. 2004. *I Die with My Country: Perspectives on the Paraguayan War, 1864–1870.* Lincoln: University of Nebraska Press.

Laíno, Domingo. 1976. *Paraguay, de la independencia a la dependencia: Historia del saqueo inglés en el Paraguay de la posguerra.* Asunción, Paraguay: Ediciones Cerro Corá.

Lambert, Peter, and Andrew Nickson, eds. 1997. *The Transition to Democracy in Paraguay.* New York: St. Martin's Press.

———. 2013. *The Paraguay Reader: History, Culture, Politics.* Durham, NC: Duke University Press Books.

Lamphere, Louise. 1985. "Bringing the Family to Work: Women's Culture on the Shop Floor." *Feminist Studies* 11(3): 519–40.

Lazar, Sian. 2004. "Education for Credit Development as Citizenship Project in Bolivia." *Critique of Anthropology* 24(3): 301–19.

Lemire, Beverly, Ruth Pearson, and Gail Grace Campbell. 2002. *Women and Credit: Researching the Past, Refiguring the Future.* Oxford: Berg.

Lépinay, Vincent Antonin. 2011. *Codes of Finance: Engineering Derivatives in a Global Bank.* Princeton, NJ: Princeton University Press.

Lewis, Daniel K. 2006. *A South American Frontier: The Tri-Border Region.* Arbitrary Borders. New York: Chelsea House.

Leyshon, Andrew, and Nigel Thrift. 1999. "Lists Come Alive: Eletronic Systems of Knowledge and the Rise of Credit-Scoring in Retail Banking." *Economy and Society* 28(3): 434–66.

LiPuma, Edward. 2004. *Financial Derivatives and the Globalization of Risk.* Durham, NC: Duke University Press.

MacCormack, Carol P., and Marilyn Strathern. 1980. *Nature, Culture and Gender.* Cambridge: Cambridge University Press.

Marx, Karl. 1993. *Capital: A Critique of Political Economy.* Vol. 3. Trans. David Fernbach. Reissue. London: Penguin Classics.

Masi, Fernando. 2000. "Desigualdad de los ingresos familiares en Paraguay." In *Pobreza, desigualdad y política social en América Latina,* ed. Centro de Análisis y Difusión de la Economía Paraguaya, 225–58. Asunción, Paraguay: CADEP.

Massumi, Brian. 1992. *A User's Guide to Capitalism and Schizophrenia: Deviations from Deleuze and Guattari.* Cambridge, MA: MIT Press.

Maurer, Bill. 2005. *Mutual Life, Limited: Islamic Banking, Alternative Currencies, Lateral Reason.* Princeton, NJ: Princeton University Press.

———. 2006. "The Anthropology of Money." *Annual Review of Anthropology* 35(1): 15–36.

———. 2012. "Payment: Forms and Functions of Value Transfer in Contemporary Society." *Cambridge Anthropology* 30(2): 15–35.

McKinnon, Susan. 2001. "The Economies in Kinship and the Paternity of Culture: Origin Stories in Kinship Theory." In *Relative Values: Reconfiguring Kinship Studies,* ed. Sarah Franklin and Susan McKinnon, 277–301. Durham, NC: Duke University Press.

MixMarket. 2009. "Report and Audit for Fundación Paraguaya de Cooperación y Desarrollo: MFI in Paraguay." www.mixmarket.org/mfi/fundaci%C3%B3n-paraguaya/files. Accessed April 15, 2012.

Miyazaki, Hirokazu. 2003. "The Temporalities of the Market." *American Anthropologist* 105(2): 255–65.

———. 2012. *Arbitraging Japan: Dreams of Capitalism at the End of Finance.* Berkeley: University of California Press.

Moodie, Megan. 2008. "Enter Microcredit: A New Culture of Women's Empowerment in Rajasthan?" *American Ethnologist* 35(3): 454–65.

———. 2013. "Microfinance and the Gender of Risk: The Case of Kiva.org." *Signs: Journal of Women in Culture and Society* 38(2): 279–302.

Mosse, David. 2005. *Cultivating Development: An Ethnography of Aid Policy and Practice.* Anthropology, Culture, and Society. London: Pluto Press.

———. 2013. The Anthropology of International Development. *Annual Review of Anthropology* 42(1): 227–46.

Mosse, David, and David Lewis, eds. 2005. *The Aid Effect: Giving and Governing in International Development.* Anthropology, Culture, and Society. London: Pluto.

Muehlebach, Andrea. 2012. *The Moral Neoliberal: Welfare and Citizenship in Italy.* Chicago: University of Chicago Press.

Munn, Nancy D. 1992. *The Fame of Gawa: A Symbolic Study of Value Transformation in a Massim Society.* Durham, NC: Duke University Press.

Musaraj, Smoki. 2011. "Tales from Albarado: The Materiality of Pyramid Schemes in Postsocialist Albania." *Cultural Anthropology* 26(1): 84–110.

Nickson, Andrew, and Peter Lambert. 2002. "State Reform and the 'Privatized State' in Paraguay." *Public Administration and Development* 22(2): 163–74.

Nussbaum, Martha. 2002. "Capabilities and Social Justice." *International Studies Review* 4(2): 123–35.

———. 2011. *Creating Capabilities: The Human Development Approach.* Cambridge, MA: Belknap Press.

Ong, Aihwa. 2006. *Neoliberalism as Exception: Mutations in Citizenship and Sovereignty.* Durham, NC: Duke University Press.

Orta, Andrew. 2013. "Managing the Margins: MBA Training, International Business, and 'the Value Chain of Culture.'" *American Ethnologist* 40(4): 689–703.

Paley, Julia. 2001. *Marketing Democracy : Power and Social Movements in Post-Dictatorship Chile.* Berkeley: University of California Press.

Parry, Jonathan P., and Maurice Bloch. 1989. *Money and the Morality of Exchange.* New York: Cambridge University Press.

Pascale, Richard, Jerry Sternin, and Monique Sternin. 2010. *The Power of Positive Deviance: How Unlikely Innovators Solve the World's Toughest Problems.* Boston, MA: Harvard Business Review Press.

Patterson, Joseph Grenny, David Maxfield, Ron McMillan, and Al Switzler Kerry. 2008. *Influencer: The Power to Change Anything.* New York: McGraw-Hill.

Paxson, Heather. 2012. *The Life of Cheese: Crafting Food and Value in America.* Berkeley: University of California Press.

Pedrozo, Mariano Celso. 2003. *La religiosidad popular paraguaya y la identidad nacional.* Asunción, Paraguay: Imprenta Salesiana.

Peebles, Gustav. 2010. "The Anthropology of Credit and Debt." *Annual Review of Anthropology* 39(1): 225–40.

———. 2012. "Whitewashing and Leg-Bailing: On the Spatiality of Debt." *Social Anthropology* 20(4): 429–43.

———. 2013. "Washing Away the Sins of Debt: The Nineteenth-Century Eradication of the Debtors' Prison." *Comparative Studies in Society and History* 55(3): 701–24.

Pitt, Mark M., Shahidur R. Khandker, and Jennifer Cartwright. 2006. "Empowering Women with Micro Finance: Evidence from Bangladesh." *Economic Development and Cultural Change* 54(4): 791–831.

Pocock, J. G. A. 1975. *The Machiavellian Moment: Florentine Political Thought and the Atlantic Republican Tradition*. Princeton, NJ: Princeton University Press.

Poon, Martha. 2009. "From New Deal Institutions to Capital Markets: Commercial Consumer Risk Scores and the Making of Subprime Mortgage Finance." *Accounting, Organizations and Society* 34(5): 654–74.

Poovey, Mary, ed. 2003. *The Financial System in Nineteenth-Century Britain*. Victorian Archives. New York: Oxford University Press.

Porter, Katherine. 2012. *Broke: How Debt Bankrupts the Middle Class*. Stanford, CA: Stanford University Press.

Postero, Nancy Grey. 2007. *Now We Are Citizens: Indigenous Politics in Postmulticultural Bolivia*. Stanford, CA: Stanford University Press.

Rabossi, Fernando. 2003. *En las calles de Ciudad del Este: Una etnografía del comercio de frontera*. Asunción, Paraguay: Centro de Estudios Antropológicos de la Universidad Católica.

———. 2010. "Made in Paraguai: Notas sobre la producción de Ciudad del Este." *Papeles de Trabajo—Revista Electrónica del IDEAS* (Buenos Aires) 6. www.idaes.edu.ar/papelesdetrabajo/paginas/Documentos/7%20Rabossi .pdf.

———. 2012. "Ciudad del Este and Brazilian Circuits of Commercial Distribution." In *Globalization from Below: The World's Other Economy*, ed. Gordon Mathews, Gustavo Lins Ribeiro, and Carlos Alba Vega, 54–68. New York: Routledge.

Rahman, Aminur. 1999. *Women and Microcredit in Rural Bangladesh: Anthropological Study of the Rhetoric and Realities of Grameen Bank Lending*. Boulder, CO: Westview Press.

Rajan, Kaushik Sunder. 2012. *Lively Capital: Biotechnologies, Ethics, and Governance in Global Markets*. Durham, NC: Duke University Press.

Rankin, Katharine N. 2001. "Governing Development: Neoliberalism, Microcredit, and Rational Economic Woman." *Economy and Society* 30(1): 18–37.

———. 2002. "Social Capital, Microfinance, and the Politics of Development." *Feminist Economics* 8(1): 1–24.

Riles, Annelise. 2010. "Collateral Expertise: Legal Knowledge in the Global Financial Markets." *Current Anthropology* 51(6): 795–818.

———. 2011. *Collateral Knowledge: Legal Reasoning in the Global Financial Markets*. Chicago Series in Law and Society. Chicago: University of Chicago Press.

Rist, Gilbert. 2002. *The History of Development: From Western Origins to Global Faith*. London: Zed Books.

Rivlin, Gary. 2010. *Broke, USA: From Pawnshops to Poverty, Inc.: How the Working Poor Became Big Business*. New York: Harper Business.

Rofel, Lisa. 2015. "Capitalism and the Private/Public Division." *Fieldsights - Theorizing the Contemporary, Cultural Anthropology Online*, March 30. www.culanth.org/fieldsights/653-capitalism-and-the-private-public-division.

Roitman, Janet L. 2005. *Fiscal Disobedience: An Anthropology of Economic Regulation in Central Africa*. Princeton, NJ: Princeton University Press.

Rosaldo, Michelle Zimbalist, Louise Lamphere, and Joan Bamberger. 1974. *Woman, Culture, and Society*. Stanford, CA: Stanford University Press.

Ross, Andrew. 2014. *Creditocracy: And the Case for Debt Refusal*. New York: OR Books.

Roy, Ananya. 2010. *Poverty Capital: Microfinance and the Making of Development*. New York: Routledge.

———. 2012. "Subjects of Risk: Technologies of Gender in the Making of Millennial Modernity." *Public Culture* 24(1): 131–55.

Rubin, Gayle. 1975. "The Traffic in Women: Notes on the 'Political Economy' of Sex." In *Toward an Anthropology of Women*, ed. Rayna R. Reiter, 157–210. New York: Monthly Review Press.

Rudnyckyj, Daromir. 2014. "Economy in Practice: Islamic Finance and the Problem of Market Reason." *American Ethnologist* 41(1): 110–27.

Sahlins, Marshall. 1972. *Stone Age Economics*. Chicago: Aldine-Atherton.

———. 2011. "What Kinship Is (Part I)." *Journal of the Royal Anthropological Institute* 17(1): 2–19.

Salzinger, Leslie. 2003. *Genders in Production: Making Workers in Mexico's Global Factories*. Berkeley: University of California Press.

———. 2004a. "From Gender as Object to Gender as Verb: Rethinking How Global Restructuring Happens." *Critical Sociology* 30(1): 43–62.

———. 2004b. "Revealing the Unmarked: Finding Masculinity in a Global Factory." *Ethnography* 5(1): 5–27.

Sanyal, Paromita. 2009. "From Credit to Collective Action: The Role of Microfinance in Promoting Women's Social Capital and Normative Influence." *American Sociological Review* 74(4): 529–50.

Schneider, David M. 1980. *American Kinship: A Cultural Account*. Chicago: University of Chicago Press.

———. 1984. *A Critique of the Study of Kinship*. Ann Arbor: University of Michigan Press.

Schuster, Caroline E. 2010. "Reconciling Debt: Microcredit and the Politics of Indigeneity in Argentina's Altiplano." *PoLAR: Political and Legal Anthropology Review* 33(1): 47–66.

———. 2014. "The Social Unit of Debt: Gender and Creditworthiness in Paraguayan Microfinance." *American Ethnologist* 41(3): 563–78.

———. 2015. "Your Family and Friends Are Collateral: Microfinance and the Social." *Fieldsights—Theorizing the Contemporary, Cultural Anthropology Online*, March 30. www.culanth.org/fieldsights/660-your-family-and-friends-are-collateral-microfinance-and-the-social.

———. 2016. "Repaying the Debts of the Dead: Kinship, Microfinance, and Mortuary Practice on the Paraguayan Frontier." *Social Analysis* 60(2).

Schumpeter, Joseph A. [1942] 1975. *Capitalism, Socialism, and Democracy*. New York: Harper.

Schwittay, Anke. 2011. "The Marketization of Poverty." *Current Anthropology* 52(S3): S71–S82.

———. 2014. *New Media and International Development: Representation and Affect in Microfinance*. London: Routledge.

Sen, Amartya. 1999. *Development as Freedom*. New York: Knopf.

Sikkink, Kathryn. 1988. "The Influence of Raúl Prebisch on Economic Policy-Making in Argentina, 1950–1962." *Latin American Research Review* 23(2): 91–114.

———. 1997. "Development Ideas in Latin America: Paradigm Shift and the Economic Commission for Latin America." In *International Development and the Social Sciences: Essays on the History and Politics of Knowledge*, ed. Frederick Cooper and Randall Packard, 228–56. Berkeley: University of California Press.

Silverstein, Michael. 2005. "Axes of Evals." *Journal of Linguistic Anthropology* 15(1): 6–22.

Simmel, Georg. 2011. *The Philosophy of Money*. Trans. Tom Bottomore and David Frisby. New York: Routledge.

Smith, Adam. 2000a. *The Theory of Moral Sentiments*. Amherst, NY: Prometheus Books.

———. 2000b. *The Wealth of Nations*. Modern Library Classics. New York: Modern Library.

Stallybrass, Peter. 1998. "Marx's Coat." In *Border Fetishisms: Material Objects in Unstable Spaces*, ed. Patricia Spyer, 183–207. New York: Routledge.

Stoll, David. 2012. *El Norte or Bust! How Migration Fever and Microcredit Produced a Financial Crash in a Latin American Town*. Washington, DC: Rowman & Littlefield.

Stout, Noelle M. 2014. *After Love: Queer Intimacy and Erotic Economies in Post-Soviet Cuba*. Durham, NC: Duke University Press.

———. 2015. "Generating Home." *Fieldsights—Theorizing the Contemporary, Cultural Anthropology Online*, March 30. www.culanth.org /fieldsights/655-generating-home.

Strathern, Marilyn.1990. *The Gender of the Gift: Problems with Women and Problems with Society in Melanesia*. Berkeley: University of California Press.

———. 2004. "The Whole Person and Its Artifacts." *Annual Review of Anthropology* 33: 1–19.

Straub, Stéphane, and Horacio Sosa. 2001. "Ensuring Willingness to Repay in Paraguay." In *Defusing Default: Incentives and Institutions*. Washington, DC: Inter-American Development Bank.

Sverdlick, Ana R. 2005. "Terrorists and Organized Crime Entrepreneurs in the 'Triple Frontier' among Argentina, Brazil, and Paraguay." *Trends in Organized Crime* 9(2): 84–93.

Thayer, Millie. 2010. *Making Transnational Feminism: Rural Women, NGO Activists, and Northern Donors in Brazil*. Perspectives on Gender. New York: Routledge.

Tomz, Michael. 2007. *Reputation and International Cooperation: Sovereign Debt across Three Centuries*. Princeton, NJ: Princeton University Press.

Triffin, Robert. 1946. *Monetary and Banking Reform in Paraguay*. Washington, DC: Board of Governors of the Federal Reserve System.

Tsai, Kellee S. 2004. *Back-Alley Banking: Private Entrepreneurs in China*. Ithaca, NY: Cornell University Press.

Tsing, Anna. 2000. "Inside the Economy of Appearances." *Public Culture* 12(1): 115–44.

————. 2005. *Friction: An Ethnography of Global Connection*. Princeton, NJ: Princeton University Press

————. 2009. "Beyond Economic and Ecological Standardisation." *Australian Journal of Anthropology* 20(3): 347–68.

————. 2015. "Salvage Accumulation, or the Structural Effects of Capitalist Generativity." *Fieldsights—Theorizing the Contemporary, Cultural Anthropology Online*, March 30. www.culanth.org/fieldsights/656-salvage-accumulation-or-the-structural-effects-of-capitalist-generativity.

Tucker, Jennifer. n.d. "City-Stories: Narrative as Diagnostic and Strategic Resource in Planning Practice of Ciudad del Este, Paraguay." Unpublished manuscript.

Villarreal, Magdalena. 2014. "Regimes of Value in Mexican Household Financial Practices." *Current Anthropology* 55(S9): S30–S39.

Wagner, Charlotte. 2012. "From Boom to Bust: How Different Has Microfinance Been from Traditional Banking?" *Development Policy Review* 30(2): 187–210.

Wagner, Charlotte, and Adalbert Winkler. 2013. "The Vulnerability of Microfinance to Financial Turmoil: Evidence from the Global Financial Crisis." *World Development* 51: 71–90.

Warren, Harris Gaylord. 1965. "The 'Lincolnshire Farmers' in Paraguay: An Abortive Emigration Scheme of 1872–1873." *The Americas* 21(3): 243–62.

————. 1989. "An Interview with Harris Gaylord Warren: From the Borderlands to Paraguay." *The Americas* 45(4): 443–60.

Weber, Heloise. 2002. "The Imposition of a Global Development Architecture: The Example of Microcredit." *Review of International Studies* 28(3): 537–55.

Weiner, Annette B. 1976. *Women of Value, Men of Renown: New Perspectives in Trobriand Exchange*. Austin: University of Texas Press.

————. 1980. "Reproduction: A Replacement for Reciprocity." *American Ethnologist* 7(1): 71–85.

————. 1985. "Inalienable Wealth." *American Ethnologist* 12(2): 210–27.

————. 1992. *Inalienable Possessions: The Paradox of Keeping-While-Giving*. Berkeley: University of California Press.

Weiss, John, and Heather Montgomery. 2005. "Great Expectations: Microfinance and Poverty Reduction in Asia and Latin America." *Oxford Development Studies* 33(3–4): 391–416.

Weston, Kath. 2013. "Lifeblood, Liquidity, and Cash Transfusions: Beyond Metaphor in the Cultural Study of Finance." *Journal of the Royal Anthropological Institute* 19(S1): S24–S41.

Whigham, Thomas L., and Barbara Potthast. 1999. "The Paraguayan Rosetta Stone: New Insights into the Demographics of the Paraguayan War, 1864–1870." *Latin American Research Review* 34(1): 174–86.

————. 2002. "Refining the Numbers: A Response to Reber and Kleinpenning." *Latin American Research Review* 37(3): 143–48.

White, John Howard. 2010. "Itaipu: Gender, Community, and Work in the Alto Parana Borderlands, Brazil and Paraguay, 1954–1989." PhD diss., University of New Mexico. http://search.proquest.com.proxy.uchicago.edu/pqdtft

/docview/8536485 10/abstract/13800344B864350169D/1?accountid=
14657. Accessed July 18, 2012.

Wilber, Ken. 2001. *A Theory of Everything: An Integral Vision for Business,
Politics, Science and Spirituality*. Boston: Shambhala.

Wright, Melissa W. 2006. *Disposable Women and Other Myths of Global Capitalism*. New York: Routledge.

Wu, David Y.H. 1974. "To Kill Three Birds with One Stone: The Rotating
Credit Associations of the Papua New Guinea Chinese." *American Ethnologist* 1(3): 565–84.

Yanagisako, Sylvia. 2002. *Producing Culture and Capital: Family Firms in
Italy*. Princeton, NJ: Princeton University Press.

Yanagisako, Sylvia, and Jane Collier, eds. 1987. *Gender and Kinship: Essays
toward a Unified Analysis*. Stanford, CA: Stanford University Press.

Zaloom, Caitlin. 2006. *Out of the Pits: Traders and Technology from Chicago
to London*. Chicago: University of Chicago Press.

Zelizer, Viviana A. Rotman. 1997. *The Social Meaning of Money: Pin Money,
Paychecks, Poor Relief, and Other Currencies*. Princeton, NJ: Princeton University Press.

———. 2005. *The Purchase of Intimacy*. Princeton, NJ: Princeton University
Press.

———. 2010. *Economic Lives: How Culture Shapes the Economy*. Princeton,
NJ: Princeton University Press.

Index

gentekuera, 167
gestionando, 144–45, 148, 150, 171, 236n10
gift exchange, 53, 203
global financial crisis: and Chinese Credit, 84; and collateral, 216n9; default in wake of, 159; and Fundación Paraguaya organization, 22, 146; overlapping liabilities in, 164
González Torres, Dionisio, 189
Graciela, 87–90, 93–94, 96–97, 99
Graeber, David, 16, 72, 211, 220n37, 236n3
Grameen Bank, 9, 35, 112, 217n16, 218n29, 225n6, 235n33
grocers. *See* shopkeepers
group-based loans: accidental value of, 86–87; creditworthiness of, 120; and death, 177, 200; and economic agency, 67; Fundación Paraguaya beginning, 112–13; and group cohesion, 125; from Kiva.org, 117; for men, 132; repayment of, 139, 157; requirements for, 115; size of, 61; and social collateral, 18, 51; social unit of debt in, 129
guarantors: credit reports on, 186; in microcredit, 107, 113, 115, 120
Gustavo, 7, 178–88, 242n12
Guyer, Jane, 195, 218n24

Han, Clara, 19, 221n52
Hart, Keith, 5, 233n42
having, conditions of, 106, 111
HDI (Human Development Index), 47
heterosexuality, compulsory, 220n39
Hetherington, Kregg, 23, 215n3, 219n32, 222n55, 223n64, 223n68, 232n31, 236n4
human capacities, 45
human development turn, 39–40
human economies, 211–12, 233n42
hyper-obligation, 26, 97
hypersociality, 64, 208

Ikatú initiative: and entrepreneurialism, 38, 46–48, 63; and microcredit as development, 36; personhood in, 52, 95; poverty indicator analysis in, 48–50, 52, 56, 59; setting up, 35
IMF (International Monetay Fund), 160–61, 232n24, 238n28, 239n29, 240nn39,41; liquidity problems and, 160–61
imobiliaria, 243n20
imperialism, 73, 77, 83
import substituting industrialization (ISI), 42

IMTFI (Institute for Money, Technology and Financial Inclusion), 9, 216n12
indebtedness: conditions of, 19, 85, 158; in contemporary capitalism, 174; exit from, 241n8; kinship and death, 176, 205; mutual, 67, 111, 177, 205; polemics about, 143
India, microfinance and gender in, 215n5, 218n29
individuality: coherence of, 50, 131; and credit relationships, 228n24
individual loans: class dimension of, 115; and creditworthiness, 131, 134, 136; social effluvia of, 116
The Influencer, 50
informal economies: central task of, 5; costs of enforcement in, 158–59; incomes in, 234n15; in Paraguay's financial sector, 160; women's work in, 110, 116, 120
information, flow of, 146
information problems, 235n33
Informconf: in advertising, 184*fig.*; creation of culture, 185; credit reports from, 6–7, 129–31, 133, 142, 177–79, 183–88, 242, 242n9; president of, 6. *See also* Gustavo; seminars by executives, 7, 178–79
innovation, rhetoric of, 30–31, 38
Insfrán Pelozo, José Aníbal, 160
integral theory, 46, 50, 228n27
Inter-American Development Bank, 15, 56, 148, 225n9
interdependency: in Ciudad del Este, 13; cultural politics of, 137; encumbering and enabling, 205; entrepreneurship and liability as, 33, 67; in financial relations, 11, 26, 114, 157–58; and Fundación Paraguaya, 136–37; knitting and unravelling of, 33, 111, 210; and social networks, 208; use of term, 220n37. *See also* economic interdependency; politics of interdependency; social interdependency
interiorization, 47, 50
Internet, NGO access to, 144
Internet, training via, 61
Itaipú Dam, 109

Jesuit training, 178, 181
joint liability: banality of, 89, 213; challenges to, 210; and deaths of members, 175, 192, 194; and distributional justice, 67; documentation of, 104, 119; and entrepreneurialism, 15, 209; and gender, 136; intimate economic